MW00475425

Crosses in the Sky

By
Paul D. Bagley

Eloquent Books

Eloquent Books
An imprint of Strategic Book Group
P.O. Box 333
Durham, Ct. 06422
www.StrategicBookGroup.com

ISBN: 978-1-60911-358-2

Printed in the United States of America

Book Design: Prepress-Solutions.com

Dedications

This work is dedicated to America's citizen soldiers—men and women who have in the past, who are currently, and who will in the future serve this nation by leaving hearth and home to stand a post in defense of the freedoms that we all enjoy and that we all too often take for granted.

To Jim,

My warmest regards and my deepest respect for your service to our country and the cause of freedom. Thank you, fellow veteran.

Paul [illegible]

Nov. 2010

Table of Contents

Introduction vii
CHAPTER 1—Tobey Hall 1
CHAPTER 2—I Chose To Be an American 9
CHAPTER 3—Discipline and Training 28
CHAPTER 4—Lord, Make This a Good Flight 43
CHAPTER 5—War Wounds 53
CHAPTER 6—The Gift of Wife 59
CHAPTER 7—Parlez-Vous Français? 71
CHAPTER 8—The Civil Rights Movement of 1945 90
CHAPTER 9—A Cohesive Mob 100
CHAPTER 10—43-38711 114
CHAPTER 11—Navigating and Nancy 128
CHAPTER 12—Scotland or Bust! 147
CHAPTER 13—Thurleigh 162
CHAPTER 14—Newla D-Dog – Lassie Come Home 180
CHAPTER 15—The Legend of Old Dobbins 187
CHAPTER 16—Medals 207
CHAPTER 17—Crosses in the Sky 219
CHAPTER 18—10th Mission Went Haywire 232
CHAPTER 19—ME262s 239
CHAPTER 20—Combat Rations 246
CHAPTER 21—Flak Jackets and Bales of Hay 258
CHAPTER 22—Fran 266
CHAPTER 23—Hanging on the Props 275

CHAPTER 24—Thirty-Five 293
CHAPTER 25—Punctuation Marks 302

Introduction

This is a story of resurrection … of deliverance. It is the tale of one man's struggle, amid a world gone insane with war, to maintain the strength of his convictions through his devotion to duty and by the maintenance of his faith. It is the account of his bomber crew, a crew that was truly blessed by a Divine Providence that watched over their lives and shielded them from harm. It is the legend of *Lassie Come Home*, one of the many aircraft of the 368th Bomb Squadron—the "Eager Beaver Squadron"—of the 306th Bomb Group. The 306th were "The Reich Wreckers," assigned to Station 111, Thurleigh, England in 1945. They are legendary because this crew was among the very few that flew the required number of missions without anyone being captured by the enemy, without any deaths, and without a single wound among the nine men. Above all, this is yet another story of man's indomitable spirit, his willingness to sacrifice that which he holds most dear for a greater good for others. It is a portrait of mankind's determination to overcome the afflictions which beset it and tackle the challenges before it through simple and utter faith in something greater than one's self.

Throughout the 1930's the United States of America, still gripped by the siege of a crippling economic depression, was struggling to rebuild herself into a nation of prosperity and opportunity. A new administration had assumed the mantle of power in Washington—an administration that somehow foresaw the bleak road ahead and plotted a course that toughened America and prepared it to endure the horrors and rigors of a war in which it would soon be embroiled. It took little for President Franklin Roosevelt to realize that hungry people eventually and inevitably reject the conditions of their poverty and turn to insurrection in order to fill their empty bellies. The United States may have been conceived in liberty, but it was born through revolution—and revolution is a condition that no presidential administration ever wants to exist during its watch. In a preemptive move to defeat any potential uprising, the newly elected president began rebuilding the American infrastructure with a furor that became the hallmark of progressivism. He started with the White House, reconstructing the West Wing and, as a sign of an awakening awareness in America of the value of every human being (an awareness that was not shared by the Axis powers that were in the midst of building their coalition), the West Wing housed the first handicapped-accessible office in the federal government. The first occupant of that accessible office, the Oval Office, was living testimony to the fact that a man confined to a wheelchair could not only contribute to American society, he could lead it as well.

It was during these prewar years that the Works Projects Administration (WPA), the Civilian Conservation Corps (CCC), and the Tennessee Valley Authority (TVA) were born—all monumental civil works projects designed to put muscle on America's bones so that it could eventually shoulder the awesome responsibility and weight of a worldwide war. Any scholar of the Great War (World War I) could unmistakably envision that seeds were sown at Versailles for a second installment of the hostilities. The inevitability, in retrospect, was as clear as crystal. But hope in America has always sprung eternal, and it remained the prevailing attitude throughout the years leading up to Pearl Harbor, despite all evidence to the contrary. Even if America was not destined to participate in the global conflict, she still needed to prepare for the future, and change—systemic change—swept across the land like a strong wind, touching everything.

Roads, bridges, dams, parks, schools, and public buildings of all dimensions and descriptions began to rise up across the nation, transforming a predominantly agrarian culture into a burgeoning cosmopolitan society. Roads that were once discernible only by the ruts that remained after a train of wagons passed over them were suddenly being paved with an aggregate mixture of sand and hot tar. Some were fashioned with the setting of slabs that formed a solid ribbon of concrete that would stretch for hundreds of miles, seemingly without end. Rivers were blocked by dams and water was harnessed to generate electrical power—much-needed power that would be used by the factories that would spring to life in abundance, for the very first time, far from the banks of rivers where they previously had been contained. High-tension transmission lines would carry alternating electrical current to remote places where the inhabitants had scarcely conceived of electrification, much less anticipated it becoming a reality in their lifetime. National parks were suddenly no longer wilderness refuges, where a pioneering spirit and agility with an ax and a knife were essential for basic survival. There were now trails and campgrounds—places where Americans could seek family relaxation in an as-yet unspoiled environment. The clapboard-covered schoolhouse in most communities, with its gossamer-thin walls and cramped spaces, now gave way to the WPA's new box structures of terracotta brick and mortar, with central corridors and high ceilings on two or three floors. Their solid foundations and rigid construction were themselves a metaphor for the national metamorphosis that was taking place.

The quiet complacence in international affairs that had marked America's years after the Great War was steadily eroding away into a new national strength of character and commitment to the causes that were of interest to all mankind. The United States had seemingly not sought the mantle of world leader, but accepted it once it was thrust upon her. Unlike any other nation in 1941—with the possible exceptions of Germany and Japan—America was fairly well prepared for the struggles that lay ahead with foreign powers, thanks to the internal struggles that she had endured in overcoming her own economic weaknesses. From the beginning of the Great Depression, America was growing in strength every day. Like a person debilitated by a crippling injury or disease, America gradually exercised her muscles each day to get back into shape. And, like the scar tissue that marks the location of a deep wound, that which had before been weakest in America—her economy—had grown back tough and rigid; a visible reminder that the skin of the nation had once been broken there. The United States of America bore that scar tissue with both humility and pride: pride in the fact that it had endured and prevailed, overcoming the doom and despair of depression; humility in the fear that it could and might happen again. America had helped win World War I in 1918—the "war to end all wars"—but it somehow managed, with her allies, to lose the peace. Fear itself, sparked by the sting of economic depression, was rapidly evolving into a national credo when President Roosevelt identified it as the only thing that needed to be feared. Anything else could be overcome through determination and ingenuity, if only Americans maintained faith in something beyond themselves—in God, in their country, or in the concern for the more devastating plight of others in distant lands.

It is amidst this backdrop that we paint the portrait of a young man who was representative of most young American men in the late 1930s and early 1940s. He was a businessman, a tradesman, and a patriot. Like that of most people, his life was not a simple stamped-out impression of some machined mold, with sharp edges and precisely defined lines. Instead, it was an intricate lace pattern of embroidery with subtle curves, peaks, and depressions, clearly defined in one place and fuzzy in another. His life was truly a tapestry of many threads. And the common threads that ran through every inch of that fabric were his faith in God and his belief in Jesus Christ as his personal savior. It was this faith alone that Bill Witcomb, resting in his retirement beyond the age of 80, would attribute for his good fortunes in war. It was an abiding conviction to his spiritual beliefs that sustained him through the din of battle, through the endless bitter cold nights of the war, and throughout the longer personal battles that would come upon the heels of World War II. And it is here, midst the years of post-World-War-II prosperity and peace, when America was relaxed and tranquil, that Bill Witcomb's story truly begins.

CHAPTER 1

Tobey Hall

He stared intently through the window at the intricate web being crafted by a spider on the oversized sill just beyond his bed. It had been a foreboding fall, austere and cold in many respects, fraught with one thunderstorm after another—three in just over a week. It was reminiscent of the English winter and spring he had endured so long ago. He watched as the sun rose beyond the window and transformed the silver strands of web into gold and, just as quickly as they had changed color, they seemed to disappear into the glass, absorbed by the gray sky and the darkness of the room. All that was left to view was a dirty window now, and the barren yard beyond. As desolate as the world may have been outside, it was not nearly as bleak as the existence inside the walls of Tobey Hall. It was not a place of choice, even though he—unlike his fellow roommates—had chosen to be there.

A middle-aged orderly trudged past him pushing a bucket with a mop, detailed to scrub a floor on the ward or swab down the remains of some patient's convulsive episode. It was commonplace to hear patients heaving their guts, or hacking with persistent coughs that would cause one's own chest to rumble from the vibrations. There were those who wandered the ward both day and night, talking in above-normal tones to themselves and purposely invading the space of others. There was the occasional scream from another inmate, or the obtuse bellowing of instructions from a nurse or an orderly to an unruly patient. If the symptoms of mental illness were subtle or latent to the layperson, the sounds certainly were not. The anguish of a human being caught in the vise-grip of internal emotional upheaval was as devastating and demanding as any eviscerated patient in an emergency room. Yet, no one here seemed to care whether or not a patient got well. This was not a treatment facility as much as it was a warehouse.

Bathrobes of thin terrycloth, hospital Johnnies of pale cotton, and slippers brought from home were the only things that helped stave off the chill of the hard polished concrete floors and the dank drafts that pervaded the ward. The warmth beneath the covers remained the only true refuge from the frigid existence at Tobey Hall. Bill sat in his bed, wrapped completely in his robe; his feet hidden beneath his blanket. He constantly stared at that dirty window. Although it would be easy to look upon the landscape beyond and dream of freedom, or of a miracle cure for whatever it was that ailed him, he, instead, stared at the dirt. He was transfixed by it. It's not as though he was fastidious about cleaning. It just seemed to be common sense to him. *How could a hospital—even a mental hospital!—allow windows to get that dirty?* he thought. *What would it take to clean them once in awhile?*

As the orderly trundled his equipment toward the mop sink in the janitor's closet and back past the row of beds, Bill leaned over the metal railing at the foot of his bed and begged a question of the man in white. Would it be possible for the orderly to let him clean the window? After all, it wasn't as though he was asking the orderly to do the work for him. Bill was anxiously willing to provide the labor, if only the orderly would provide the permission and the supplies. Leaning on the mop handle for a moment, the orderly paused in contemplation.

"Come on," said Bill with a whine, "even a nut can wash windows!" The orderly pondered the statement a bit, then deigned to let the mental patient demonstrate his mettle by scrubbing away the years of dirt that had accumulated upon the only link that Bill Witcomb had to the world outside. He handed Bill a thick tan sponge that looked as though it had just been plucked from the ocean floor, and a bucket filled with warm water that he anointed with a healthy splash of ammonia concentrate. There were towels in the hamper that had been destined for the laundry, but could still serve as polishing cloths when the scrubbing was finished. Despite the risk of contamination from the soiled goods, Bill burrowed into the job, scrubbing those windows absolutely spotless with the vaporous solution and stained linens. He started with the one closest to his own bed, although it mattered little where he began. After all, he had all the time in the world. Despite there being no demand upon him to finish rapidly, he was done in what seemed like no time at all. Left with only a clear view of the browning lawn beyond, all that remained was to sit and stare. Here there was no rehabilitation, only time to sit and think … time to listen to those hacking coughs, to that wrenching heaving, and to the inane chatter of fellow patients who were in truly a different place than he. There was nothing but time available to him with which to think … to remember … to reflect.

After a week or so of washing windows, Bill and another patient began assuming more of the ward cleaning chores, relieving their orderly for other duties. Of course, the orderly had no other duties, and was more than content to let the patients carry his load. Even though Bill realized from the start he was being exploited, he didn't care. He had something constructive to do each day, a function—a true purpose. It was his reason to get up and out of bed each morning. That was what virtually all of the men on the ward lacked—purpose.

This custodial routine lasted only a short time before Bill began questioning in his own mind why he was even there at all. It's not that he minded the work—in fact, he rather enjoyed it. He recalled having signed the voluntary commitment papers, so it wasn't a question of how he got there, like it was with so many of the patients on the ward. His concern was why he remained there after all this time. Yes, there were drugs each day, to keep the patients quiet and complacent, but there was no evidence of ongoing treatment, no therapy, not even diagnosis, and without those components, there certainly could be no hope for change.

Bill leaned on the mop as he finished up the floor of the latrine and grinned at the orderly who was overseeing his work. The orderly grinned back at him, pleased that the room sparkled.

"How do I get out of here?" asked Bill matter-of-factly.

"You wanna get out of here?" replied the orderly, astonished at such a thought.

"I didn't come here to live," said Bill in amazement.

"Well, the best way is to write a letter to the doc. Tell 'im you're all better," said the man in white.

Bill paused, he then quietly asked, "Can I get some writing paper and a pen?"

– – –

"So," said the doctor, as he reclined in his chair and perused the file before him. "I see that you've written a letter stating that you believe you're all better now. Is that true?" asked the clinician peering over his half-frame glasses at the man in the bathrobe.

"I believe that I am better," replied Bill.

"Are you sure you're *all* better?" asked the doctor.

"I didn't say I was *all* better. I don't think anyone who's ever been in here can say that," explained the patient. "I said I'm better than I was, meaning I'm better than I was when I signed myself in here."

"You think you're ready to go back into the world and face all those things that drove you to us in the first place?"

"I do."

"What has changed?"

"I have," answered Bill.

"How?" asked the doctor.

Bill spent the next hour or so talking about the revelations that had come to him over the course of his hospitalization. When he had checked himself in to the New Hampshire State Hospital, even he would have described himself as a basket case. It was the logical result of everything that had accumulated to that point in his life. Born between the two World Wars; raised in the wake of the Great Depression, and on his own before the first Japanese aircraft carrier ever set out for Pearl Harbor, Bill Witcomb had seen much and weathered much. By the time America was bearing the social turmoil of the civil rights movement, Bill Witcomb was a well-established businessman, a husband and father, and a decorated veteran of two military theaters. The emotional and psychological traumas he had endured during his active participation in both the war in Europe and the Korean Conflict had been put on the back burner of his mind. There, those traumas simmered. From time to time, additional bitter ingredients were added, allowing it all to ferment into an indigestible psychological stew. By the time Lyndon Johnson was reinstalled as the Commander-in-Chief for his own term, Bill's emotional state was nearly out of control. His depression was profound, and his focus was gone. Bill was no longer able to cope with the day-to-day stresses that confront parents, husbands, and business people all the time. His family and close friends were all aware that something was different, but none could put their finger on it. His wife Frances knew of the changes, better than anyone, and she couldn't make sense of them. There had been the endless nightmares and the bed sweats. There had been countless times that she had awakened in the middle of the night, not knowing what was wrong, only to find Bill awake, sitting in the dark, in a remote and untouchable solitude which was accompanied by a deafening silence.

The depth of Bill Witcomb's depression was common. So, too, was the cause. Although it would be another decade before the syndrome would acquire official recognition by clinicians as *post-traumatic stress disorder*, the lack of a moniker made it no easier to treat, and certainly no easier to endure.

After days of intense discussions with the psychiatrist at the state hospital, Bill Witcomb was pronounced ready for a return to his home and his job. Although little was seemingly undertaken by the hospital staff to treat Bill's condition, the brief time-out that he had taken from the emotional pain that had pervaded his adult life had worked. He was apparently back to normal, so far as the doctors could see. But then, their involvement in his treatment was marginal at best and their observations cursory in every way.

Coming face-to-face with the ghosts of his past finally brought him to the point where he could begin the path to recovery. Bill Witcomb had wrestled those ghosts and won this round—or he had at least brokered a truce. He managed to come to the realization that not everything that happened to those in his past was attributable to him, and that he need bear only his share of guilt about the fate of his comrades and the enemy during the war. Bill now felt wonderful about himself and about life. The ghosts were still there, but contained in their proper place for now. It was time to get back into the game.

Upon reflection later in life concerning his thirty-five day stay in 1965 at the New Hampshire State Hospital, Bill Witcomb was crystal clear concerning two things only. The first was that he demanded and obtained a letter of discharge from the psychiatrist that Bill proudly carried alongside his multi-engine pilot's license for the remainder of his life. The second was that it was there, amid the noise and anguish of others, surrounded by the smells and sounds and sights of mental illness, and trapped in a self-imposed domestic captivity, that he grappled for the first time with the demon which plagues all veterans. It was there, within those dingy walls of Tobey Hall, that Bill Witcomb moved himself closer to healing the wounds that no one could see. It was there that he finally managed to consume that bitter stew, and keep it down. "We are all in recovery all of the time," Bill waxed philosophical one day, but spoke with the wisdom and conviction of someone who knew that to be absolutely true. It was spoken by someone who lived that truth every day for decades.

It is said that there are only two kinds of people who serve their country in wartime: those who are killed in action, and those who ever after feel a deep guilt that they were not among those who were killed in action. Survivor's guilt is often associated with human beings that manage to escape the jaws of death while others are consumed by them. It happens in plane crashes and in shipwrecks, in modern school massacres and in terrorist attacks, in earthquakes, tornadoes, and hurricanes. Yet, it is somehow more palatable and understandable in American society in any of those situations than when it manifests itself in the shock and nightmares of military veterans, who carry with them always the inner scars of battles that they have endured. While pondering the dirt and the dust caked upon the ward windows of Tobey Hall, Bill Witcomb pondered his life up to that point, and he weighed the value of his contribution against the ultimate sacrifice of his comrades. He grappled with the horrors that he had survived almost a quarter of a century before and struggled with the visions of humanity engaged in the near self-immolation that was World War II. Amidst all this, Bill pondered his faith in God, and his position in relation to the outline handed down to him by God through the Bible. The obligations of Christianity were awesome indeed, and it was difficult to rationalize the acts of a citizen soldier with the rules of religion and the tenets of his faith.

It was impossible for Bill Witcomb to make sense of it all, because wars, by definition, are one human endeavor that rarely makes any sense for those who must fight them. He sat day after day, trying to remember every detail of his existence, trying in vain to find the point where the fabric of that life began to unravel. He stretched his mind back to his childhood, to when he was a boy, then a young man, and back to those endless days when he was a pilot—a flying soldier—a warrior with wings. It was a different world then. Mankind had not yet envisioned many things. Penicillin and plastic were only concepts. Nazism and death camps hadn't yet been articulated. A loaf of bread cost only 8¢. Bill remembered much of it—particularly that loaf of bread. In fact, he remembered much of it all too well …

CHAPTER 2

"I Chose To Be an American"

Britain was a highly competitive land toward the end of the industrial revolution. The Gilded Age had been a period characterized by the creation of ornate furnishings and detailed crafts of fine silver and gold. It was also a time when the metamorphosis of society was bringing to a close the distinctive caste system that had pervaded most western cultures. Men and women of all socioeconomic levels were now increasingly more demanding of all the freedoms that being part of the western democracies offered, despite the efforts of the propertied upper classes to maintain a status quo. Those in the working classes were no longer content with mere existence. They wanted a greater share in the opulent prosperity that was the hallmark of the new century in England and abroad. Therein lay the seeds for a social upheaval.

This desire for acquiring more was indicative of the skilled tradesmen: accomplished perfectionists providing superior products and commanding premium prices. Glass blowers and crystal cutters, furniture builders and silversmiths were all numbered among the ranks of the highly skilled artisans and guild members, with their handcrafted wares of wood, precious metals, and crystal glass fetching increasingly higher prices with each passing day. But industrialization found its way into the trades, and many artisan products were now being mass-produced—many offering almost the same level of exquisite workmanship as those previously made only by hand. This was so partly because the skilled tradesmen of the day were instrumental in developing the methods and means of mass production. It was for this very brief period that both the artisan and the industrialist coexisted equitably.

Divergent forces were at play, however. And, like the law of physics that says for every action there is an equal and opposite reaction, social upheaval was the inevitable reaction to the mechanization of the workplace. Industrialization forged the way for a new form of consumerism, and working-class people—including the artisans—wanted a greater share in what would become the industrialized nations of the world. This rapidly changing social and economic climate would lead to predictable recessions, and eventually depressions, in both America and Germany. Yet, in England, the tradition of economic stability had been world renown. A world economy was now the rule, and the famed stalwart British pound sterling was affected, along with the rock-solid Anglo-colonial economy abroad. England was forced to recognize the laws of global supply and demand amid a burgeoning new world market. Fierce competition from foreign vendors was changing the paradigm.

A drop in the demand for fine wares at the passing of the Gilded Age was to be expected. When the RMS Titanic plummeted to the depths of the Atlantic in the chill of April 1912, so too did the demand for fine sterling silver ornaments in the British Isles. Suddenly, after the tragic loss of Britain's premier ocean liner, British life took on a little more meaning than just having property, and a new energy was being applied toward the tools and gadgets that would save humanity from the clutches of such disasters. Fancy frills, elaborately carved furnishings, and gilt-edged baubles were soon to give way to new streamlined utilitarian and art-deco designs. Women's fashion began to reveal more of the splendor of the female form, heralding a new diversity and permissiveness in morality, both in Europe and North America. The concept of a forty-hour work week was now almost commonplace on both continents. And in England, there were bustling trade opportunities in many new fields of endeavor, relegating many of the time-honored trade guilds to near extinction.

High on the top of the list of these trades was that of the silversmith. Among the corps of young silversmiths who had faithfully plied their craft in Britain was a Birmingham journeyman named Clarence William Witcomb. Witcomb had served a brief time in the uniform kilts of the Coldstream Guards during the war to end all wars—the branch chosen primarily due to his fondness for the kilts. But he was quickly whisked back into industry when his much-needed skills were necessary for the production of precision military airplane parts. He had studied his craft and elevated it almost to an art by honing his talent to a professional edge. As a true craftsman, his skills would always be in demand at some level in England, and after the war he went to work for Mappen & Webb, Ltd., a blossoming young company with great promise. It was here that he found Elsie Bates working as clerical support in the company offices. Elsie was something very unusual, and very special.

There was a predictable economic downturn after the World War that had crippled much of the world. England was not spared this depression. Recognizing that it was only a matter of time before the ebbing demand for fine silver goods consumed his employment relationship with this now-established firm in England, Witcomb began to scour the planet for a place where true silversmiths were still in demand. He found such a haven in Canada, where Mappen & Webb was opening an expanded operation in a Crown colony. The company was speculating that an abundant untapped market lay on the North American continent, and had decided to cash in on it. The choice to move to the colony was a natural leap for the company, even though it was a labored decision for Witcomb. But the economic trend was clear: Canada offered more to him at a time when he needed more. At the age of 24, Witcomb married 25 year-old

Elsie Martha Anny Bates in 1920. A short time later, they found themselves bound for Canada aboard a steamship.

– – –

As Witcomb and his pregnant bride strode along the railing of the ship bound for Halifax, Nova Scotia, England slipped from view astern of the vessel. Unlike so many Europeans, who had either escaped a politically oppressive birthplace or who abandoned an economically deprived homeland for the promises of America, the Witcombs perceived their actions as merely helping populate one of the Crown's premier colonies and serving the interests of their firm at the same time. His uncle Arthur Witcomb, a famed Royal coronet musician, had himself left the renowned Coldstream Guards and accepted a posting with the United States Marine Corps band in Washington, DC. When someone once spelled his last name Whitcomb, he corrected them politely by saying, "There is no *H* in my name. That's where the *wit* comes in."

But Clarence Witcomb, or Bill as he was known to family and friends, was still very much an Englishman, and still very proud to be a subject of His Majesty King Edward. Living and working within the dominion of a royal Edwardian regime was not only tolerable for him, it was preferred in many ways. The caste system in Britain was deemed unfair by many of the lower echelons. But, after all, it was that very caste system, which millions of his fellow countrymen had abhorred—with its money-rich gentry who bought fine silver goods—that made Witcomb's stock in trade so profitable. With the rapid erosion of the English caste system, coupled with the progressive social and technical alterations in Britain, the demand for fine silver was on the wane. The time had been right for the company to find a new niche market and for the young Witcomb newlyweds to establish a new home.

– – –

Now firmly entrenched in the Canadian culture, and committed to life on the new American continent, Witcomb and his bride were in the throes of creating their family. Although an ocean away from everything and everyone they knew, Bill and Elsie had established a reasonable living for themselves, despite the economic hard times that befell much of the world. Charles William Henry Witcomb sprang into the world on February 6, 1921. He would always be called Bill, like his father. By the time he had grown beyond the toddler stage, a second Witcomb son, Kenneth Arthur, was born in 1925.

The Witcomb boys grew up like virtually all other Canadian children living in and around Montreal. They attended church with their parents, they did their chores (what few they had at such young ages), and they minded their parents. They were seldom caught in mischief that could have led them to real trouble. They were good young boys. They were nice young boys.

By the time the younger Bill was five, the economic climate in and around Montreal—like the rest of the industrialized world—had eroded considerably, but had not yet disintegrated completely. Regardless of positive financial forecasts, Mappen & Webb announced they would return to Birmingham and abandoned all operations in Canada. Bill senior was now searching the landscape once again for greener pastures in which to work. He knew England had little to offer him, since few changes had occurred in the silversmith industry since he had immigrated to Canada. The Canadian Pacific Railway Company offered him a job that put him in charge of all the silverware that it maintained on their trains. Despite the economic hard times that had engulfed the western world in the previous decade, pure silver was a tradition aboard their trains and the CPRR was determined to maintain standards. Witcomb wanted to remain in Canada, but Elsie was not willing to have her husband traveling regularly, which would have been a forgone requirement in that position. He kept looking for something better.

Bill senior wrote a letter to a man in the United States

named Rupert Nock, the president of the Tolle Manufacturing Company, applying for a position. Nock (a fellow Englishman) replied swiftly with a job offer. Nock required a skilled silversmith who could oversee certain manufacturing operations and Bill Witcomb was just the man for the job. Witcomb was an accomplished silversmith who fully understood the methods of modern mass production, and he would be most likely to impart both the industrialist's need for volume and the artisan's demand for quality to Tolle's existing workforce. Once again Bill and Elsie founded a new home in another country, this time in the United States. In the seaport community of Newburyport, Massachusetts, the Tolle Manufacturing Company offered outstretched arms to accomplished silverworkers who came to establish its new mechanized operation. Newburyport was a bustling little community situated on the Merrimack River, right in the shadow of Plum Island. It was a fishing community, a boat-building community, and now a fine silver producing community. Large boats, small ships, and railroad trains, laden with tin, zinc, copper, and silver were frequent visitors, and the Tolle Company had a constant supply of the raw materials necessary for producing their fine wares.

Bill Witcomb moved his young family south from Montreal to Newburyport at a time when major U.S. immigration quotas had yet to be imposed. He was a skilled tradesman in a highly competitive field, a family man with strong Protestant convictions, and a most-desirable addition to any New England community. Besides, the president of Tolle Manufacturing wanted Bill. He was a transplanted Englishman himself, and he liked the idea of having a fellow countryman at his side. They could speak the same language—the King's English.

– – –

The Witcomb family moved into their new home at 11 Tyng Street in Newburyport in 1926, and into a new life that would forever establish the destiny for both young Bill and Ken. At the age of five, Bill junior had been raised on Episcopal doctrine in Canada. The two brothers had always attended church weekly with their parents. But in Newburyport, their home sat but a stone's throw down the street from a Congregational Church. Whether from convenience or conviction, the Witcomb family soon became parishioners of that congregation, and Bill junior was now paying heed to a new strain of Christianity. Regardless of the specific tenets or rituals of any particular religion, Bill was first and foremost a Christian; a distinction in his character that he would use to describe himself throughout life. His faith in Jesus Christ was always part of the very composition of his being, even from the earliest days of his understanding, and no secular delineation would alter the depth of his convictions toward the basic nature of his faith. The Holy Bible was his only roadmap.

Throughout their childhood, Bill and Ken were not as close, perhaps, as brothers could be. Elsie doted on Bill, her favorite, and Bill senior seldom interfered. Young Bill was an excellent student; Ken was more the daydreamer and mediocre scholar. Bill was older, the more outgoing and responsible son; Ken the younger, more itinerant, and inwardly focused. Elsie didn't mean to build barriers between the two brothers, but their age separation of more than four years helped expand the distance between them. Put simply, they were each in different places in their lives.

The boys had the quiet, almost lazy Merrimack River to watch each day at the end of Tyng Street. Around the corner onto Merrimac Street and down a block or two, they would watch the trains crossing the turntable trestle that sat in the middle of the river. When the large boats and small ships would move up or down the Merrimack, the trestle would swivel out of the way, creating a passageway for vessels on each side of its axis. The boys especially loved to watch the locomotives as they chugged their way across. They pondered the people in the passenger cars, their destinations, and their reasons for traveling. They considered the varied cargoes in the many freight cars they saw, and were quick to count the coal cars that hauled their black gold north to Portsmouth, Portland, and beyond.

The Tyng Street house was a simple abode—two floors of wooden clapboards on a brick foundation, capped with a full attic and acute angled roof. There was a narrow yard along the side of the house, and a smaller one in back. Shutters painted black adorned the windows, although the shutters were never closed, and the corner moldings on the house were crowned by flared capitals that created the impression of Ionic columns on both sides of the front façade, as though drawn from some classic Greek or Roman architectural design. It was a sturdy little house, with its mirror image built right next door.

Tyng Street was a good neighborhood in which to grow up. Bill's best friend lived a few doors away, and the *No-yes* brothers (a family named Noyes) were there as well. Small and large houses mixed together in a somewhat logical pattern of streets and roads—certainly most logical for a colonial New England town. Most of the structures dated to the middle of the nineteenth century; many stretched back to the eighteenth. There was an unusual socioeconomic mixture in Newburyport. Certainly, the mansions of the old sea captains that lined High Street would normally be considered an exclusive neighborhood. But many of these fine homes were adjacent to the little streets that led down toward the river, where smaller dwellings lay. These were the homes of working-class people. Scattered amongst them were moderately sized houses, belonging to businessmen, shop owners, and professionals of all sorts. The result was that no one neighborhood was a ghetto, and no single area of town was considered the "good" part of town. Newburyport had achieved for itself, seemingly through a natural evolution, that for which America was famous: the equal sharing of space by all levels of society. It was truly heterogeneous in composition but homogeneous in attitude, and this served as an important model during the formative years of the Witcomb boys.

Young Bill had constructed coops in the back yard, where he raised chickens and collected their eggs each day. When the other kids in the neighborhood were playing hide-and-go-seek or kick-the-can, Bill was caring for his flock, gathering the fresh eggs, and selling them to the neighbors. Each spring and fall he would test the old saying that an egg could be stood on end at the precise moment of the vernal or autumnal equinox. He would sit poised with a fresh jumbo egg at the kitchen table and wait for the exact moment that the sun rose to cross the prime meridian. He never did get that egg to stand on end, for he had discounted all the other factors that were involved: the levelness of the table, the amount of vibration from the nearby factory where his father worked, the steadiness of his own hand. Such things were beyond his grasp at that age, but he would learn, in time, to take everything into consideration when dealing with science, mechanics, and physics. Throughout his life, eggs would always be a part of his diet, even when they were scarce. He learned to tell the good ones from the bad early in life, an acuity that would serve him well in command situations. And he learned to savor the taste of fried eggs very early as well.

The distance between the two Witcomb brothers grew wider with time. Elsie continued to favor Bill, and Ken managed to make do with his share of attention, positive and negative. While Bill was diligently studying for high school exams, Ken would be upstairs in the attic making a racket with model airplane engines that sputtered and crackled. In the twilight of his life, Bill would recognize the irony of Ken playing with those model airplanes, yet it was he who eventually took to the air during the war. A different fate indeed awaited Ken.

When the Great Depression hit America, silver was no longer the hot commodity that it had once been. People wanted and needed food and jobs, and both were in short supply. Bill Witcomb senior was no exception. His hours were cut back from a regular forty-hour week; first to thirty, then twenty. When work shriveled to only two days a week, there was no way for him to provide for his family. The result was that he left Tolle Manufacturing temporarily and went to work in a grocery store. The superintendent of the First National Store, Jim Clancy, offered him an opportunity to start at the bottom and work his way up through management. He was warned that such a rise would take considerable time. It wasn't what he wanted, but money was scarce, and jobs even scarcer. Determined to make this a profitable move, he burrowed into the job of store clerk with all his might and, within two weeks, was promoted to store manager by the man who had hired him. Within a year, Bill senior had been made regional manager for all the First National Stores in the Newburyport area. Although not inclined through personal preference toward mercantilism, Bill showed an amazing aptitude for it and rose through the internal ranks at a meteoric rate. As regional manager, he was able to introduce his eldest son to the working world for the first time.

At his side, Bill the younger, during the summers and whenever he wasn't in school, was an able assistant stocking shelves, bagging groceries, and tending to customers. A loaf of bread would sell for eight cents, but Mr. Witcomb would tell his customers that the special was three loaves for a quarter. Without thinking of the arithmetic involved, shoppers would scoop up three loaves and pay over their quarter, not realizing they were paying more, not less. The younger Witcomb would then meet them at the door with a shiny new penny in change and a bright smile, and father, son, and their customers would have a good-hearted laugh at the whole thing. It was that kind of natural charm that made both the Witcombs natural businessmen.

It was at the store on Plum Island, only a few miles on a bicycle from Tyng Street, amid the sand dunes and hardy marsh grass, that Bill junior prepared the produce for sale each day. Cleaning out the vegetable display and dumping the spoiled goods over the embankment behind the store seemed to have no consequence at first. After all, the gulls routinely made short work of anything edible. They would swoop down at an alarming speed, then, with a flare of their gray and white wings, they would rock backwards as they slowed themselves down, and extend their legs as though lowering a retractable landing gear. He often witnessed the gulls from the back door of the store, rooting around in the sand at low tide for clams that were close to the surface. They'd snatch one of the tasty crustaceans and fly toward the parking lot of the store. There, high over the concrete slabs, they would let their prey go to be smashed on the hard surface of the driveway. They would then fly down and feast on the tender clam meat that was now exposed to them. This was Bill's first exposure to precision daylight bombardment.

One day, while watching the carnivorous gulls, Bill noticed sprouts appearing in the sandy soil out back. He looked closer to find that there were tomato plants coming up where the spoiled goods had been dumped. Apparently the seeds of a discarded tomato had taken root, and the healthiest stocks he had ever seen were growing up at an alarming rate. Bill decided to cultivate the plants and staked them up so they would remain upright while bearing heavy fruit. In time, luscious large beefsteak tomatoes were clinging to the vine, making the change from green to red in the late summer sun. Finally the day came to pick them, and Bill dutifully cut them from their stalks, brought them into the store, and washed away the island dust from their skin. This was going to be a double treat: Bill loved nothing better than a good tomato, and these had the added benefit of being, for all intents and purposes, free. An accident had brought them forth, Bill thought, but that could mean some real profits for him and his family. During the economic crunch in the wake of the Depression, everyone was looking for ways to turn simple things into cash, and he knew they could sell whatever they didn't eat.

Bill sat at the makeshift table in the back room of the store and laid one of the juicy red orbs on a plate before him. Alongside was a saltshaker. That first tomato was succulent, red and ripened to perfection. If a Madison Avenue ad agency had seen that tomato, they would have surely snatched it up for a photo layout to advertise tomato soup in a color magazine, or for the bright new label on a can of stewed tomatoes. Bill pierced the skin of the tomato with a sharp knife and quickly sank his teeth into one of the halves he had cut. The juice was abundant, the texture perfect. But there was a problem. Plum Island was a virtual sand bar in the Atlantic Ocean. Dotted with cottages and a road or two, it existed primarily for the casual beachgoers who enjoyed the beautiful white sand beaches that surrounded it. The beautiful white sands of Crane's Beach lay just across the mouth of the Ipswich River. Plum Island wasn't part of an estuary in any way; it was a tidal area along the Parker and Ipswich Rivers, and virtually all the groundwater that existed in and around the store was actually seawater. It was in this estuary that the famed Ipswich clam beds lay, where saltwater clams known the world around were harvested. Bill's tomatoes had assimilated the ocean's salt, just as the clams did. In his youthful mind, though, he had grown what he perceived to be the perfect tomato. It was already salted, naturally, which is exactly how he liked his tomatoes. His dreams of big profits were gone. But he had a stash of tasty treats for himself for a brief time, and he was satisfied with that. He made the best of it. Later in life, making the best out of a bad situation would become important. In fact, it would become commonplace and even essential for survival.

– – –

In 1938, the Town of Newburyport had completed construction of a new high school, Mount Rural, only a short walk up Tyng Street from his home. Young Bill Witcomb was a member of the first graduating class. As he was completing his studies, Adolph Hitler was just completing his occupation of Austria. Destined to venture out and change a world that seemed bent on a course of self-destruction, those 1938 graduates had little notion of the tests that would come their way much too soon. War was barely in their vocabulary. They had studied in U.S. history class the

Revolutionary War, the War of 1812, the Civil War, the Spanish-American War, and the Great World War. But a modern war was not on their horizon. Not yet, anyway. If there was war in the world, it was in China, or Slavic Europe, or Spain and of little concern to high school kids from Massachusetts.

Bill Witcomb had been singled out before graduation by the American Legion post in Newburyport. Each year, the Legion members would select the high school senior they deemed to be the most patriotic, and Bill—according to his classmates and teachers—was the logical choice in 1938. At a school assembly, he received a certificate denoting this distinction and quickly rushed home to show his parents. His father was startled and perplexed.

"You're not even an American," he said matter-of-factly to his son. He was right. Bill had never thought of that. For the first time in his life, he faced the stark reality that he was a Canadian by birth and never formally naturalized. This was something he was bound to remedy himself, and the younger Bill Witcomb proudly became a citizen of the United States that same year. He would, from that day forward, boast that he was conceived an Englishman, born a Canadian, but he chose to be an American.

The graduating class of Mount Rural had a tough road ahead of it just finding jobs. Despite the economic recovery of the nation under Roosevelt's New Deal, jobs were still scarce, and really good jobs were nearly impossible to find. Bill Witcomb had known a man in Newburyport who was part of the hierarchy of the F.W. Woolworth Company. He had taken a liking to Bill and had seen him at work in the grocery stores managed by his father. He knew a young man with that kind of drive and customer appeal would do well in any retail environment, and he wanted Bill on his team. He offered Bill a position in the company's premier store on Washington Street in the heart of downtown Boston.

"You'll have to start at the bottom," he told the young Witcomb. "But with John Brown teaching you the business, you can go far." John Brown was the manager of the Boston store, and was known in the retail world for his ability to turn five- and ten-cent sales into big dollars for the stockholders. He was a man made from pig iron and forged in a mold that was doubtlessly destroyed immediately afterward. Boston's store was profitable not only because it carried a wide array of items, but also because it was centrally located downtown, just steps from the subway entrance on Washington Street. This made it accessible to virtually the entire city and extremely accessible for people to slip in and out and purchase their needs in one place, rather than having to travel to several smaller shops around town.

Bill Witcomb started as a stock boy in Boston, commuting from Newburyport on the Boston and Maine Railroad. Each day, the train would leave Newburyport station and travel along the coast through Ipswich, Wenham, Beverly, Salem, and eventually into Boston. It was a long ride both ways, with many stops along the way. It was exhausting. Often, when he worked late to prepare the store for the next day, he would miss the last train north. Bill would curl up on a counter at the store, or on the floor, and sleep there for the night. In the morning, he'd make a quick dash down Washington Street before opening, for coffee and a muffin, then back to the arduous toil. John Brown worked Bill hard, but within a year, young Witcomb was promoted to assistant store manager. The promotion had little to do with Bill's relationship with his highly placed benefactor back in Newburyport, and more to do with his dedication to his job and the people with whom he worked. Just like his father, Bill rose quickly in the Woolworth organization. Brown had immediately seen his potential when he was assigned as a stock boy and quickly put young Bill in charge of eight girls—management still being the exclusive domain of the male gender in 1939. But Bill Witcomb would have risen to it in time regardless. He was a natural leader, dedicated to getting a job done. The girls under him found him easy to look at as well, with his tall slender frame, square shoulders, and swarthy good looks. Bill embodied the fashionable term of the day: tall, dark and handsome. He was a tough taskmaster, but his looks and charm, and the fact that he was an eligible bachelor, combined to make him more than tolerable. The work got done and Bill's department shone. It wasn't long until Brown made him his second in command.

Witcomb gave up commuting each day and moved into an apartment at 11 Walnut Street on Beacon Hill. He rented space at Mrs. Parmerlee's rooms on the third floor and soon became what she called her "star" boarder. He was a tidy young man who attended church each week, and who always had a broad smile and a soft comment for Mrs. Parmerlee when he came into or left the house each day. He got on with the other boarders as well, which made running a boarding house in Boston easier all around.

He would walk past the Massachusetts State House each day, right outside the governor's office window, turn from Beacon Street down to Tremont, then duck down the alley off Tremont across from the Boston Common which led to Washington Street—a mere block from where the Sons of Liberty had rallied around the Liberty Tree a century-and-a-half before. He noticed the smells of the city, different with each season. Summer was, indeed, the most unusual. In the nineteenth century, the harbor was much closer to what is now downtown Boston. A systematic dredging and filling-in of the harbor occurred over a hundred-year period, and land and buildings were now occupying space where square-rigged ships once berthed. In the 1800s there was a thriving molasses industry in Boston, which accounted to some degree for the famed Boston baked beans (molasses being an obligatory ingredient). One such company had a huge vat of molasses give way one day, unleashing a tidal wave of the sticky goo that washed toward the harbor, absorbing everything and everyone in its path. Once it reached the harbor, it actually sank a ship tied alongside by capsizing it when molasses flowed over the decks. The city was never able to remove all the molasses from the cracks and crevices, and toward the end of each summer, the streets and sidewalks around Milk and Tremont Streets would still ooze some of the sugary substance into the air. It was a bittersweet smell, a preposterous mixture like candy and dirt—an incongruity at best.

John Brown had urged Bill from the beginning to get some formal management training, so Bill decided to enroll at Boston University (B.U.), where he attended a class in salesmanship two nights a week. It was hardly a conventional college education, but it was schooling, and Bill dug into it like he had in high school. He excelled in the course. But then, the instructor was preaching to the choir with Bill. His natural abilities as a businessman and salesman far exceeded anything the class had to offer. The only tangible things Bill took from the course were the certificate of completion and the college credits.

In 1940, he was transferred out of Boston to the Chelsea store. This meant commuting again (although a much shorter distance than from Newburyport to Boston). He walked a portion of the trip at both ends and took the subway in the middle. It didn't add that much to his day, but Chelsea lacked the convenience to his room on Beacon Hill that the downtown store offered. Chelsea also offered Bill less chance for advancement. It was not a showcase operation like the Washington Street store. Bill longed to move back home to live. Commuting from any distance was still commuting, and the costs of commuting and living on Beacon Hill were stretching his meager means.

It was during this time that Bill was becoming increasingly more familiar with what was happening in the world outside of America, especially in England. An actual war was now being waged in Europe, a war in which America was to play no immediate role. After all, America had the Neutrality Act, enacted in 1936, and American involvement in foreign hostilities was not an option under the law. Regardless, Bill Witcomb's fervent loyalty and patriotism consumed him. He foresaw a time in the not-too-distant future when America might be entwined in the tentacles of war, and he wanted to serve his newly adopted country. He estimated that he would be better off if he entered military service before a war, in order to get properly trained. His parents felt otherwise. In fact, his mother Elsie was diametrically opposed to military service of any kind as an option for either of her sons. Even though she spent considerable time and expense preparing and shipping Bundles for Britain to family and friends enduring the German Blitzkrieg in England, her sons were not soldiers in her mind. In the caste system in England, the enlisted ranks were the exclusive domain of the lower classes, and officer commissions were offered only to middle- and upper-class individuals. Elsie was going to have nothing to do with her sons enlisting in any army that would condemn them to enlisted ranks, for this was beneath the station to which they were born. She and Clarence had forged their position in the middle class, and nothing—including the patriotic whim of her eldest son—was going to compromise that.

Secretly, Bill met with a Marine Corps recruiter who was delighted at the prospect of having this sturdy young man join his beloved corps. The only obstacle to his induction was his age. In 1940, a military recruit in any service branch had to be twenty-one years of age or have his parent's written permission. At 19, Bill was confronted with the difficult task of having to face Elsie and his father for their consent in order to become a Marine. The answer was a flat, harsh, and resounding *no*!

Having failed to win his relentless argument with his parents over his enlistment in the armed forces, Bill's attention was soon swayed in a new direction. He began courting the young woman who would eventually become his bride. Eleanor Atkinson had been a year behind Bill at Mount Rural, and her father, Willis Atkinson, was owner and proprietor of the Atkinson Lumber Company in Newburyport. While Eleanor saw a dashing young businessman with a bright future with the F. W. Woolworth Company, her father saw something more. Atkinson saw a potential heir to the family business which he had built. Bill Witcomb's work ethic was well established by now, and apparently just as well known. His business potential was obvious to any entrenched businessperson. Willis postulated to himself that this young man could not only be the key to his daughter's happiness, but he could fit in very nicely with the family company. Atkinson offered Bill a job—once again, starting at the bottom—but filled with a foreseeable potential that Woolworth's could never match. Bill would rise through the ranks quickly as he applied his talents to the job. He never once considered that one day he could own and become sole operator of Atkinson Lumber, one of only two major rival firms in the Newburyport area. The job interested him for other reasons.

Bill took the job in a flash. He was able to move back to 11 Tyng Street and stop his commuting between Newburyport and Chelsea, which made the transition to a lower salary seem almost like a raise. The work was tough. He would unload freight cars filled with bags of concrete mix, square off stacks of cut lumber, and generally handle anything that came his way. While his muscles were being strengthened by the arduous labor in the yards, his future bride was attending proper finishing schools at Colby College in New Hampshire, and eventually Wellesley College outside of Boston. Willis Atkinson watched the young former Canadian with a keen eye, realizing that there was more to this young man than simple brawn. His business acuity clearly showed in the way he dealt with the customers and his coworkers, and Bill was quick to offer sound suggestions to his bosses on how to improve the retail operations and turn bigger profits for the company. As he had done at F.W. Woolworth's, Bill did very well at Atkinson Lumber. He went from a common laborer to the assistant treasurer of the company in a year-and-a-half—partially because of his relationship with the boss's daughter, but mostly because of his own initiative and ability. It would have been considered something miraculous, had it not been Bill Witcomb doing it. But he was truly a natural. He had leadership qualities and a sense for straightforward business dealings that drew people and customers toward him like a magnet. Willis Atkinson sat back and counted his blessings, as well as his profits.

As dazzling as his rise was within the company, he remained the humble tradesman that his father had taught him to be back in the grocery store on Plum Island. Bill always believed that service to customers was the thing that brings about repeat business, and the long-term dollar far outshone the short-term profit schemes that cost much and offered little to the consumer. Bill's Christian charity and sense of fair play were the controlling forces within him. He had been reared on the Golden Rule, and he had tried to live by that standard each day. As a result, he and his company prospered. But all that would change abruptly one Sunday afternoon in December, when he and the nation learned the worst. A remote paradise that he'd only read about in school books and seen photographed in the *National Geographic* magazine had been suddenly and deliberately attacked by naval and air forces of the Empire of Japan. America was officially at war the next day, and the gauntlet thrown down by President Roosevelt to provide the American people with the ultimate and complete victory was at hand. There was no way that Elsie could stop her eldest son now. The rules that controlled American society had all been blown away with the bombs that fell on Hawaii. Bill was going to enlist. Thus, he began his longest journey.

Chapter 3

Discipline and Training

The Pearl Harbor disaster was the most shocking and alarming call-to-arms that America had ever experienced up to that point in time. A prosperous democracy at peace was suddenly thrust into the plume of a flame that was a world war. Life, as most Americans knew it, was inexorably altered. Sunday—traditionally a family day of rest—would never again be a time when all Americans would sleep peacefully. The map of the world would never again look the same. A new American paradigm emerged that placed demands upon every mother's son, and Elsie Witcomb's sons were no exception. Before the Germans and the Japanese would capitulate three-and-a-half years later, the bonds and boundaries of her motherhood, like all American mothers, would be sorely tested.

December 1941 was a perilous time, fraught with terrible consequences for each and every decision that was made. Soldiers, sailors, and airmen who were part of the United States armed forces at that time were confronted not only with the prospects of fighting a global war on two fronts, but also were charged with the responsibility of getting the new army, navy and army air force properly prepared to participate in that war. Bill Witcomb had been right in his thinking that those who were in the military prior to America's involvement in the hostilities would be better prepared and positioned for the job ahead. But the future preparedness of America's military hinged upon a single point—those soldiers and sailors had seen the level of preparedness of the U.S. military before Pearl Harbor, they vowed to move forward, and they never looked back. The armada of ships and planes, and vastness of the ground, sea, and air forces that would be needed to defeat the Axis powers, would so overshadow the standing American military of pre-December 1941 that America would from that point forward be known as a military superpower. The Arsenal of Democracy would be a difficult entity to create before it would be poised to unleash a juggernaut upon a world map. Elsie's eldest son was destined to play a significant role in developing a portion of it.

Bill marched himself to the recruiting station in Haverhill, Massachusetts where he and his neighbors lined up to enlist on Monday, December 8th. His patriotism and convictions hadn't wavered for an instant. Like most young Americans, not once did he consider not serving. The only question before him was how he was going to serve. In his youth, he had always envisioned himself a soldier—that's why he had chosen the Marine Corps in his ill-fated attempt at enlistment a year-and-a-half earlier. It had been his little brother Ken who had shown a fascination for airplanes. But faced with the decision of which branch of the military to serve in, Bill elected to join the Army Air Force (AAF). (The Air Force did not become a separate branch of the service until 1947.) He reckoned at that time that being a trained aircraft mechanic might prove beneficial after the war was over, the presumption being that civil aviation would only grow in time. Like most enlistees, he was certain that the war would be over in six months or so, and he would be able to resume his career in no time. After enduring the routine induction physical and completing all the paperwork, Bill said his goodbyes to his family and sweetheart Eleanor Atkinson, and boarded a train to Boston to go fight a war with millions of other young Americans, each being paid at the rate of $21.00 per month. It was their duty, they reasoned, and they were going to do it.

– – –

Like most inductees, Bill Witcomb was wrenched from his home surroundings and transplanted to a part of the country that was completely unfamiliar to him. He was given an enlisted man's identity number, 11021140, as a means of specific identification. It may have been dehumanizing in one sense, but in 1941 no one made an issue of that. He did his initial, albeit short-lived, basic training at Jefferson Barracks outside St. Louis. It was a flat piece of ground, void of any charm by his way of thinking, and completely lacking an ocean like his home on the Massachusetts north shore. An ocean close at hand was essential to living the good life by Bill's standards. The only body of water close at hand was a straight drainage ditch that ran alongside the camp to channel the run off water after it rained. Despite its size, there were fish there to catch. One of the recruits from down south peered into the tiny stream and commented, "We got one a them back home—we call it a creek." Another from the Midwest stared into the water with his hands shoved deep in his pockets and said, "We call ours a brook." Still a third, with a shake of his head said in a cynical Brooklyn twang, "We got one too—we call it a sewer." And thus the drainage ditch at Jefferson Barracks quickly became the place where the men would catch what they called "sewer trout" and have the cooks fry them up for an additional protein ration above and beyond what the government provided them.

As Bill and his fellow recruits stepped off the train that delivered them to the camp, all were suffering from the worst case of diarrhea they had ever experienced. Being cramped aboard that train was the equivalent of being confined in a cattle car. The water served at meals, though obtained fresh at each whistle stop, was held in tanks aboard the dining cars, and they were seldom, if ever, sanitized, making them the perfect breeding ground for all sorts of germs and bacteria. It was a wonder that diarrhea was all the recruits had contracted. A three-day pass was offered by the commanding officer (CO) to the first recruit to have a normal bowel movement, although how the CO was going to verify this was anyone's guess. Bill and the others were trundled into a classroom at one point, and a matronly nurse spoke to all of them about hygiene, in camp and in the field. She was articulate, even graphic at times, in her descriptions and sound in her reasoning. "Fear God," she lectured eloquently, "and keep your bowels open" —words, indeed, to live by.

The recruits were outfitted with all kinds of equipment, much of it foreign to many of them. Bill and his unit were pushed through the supply building that eventually became known in the Air Force as the *green monster*. Here they were fitted for uniforms and their personal issue. On one such visit, the troops were all issued overshoes. The quartermaster personnel would place one overshoe on a recruit's foot, and the sergeant in charge would say, "Dat's a fit," and send them on their way. Bill noticed a group of troops who had all come in from South Carolina that morning. They all got their overshoes the same as the rest—if it was on your foot, it was the right size. That evening, as darkness was starting to fall over the barracks, Bill heard a great commotion coming from the green monster. It was all the South Carolina troops yelling at the sergeant that their overshoes didn't fit.

"What's the matter with them?" questioned the supply sergeant.

"They're all too big," they barked in reply.

"Try putting them on *over* your shoes," instructed the sergeant, shaking his head as he closed the door to the green monster and bolted it shut. "Damn hillbillies," he muttered to himself. Therein lay the essence of adapting to the military way of life—getting used to things that were unfamiliar to you. Southern troops had little use for overshoes, given the climate in which they lived, and few had ever seen such things. Troops from the north had difficulty adapting to the southern ways as well—Bill would eventually find Southern traditions associated with the treatment of Negroes completely unacceptable.

Thousands of young men were crammed into the camp to learn the basics of military life at Jefferson Barracks. All recruits were trained in basic cleanliness, a foreign concept for many with whom Bill served. Diarrhea was not to be the only disease that confronted the young recruits. Added to this were the casualties that could be expected from colds and pneumonia resulting from sleeping in nothing but tents in the middle of winter as snow fell outside the folded flap of canvas. A simple tiny coke stove in the center of the tent was their only source of heat. Eight men would fold themselves into the narrow confines of an umbrella tent, sleeping on canvas cots; all were reminded constantly of the bitter chill as the cold air circulated beneath them under that thin layer of comfortless canvas that was stretched taut between the wooden frame members of their cots. Many lined the tops of their cots with old newspapers in order to insulate them better from the cold air, but their efforts were futile.

Sleeping on a cot rather than in a bed was difficult to get used to at first, but the arduous days of marching, hiking, physical training, and close-order drill made it easier to accept at the end of the day. Those taut web mattresses of fabric, with no give and no warmth, were suddenly a haven for the weary troops after a forced twenty-mile hike with full field packs and Enfield rifles carried at high port. The trainees kept their full uniforms on, with overcoat, boots, and overshoes, in a vain effort to keep warm amid the winter at Jefferson Barracks.

The few showers that were practical, given the frigid weather conditions and the primitive plumbing, unlike home, were never a time for private contemplation. Trainees showered together, shaved together, and sat on toilets six and eight abreast—in some latrines, the commodes were in double lines facing each other in open rows. Modesty was maintained in the towel that cloaked the lower body. Everything else was more or less public and—in time—taken for granted.

Military meals during basic training were an adventure that most recruits would have easily forgone had it not been for the need for sustenance and, in some situations, recreation. Whether recruits considered meals a physical necessity or pure cuisine, it was a forced three-mile march each way to and from the mess hall for Bill Witcomb and his platoon. Meal trays made of cold metal were poor substitutes for Mom's oven-warmed white china, and tables surfaced with some strange composite material made of hard and impersonal linoleum-like material were no replacement for the linen or lace tablecloths that the boys had left at home. But then, these young men were not being trained to sit at a properly set table and display proper Sunday table manners. They were being trained for war. Utility was the underlying keystone to their training, and elimination of Mom's frills and fancies was essential to the task. They were no longer Mom's boys—they were the Army's men, and they were expected to behave as such.

The food was a far cry from Mom's fare as well. Creamed chipped beef on toast was served at breakfast each day, along with a dollop of scrambled eggs, a strip or two of bacon or a couple of sausages, and all washed down with the blackest coffee imaginable. Occasionally there were truly fresh eggs, a special treat for Bill Witcomb. Powdered eggs and milk were available to the military, but not yet in the abundant quantities necessary for feeding ten thousand men at once. This would change in due time. Like the training, the food was basic: lots of starch, some protein, and an ample portion of fat. For many, it was a step up. The Great Depression had left half the country hungry for over a decade, and military service for many of the recruits meant they were eating three square meals a day for the first time in years. While those from moderate and prosperous households had looked upon the food as barely palatable, others beheld a feast. This was the fundamental nature of military basic training: bringing those who are up down to a moderate level, bringing those who are down up to that same level, and keeping those in the middle roughly where they were when they started. Military food was merely a metaphor for the underlying objectives of basic training.

The recruits were compelled to take turns assisting in the preparation of the meals, and in the cleanup. This was in keeping with the military notion that everyone in the service could be called upon to do any job at any time. Kitchen Patrol, or K.P. as it was better known, was the military's way of spreading the workload around. It achieved two primary objectives: it got the work done, and it kept the recruits busy. There were just so many trained military cooks available, and their job was far too big to be handled just by them. Therefore, unskilled work—the "grunt work"—was to be provided by the recruits themselves. Lugging crates and cartons of food to preparation tables from loading docks outside the chow hall, scrubbing floors, washing pots and pans, setting the tables and, of course, peeling the mountains of potatoes were customary assignments for the rotating unskilled workforce. Cooks in white uniforms and aprons would oversee each squad in the task it was assigned, making sure that all chores were carried out the Army way. Sugar bowls, salt and pepper shakers, and napkin holders were aligned on each table, forming a perfect row. A string was strung down the length of the tables to ensure everything was in proper order. Adjustments were then made to ensure that the hall was in perfect alignment. A warrant officer would position himself so that he could look down the line of tables and eyeball the lineup of the condiments. When he once commented, "Soldier, your sugar bowls aren't dressed properly," to a man from Bill Witcomb's platoon, the soldier marched over to the head table, stared down the row of tables like a general inspecting the troops, then brought himself to full attention. With polished military bearing and precision, as though he were a drill instructor barking out orders on the parade grounds, he called out the command:

"Sugar bowls, and sugar bowls only, DRESS—RIGHT—DRESS!"

The warrant officer didn't appreciate being mocked by a mere recruit, and the man was condemned to peeling potatoes for the remainder of his stay on K.P. And, since potatoes were the mainstay of virtually every meal, there were plenty of potatoes for him to peel.

The serving lines were scrubbed down after each meal, and then replenished with fresh ice. Steam tables with stainless steel chafing trays held enormous amounts of the entrée of the day, along with the side dishes of mashed vegetables and gravies. Ladles were used to plop a portion of food onto the metal mess kit of the recruit in line for his meal. When the ladle connected with the metal mess kit, it barked out a sound that implied it was time for that recruit to move on to the next station. Second helpings were something usually only gotten at home. Slowly but steadily, like automobiles being assembled in the manufacturing plants of Detroit, the recruits moved through the chow line assembling their meals. They would then sit down on benches and wait for their table to be filled before diving into their food. That was part of the discipline—waiting to eat. A short period with all heads bowed around the table allowed each man to give thanks in his own way, then dive into the tray of calories before him. Meals at home, and even in restaurants, were different not only in taste, but in the sound. At home, one could hear the melodious sounds of silver utensils chiming against fine china. It was almost musical. The tiny tinkle of crystal wine glasses and the warmth of friendly discussion were the sounds of contentment and of fulfillment. Here, at Jefferson Barracks, it was different. Stainless steel serving utensils slamming onto aluminum alloy mess kits had replaced that music. It was a harsh and bitter chorus, almost alarming; like gunfire. And the sounds of contentment heard from family members who were enjoying a leisurely Sunday feast were replaced by hundreds of grumbling recruits with stuffed mouths who would scurry through their meal just to be done with the ordeal, while simultaneously carrying on a conversation. It was feudalistic. It was Neanderthal.

It was the ultimate responsibility of each recruit to keep his own kit clean. That meant his rifle, his laundry, his bunk area, his mess kit, and himself. It was tough enough to remain clean of body, given the infrequency of hot showers. Keeping your personal area and bunk clean was nearly impossible because of the dust, coupled with the obvious problems inherent in living inside four canvas walls with more than half a dozen roommates. Keeping your rifle clean was not optional under any circumstances. This, after all, was the Army. Keeping your laundry clean was difficult, since most of the recruits wore every stitch of clothing issued to them just to stay warm. As for the mess kits, after finishing meals, recruits would line up near two barrels of hot water—one soapy, the other clear. They would simply dunk their aluminum mess kit into the soapy water a few times, and then rinse it in the clear hot water tub. That was considered sufficient to cleanse away all the debris and all the germs that had collected on the metal. Bill Witcomb didn't buy it. Instead, he went to the Post Exchange (P.X.) and purchased half a dozen bottles of Williams' Shaving Lotion. After the ritual cleansing at the end of each meal, Bill would swab out his mess kit with the shaving lotion. The 85% alcohol content of the lotion killed off the spores and germs and kept him in the peak of health. There was a very slight aftertaste that was present with each meal, but the reassurance of knowing that it was safe to eat from the kit made it bearable for Bill. Others, who were less conscientious about cleanliness, were contracting all sorts of diseases, from simple diarrhea to dysentery.

An outbreak of spinal meningitis took its toll on the station, but offered an upside for Bill and his squad. A fellow recruit named Taber had contracted the deadly disease. The moment his case was diagnosed, the medics swooped into that portion of the camp and pulled everyone out that had been in close contact with Taber. Taber had been in Bill Witcomb's training group, so the entire platoon was removed from the tent city that had been their home and that occupied the far reaches of the training base, and was relocated into wooden two-story barracks buildings. Here Bill and his group would stay in quarantine for two-and-a-half of the coldest weeks of the year. Within those wooden walls, there was plenty of heat on the ground floor. Running water in real sinks for daily ablutions, meals were delivered hot three times a day in aluminum trays, and the dirty dishes were collected afterward. Those delivering the food would place the meals at the top steps outside the barracks door, and then run for their lives in fear that they would catch the dreaded meningitis. The only diversion for the quarantined troops was a basketball that was delivered to the barracks one day by mistake. They made the best use of it they could, creating a makeshift court on the first floor squad bay and establishing "house rules." But it was two-and-a-half weeks of boredom at best. No schooling, no drill. The food was first-rate though, and they were given as much ice cream as they could eat—a rare treat, certainly, for mere recruits. When the quarantine was up, Bill and the others were returned to the frozen tents for the remainder of their stay on the post. It was still cold, but the worst of the winter had now passed.

It was there, at Jefferson Barracks, that Bill Witcomb learned his most important military lesson. It was a lesson that he would carry with him throughout his life. He was fortunate enough to have a drill sergeant who had served in the last war, and who had trained troops ever after. The sergeant gave them two words to live by that became the watchwords of Bill's tour of duty, indeed, for his entire life. The sergeant stood before them on the first real day of training after the quarantine and addressed them like a college professor addressing an auditorium filled with undergraduates. He strutted a little, but stopped cold in his tracks when he uttered the two words.

"Men, while you are here, it's my job to teach you what you need to know to get you through this war. And I'm here to tell ya, there are only two things that will get you safely through. Those two things are *discipline* and *training*." *Discipline* and *training*—those two words would become Bill Witcomb's personal doctrine.

Throughout the weeks of basic training, Bill Witcomb and all the trainees drilled with the famous British Enfield—a .303-caliber, bolt-action rifle that, up until that time, had been the consummate military field weapon in the world. It was long and it was heavy, but it was considered among the finest military bolt-action rifles ever manufactured. It was reliable, and in early 1942 it was the only shoulder weapon available in sufficient quantities to train all the new recruits. Bill Witcomb qualified at a level sufficient to be trained as a sharpshooter. But Bill Witcomb had joined the Army Air Force, and the Army Air Force had little need for sharpshooters.

– – –

As an enlisted recruit, Bill was not destined to fly in the Army Air Force, although his desire to do so was growing with each passing day. Only officers served as pilots, and the vast majority of them were college boys, graduates of prestigious private schools or the famed military academy at West Point. Although a good student at Mount Rural High School and at Boston University night school, Bill was not considered a college boy by any stretch of the imagination. They were mostly those fortunate few who attended the Ivy League schools, or the top ten. Night school boys like Bill were pretty much always enlisted personnel, assigned to carry the load while others defined it. This was the essence of the age-old caste system employed by every military force in history. Even the location of insignia of rank was demonstrative of the philosophy behind this ancient two-tiered system. Officers wore their ranks on their shoulders, representative of the burden of command that would weigh upon those shoulders. Enlisted men wore their insignia on their sleeves, where their muscles were located, signifying their reliance upon those muscles in order to carry and use the weapons of war. Bill Witcomb was headed toward a military career in aviation, but as a mechanic, not a pilot. He accepted that with understanding, and maintained pride and dignity in the knowledge that he was serving his country. After all, that was the whole purpose of his being in the military. If the Army Air Force wanted him on the ground turning a wrench, that was perfectly acceptable to him. Although …

– – –

As his basic training ended, Bill Witcomb was trucked north to Chanute Field in Illinois for advanced training as an airplane mechanic. The Army Air Force had a variety of airplanes that it flew, and all needed maintenance regularly—some more than others. There would be plenty of work to do—of that there was no doubt.

Springtime was in full bloom when Bill arrived at Chanute Field. There was color in abundance as nature opened her closet and displayed her entire colorful wardrobe. The air was soft, offering no hint of the winter that had ravaged the Midwest that year. The bitter chill of Jefferson Barracks was behind him. Chanute Field was a complex of runways with adjacent hangars, wooden two-story barracks that badly needed painting, and yet another set of chow halls like those at Jefferson Barracks. It was a military post, a training post, nothing more, nothing less. Everything had a purpose. Nothing was for show. It was utilitarian … Spartan … military.

As he had done in high school and at B.U., Bill dove into his studies with everything he had. He learned about the inner workings of airplane engines; how the magnetos fired, how the propeller shaft was propelled by the sequential firing of the pistons, how the carburetor mixed air and fuel in the appropriate cocktail to ensure maximum combustion and power. He learned about the mechanisms that allowed for retractable landing gear, and about the cabling which connected the stick in the cockpit to the control surfaces of the airplane. He learned about hydraulics and Pascal's law of fluid dynamics: important stuff for those who repair and maintain airplanes—more important stuff still for those who fly them. Each day, Bill would reserve some time between lunch and his afternoon classes to sit outside a hangar and watch airplanes. He watched young inexperienced pilots take off and land; he watched them taxi. He couldn't fathom why one needed a college degree to pilot those airplanes. But there it was, and there he was.

With only two weeks left of his formal mechanical training, he sat on the bench one day outside hangar number four with a classmate. Bill was eating a tomato that he had smuggled out of the chow hall after lunch, and his classmate had an apple that had been given to him by a Red Cross lady the night before. It was a bright, early afternoon, with puffy wisps of clouds floating in front of a cobalt blue sky. As they sat there, admiring the grace and ease of the takeoffs and landings, a P-39 pursuit aircraft came into sharp focus before them. The pilot was attempting to land with his gear retracted. Whether or not he knew that his gear was up was not clear. What was clear is that he was going to belly land on Chanute Field. The pair of mechanic trainees winced while they watched in awe as the plane touched down on the hard black-tarred runway. The jolt of impact had apparently startled the young aviator, who reacted with too much rudder control with his left foot. The plane started veering off the runway and began sliding across the tarmac and toward hangar number four, sparks, dust, and smoke spewing from its underside. With a noise like rapidly approaching thunder, the plane skated toward Bill, twisting and yawing as it moved, wing tips flapping up and down jerkily. With a subtle but sudden quiet, like turning off a radio that was broadcasting only static, it finally came to rest a few yards from where Bill and his colleague sat eating their fruit. Bill looked at his classmate. His classmate looked at him. As the pilot emerged from the cockpit, a thin cloud of dust and smoke still climbing into the air from beneath the plane, with the propeller stationary, its three blades either bent or broken off completely, the pair of mechanic trainees both blurted out, as though singing from a hymnal, "Hell, we can do as good as that!"

The following day, Bill and that classmate were in the orderly room of the training squadron requesting applications for flight school. Both postulated that their worst screw-ups would have to furnish better results than what they had witnessed the previous afternoon, and both were determined, now more than ever, to fly. The first sergeant had other ideas. He was old-school Army. He had come up through the ranks after the First World War and saw no reason why anyone should make the quantum leap from enlisted trainee to officer candidate simply by filling out an application or passing some silly test. He bellowed at the trainees what he deemed to be the obvious:

"Those boys are *college boys*. They're *educated* boys. They went to school a long time and studied a lot of technical things in order to pass that entrance exam. You two only have high school educations. You don't know enough. You'll fail!"

"Can't we try?" asked Private Witcomb.

"What would be the sense?" demanded the first sergeant. "You'll fail, and all you would have done is waste your time and the Army's time."

"Sergeant, can't we at least try to pass the exam?" they pleaded. After much vacillation, the first sergeant reluctantly caved to their request and obtained the necessary paperwork for them to apply for flight school.

The applications were completed, and the examinations were forwarded to the squadron for administration. A hardnosed captain, a more-or-less disgruntled group adjutant, was assigned to proctor the exam, and he sat there in the classroom scrupulously observing the pair of privates who were laboring over the exam. He was familiar with the flight school entrance exam. He knew firsthand the difficult challenge before the pair of trainees. He had taken it and failed. His college education had proven insufficient for the challenge of the flight examination. The exam was laden with trigonometry, chemistry, and physics questions that could stump even a seasoned professor. Bill and his colleague bore down hard with each section of the exam. It was a come-as-you-are test, which was geared to assess what you had retained over a long period of time, not what you could cram into your head just prior to taking the exam. There was no way they could have studied for it, no way other than having acquired the appropriate knowledge before joining the Army Air Force. The six hours of examination ticked by slowly for the young captain. But for the pair of privates, it seemed like only seconds. Once completed, the pair returned to their mechanical training while the exams were scored. It took some time for the results to be posted, but both passed their examinations with flying colors. Bill Witcomb had received one of the highest grades ever recorded on the flight school entrance exam. And he did that with just a high school diploma from Mount Rural High School and a couple of college courses in salesmanship. With the exam behind him, a few days later he was headed off to flight school and a whole new set of challenges. Now *discipline* and *training* would count more than ever.

Chapter 4

"Lord, Make This a Good Flight"

More train rides were in store for Bill Witcomb before he'd see flight school, but on these occasions there would be no diarrhea. *Discipline* and *training* had already yielded great rewards. They had taught him how to monitor and control his intake, thereby minimizing his risk of disease. Of course the trains weren't as crowded as the one that had fetched him from Boston to St. Louis, nor were the rides as long. And Bill had remembered the words of that matronly nurse at Jefferson Barracks—*Fear God, and keep your bowels open.* He did just that. He scrutinized his diet, and he tried to limit his fluid intake to bottled beverages or hot coffee. Whatever he did, it worked. He arrived at Kelly and Randolph Fields in San Antonio, Texas in the crest of health, ready and eager to begin his training. There would be no reacclimation time necessary after this trip—no need for the previous inducement of a three-day pass. He was fit and ready to learn and just twenty-one years old.

It was in the shadow of the famed Alamo that Bill Witcomb would acquire a new identity number as an officer candidate, 0674074, and where he would learn the basics of aeronautics in ground school. It was there that he learned, for the first time, that he had two middle names given to him by his parents—he was actually Charles William *Henry* Witcomb—a common-enough practice in Europe and Canada at the time of his birth, but somewhat extraordinary in the United States.

The pilot trainees saw airplanes at Kelly Field, but were allowed to touch none of them. The subject of navigation, both celestial and dead reckoning, was covered in depth, including practical ground exercises for the flight cadets. They were to fix their positions on aeronautical charts using only the minimum amount of information and instrument readings they were given. The cadets were also instructed in the fundamental theories regarding airflow over and under an airfoil. The concept of lift plus thrust overcoming weight plus drag was drilled into their heads—no plane on earth could fly without satisfying that formula. They were taught about fuel mixtures and how combustion at varying altitudes is different than it is on the ground. They learned how these ratios must be precisely monitored and adjusted in flight in order to make the engines run at peak efficiency. After all, control of the power plant was the key to sustained flight. The cadets were also, parenthetically, being shown how to be officers. Bill Witcomb ranked at the top of his classes at both Kelly and Randolph Fields, where he was competing openly with college graduates. It had been easy for officials in the military to confuse schooling with education. It was clear from the training results that Bill was a highly educated man, despite the fact that he lacked formal schooling.

Within a few weeks, Bill and his fellow cadets were aboard yet another railroad train, bound this time for Spartan Aeronautics at Muskogee, Oklahoma. It was at Muskogee that many of the young American military pilots took their initial, or primary, flight training. Like Jefferson Barracks and Chanute Field, the Spartan Aerodrome was just another training base—utilitarian and barren, desolate almost to a fault. There seemed to be dust everywhere. And, for the first time, Bill was confronted on all sides with strong southern accents and protracted drawls that he often had trouble understanding, himself being a New England Yankee. Of course, the reciprocal was true as well. Bill maintained a strong north shore twang more reminiscent of a New Hampshire farmer, and his rapid way of talking was often difficult for the southern boys to follow, much less fully comprehend.

It was at Spartan Aeronautics that Bill Witcomb would meet his primary flight instructor, C. J. Wertz. Mr. Wertz, as he was always to be addressed by his students, was a civilian instructor hired by the Army to teach new pilots how to fly. He was a tough taskmaster, a square-shouldered handsome man who seemed ill-at-ease in a flight suit but perfectly natural sitting in a cockpit. He always wore a tie, but it was usually loosened at his collar button. His eyes were mere slits and his mouth seemed to exist more on the right side of his face than on his left. He seldom smiled and was perpetually reluctant to stand for photographs, deeming the process of recording historic events a colossal waste of time.

When flying with his students, Mr. Wertz would sit in the dummy seat—the front seat—of the open cockpit monoplane and instruct students through a hearing tube that ran to the pilot's seat. The students would listen to him through the ear tubes and execute the instructions he gave them. Mr. Wertz would put them through their paces and, when he was satisfied that they were ready to solo, he would light up a cigarette while they were taxiing. Just as they reached the parking spot where the other students were standing, he'd blow smoke through the talking tube. The students on the sidelines would see the smoke coming out of the ears of the student pilot, signifying that he had passed his primary and was ready to solo.

The plane assigned to Bill Witcomb was shared by another flight cadet named Weikal and bore the number 70 on the nose. It was a metal-skinned, single-engine tail-dragger that was considered by experienced pilots easy to fly. Of course, for young flight students, it was like trying to control a drunken and angry rhinoceros. Unlike tricycle landing gear, which kept an airplane in a relatively upright position and steered more or less like an automobile, tail-draggers had to be propelled into a flying position. Once they reached a certain speed, the tail would naturally lift from the ground, making the fuselage somewhat level. Depending on the critical angle of the airfoil—the angle at which optimum lift could be achieved—each tail-dragger would reach maximum lift at varying angles. A few more knots of airspeed, and the pilot could rotate the stick backward and literally launch the plane into the air. This meant that the pilot never had a clear view of what was directly in front of him when he was on the ground. He had to rely upon his ability to look outside the cockpit, and his ability to maneuver the plane slightly during taxi, takeoff, and landing. Crawling around on the ground was best achieved by weaving back and forth using the entire width of taxiways, much like a drunken driver on a deserted road. The fuselage of the airplane would be at an angle to the taxiway, allowing the student to see down its length. The student could then yaw in the other direction and see around the other side of the plane. "Old Number 70," as the plane was known, was a beast. But it was a beast that had to be mastered by Weikal and Bill Witcomb if they were to move ahead in their flying careers.

The late summer and early fall had been hot. There was an absence of stormy weather, which gave the trainees ample cockpit time to accomplish their mission of flight. Each man had to log ten hours with his instructor before he would be permitted to attempt a solo flight. Without the solo, there was no hope of ever being a pilot of any kind. Bill had ten hours, but he still ground looped virtually every time he had the controls. Ground looping is a radical direction change of the plane on the ground by an inexperienced pilot who has not learned the elements of trim and subtle adjustments that are needed to control an airplane in flight or on the ground. Mr. Wertz was not impressed.

"I'll give you two more hours, Witcomb," said the crusty instructor with a snarl, secretly hoping that the young cadet would be able to meet the minimum standards. Wertz knew that the Army was pushing these kids through fast enough, but there was nothing he could do. There was a war on, and those who would fight it had to learn their jobs in a terrible hurry. On paper, Bill Witcomb was the best of the bunch. But he tended to over-control each time he was in flight. Instead of easing the stick back gently on takeoff, he would pull back hard, causing the nose to spike upward, thus dropping the airspeed. He would then overcorrect and push forward too far on the stick, causing the plane to slam back down onto the runway, picking up momentum as it sank from the air. It was as though Bill was trying to bully the airplane into compliance rather than gently coaxing it to obey. He hadn't yet accepted the fact that airplanes prefer subtle changes in their controls, and respond somewhat slowly to those changes. It had Mr. Wertz perplexed as to how to correct the young cadet. He'd never before encountered a more natural book student and, at the same time, a worse practical one. Giving the kid two more hours of practice time might just do it, he thought. "But after that," he bellowed to Bill, "if you can't cut it, it's back to turning wrenches." Bill understood all too well.

Bill stood by and watched as his fellow cadet, Weikal, took his test flight with Mr. Wertz. While in primary, Bill had been first at everything but this final test. Weikal was a lanky beanpole who wore size thirteen boots and had a nose that seemed to run from his forehead to his chin. He was a good student and a good friend to Bill. He didn't want to outshine Bill that day, but, like Bill, he wasn't given an alternative. This was his test, and either he made the grade today or packed his bags for some military fate other than flying. The plane taxied away from the apron where Bill stood watching; Mr. Wertz in the front seat facing forward, Weikal in the rear seat glancing back at his friend over his shoulder. Bill clasped his hands in front of him and shook them in a gesture of good luck and congratulations. Weikal nodded his appreciation and Old Number 70 fishtailed back and forth on the narrow taxiway, giving the pilot alternating views of the path ahead—first portside, then starboard, and so on. It then strolled down the runway and lifted off smoothly, banking at the far end of the field and turning out of the pattern before moving on.

Twenty minutes later Old Number 70 chirped out its presence on the runway as the tires hit the tarmac and began to spin. Weikal put her down easy, cut back on the throttle, and maneuvered her to the taxiway near the patch of grass where Bill stood waiting. The other cadets stood around by the hanger or by other airplanes, awaiting either their turns or their instructors. Mr. Wertz could be seen sitting in the front seat, his mouth covered by the talking tube, his eyes obscured by a set of goggles. Suddenly, as Weikal cut the engine and the wobbly aircraft came slowly to a stop on the grass, Bill could see smoke coming out from under the earflaps on Weikal's flying cap. He had his goggles perched on top of his head, the chinstrap unbuckled, and a grin on his face that wouldn't go away. Mr. Wertz never told him that he had passed. Weikal knew because he could smell the cigarette smoke being blown through the talking tube, and he knew that he had been put on display by his instructor. Bill Witcomb grinned from ear to ear as well. He was happy for his friend. The other cadets laughed a bit, and nodded their congratulations. Mr. Wertz dismounted the airplane as Cadet Weikal restarted the engine, waited for the signal lamp from the tower, and eventually took off for his solo flight.

Spartan was like most military bases in the early 1940s. It was an encampment filled with young men. Some were still in their mid-teens; others, like Bill, were in their early twenties, and still others were slightly older. Anyone over twenty-three was considered an old man. Being at their stage of life, they were still filled with youthful energy and anticipation. Physical exercise was one thing that held them more or less in check. They played baseball and football whenever there was free time. Bill Witcomb especially liked football. There was a rugged sense of competition in football that appealed to him. Maybe it was the contact of the tackles, the rowdiness of the blocking, or the fact that it was played out on a grid that was reminiscent of an air map. Maybe it was because the passing game was akin to aerial warfare. Regardless of the subconscious reasons, Bill openly loved it and never missed a chance to join a pick-up game somewhere on the station. Toward the end of his training, when Mr. Wertz was near the end of his patience with trainees who had yet to solo, Bill participated in a game of football where he received the ball and started running for long yardage. Unfortunately, the opposing team was onto him, and tackled him with thunderous and overwhelming power. Bill hit the ground hard, clutching the ball with all his might. Several of the opposition fell on top of him as well, and, in the process, cracked several of Bill's ribs.

Bill was in agony as he emerged from the infirmary. Inside the clinic the doctors were all busy with some emergency case, so a nurse and corpsman taped him up to keep his chest movements to a minimum, thus allowing the cracked ribs to eventually heal. The tape restricted his upper body movements tremendously. Not only was football out of the question, flying appeared to be in serious jeopardy as well, even though no report of his medical condition had made it to his squadron. Today was the day for his final flight with Mr. Wertz and his final flying test. He either made it this day or he was destined to be a mechanic and never hold the controls of a military airplane again. With the help of his fellow cadets, he got himself taped up and suited up properly in his flying suit—an overall with pockets on the chest and a belt about the waist. He walked a little stiff-legged, but maybe nobody would notice.

Mr. Wertz asked if he was ready for his examination, and Bill hesitatingly said yes. Weikal helped Bill with his parachute while Mr. Wertz attended to some papers in the operations hut, then the pair walked out to Old Number 70 and prepared for the flight. Mr. Wertz climbed aboard first and got in the front seat as usual while Bill Witcomb did a preflight walk around, kicking the tires gingerly so as not to exacerbate the condition of his ribs. He pulled on the prop while Mr. Wertz sat impatiently in the cockpit. Bill scrutinized the airplane, searching desperately for a defect in the craft in the hopes that he could postpone this crucial flight, but there was absolutely nothing wrong with Old Number 70, aside from it being old and underpowered. The flight would have to go on as scheduled. He climbed into the cockpit, wincing with pain as he swung his leg over the cowling, and seated himself. Fortunately, Mr. Wertz was still facing forward. It took Bill longer than usual to strap in, given the constraints of his bandaging, and Mr. Wertz grew impatient and asked what was taking so long.

"Just checking the control linkage," said Bill through teeth clenched in pain. "I wouldn't want anything to go wrong. I like staying on the safe side."

"That's the side to be on, Witcomb," replied Wertz without turning around. "The safe side."

"Yes, sir," was all that Bill could get out. Finally seated as he should be, sitting on his parachute and strapped in by his safety belt, Bill turned on the switch and yelled, "Clear." The propeller turned slowly at first, and then burst to life with a roar. Bill adjusted the fuel mixture slightly to get the desired revolutions per minute (RPM), then motioned with his hands to the private standing by with the fire extinguisher. Bill's thumbs were pointed outward and he drew his hands apart, symbolizing that he wanted the wheel chocks pulled out for takeoff. The young private did as instructed and cleared away from the aircraft. Bill gently pushed the throttle forward and the plane began to move. Turning, pushing, and pulling the aircraft controls very gently was the best that Bill could manage. Every movement meant pain. He was trussed up like a turkey for Thanksgiving and he could barely move inside the narrow cockpit. Old Number 70 retraced the path that Weikal had taken two days before, weaving back and forth down the narrow taxiway, then out onto the active runway. Bill lined up the nose for the center of the runway, and then did one last check to make certain everything was working properly. He said a quick prayer silently—"Lord, make this a good flight"—then walked the throttle forward until it was at maximum.

The little plane rolled down the runway and the tail lifted off the ground gently, bringing Bill and the cockpit up to the point where he could see the runway in front of him. He pulled back ever so slightly on the stick and the nose barely changed position. Bill was convinced that he was going to fail. But suddenly, Old Number 70 lifted off the ground. Bill felt the wheels stop vibrating and the little metal aircraft suddenly remove itself from the surface of the earth. Bill pulled back just a touch more and executed the most perfect takeoff of his short flying career. It was as smooth a takeoff as C.J. Wertz had ever seen from a student. At the far end of the field, Mr. Wertz instructed Bill to bank left and climb to five thousand feet. Bill gently eased the stick over and gave it a little rudder pedal. The plane obediently responded, making a flawless sixty-second turn ninety degrees to port. It was a textbook maneuver. Wertz put the cadet through the usual paces—a couple of turns, a loop, and a roll. He had him stall the plane and recover at five thousand, and then head for the barn.

Bill located the field and lined himself up for his landing. The gear was extended and the flaps were down, slowing the plane down for landing. His glide slope was a little high, but it was certainly within acceptable limits for Mr. Wertz. The rest of the flight had gone off wonderfully, so using a little too much runway was not that big a problem. Bill put her down and taxied to the apron where Weikal and all the other cadets who had passed their primary waited. As Old Number 70 lumbered to a stop on the grass near the tarmac, Bill Witcomb raised his goggles to his forehead and unsnapped his chinstrap. As he did, blue-gray smoke billowed from his ears, and his mates all cheered for him.

C. J. Wertz tossed his cigarette clear of the plane and climbed out after instructing Bill through the tube to make his solo flight. Bill returned to the air after repeating his prayer, this time more confident in himself and astonished at how well the airplane responded to the subtle instructions that he had given it. That last flight with Wertz provided him with an epiphany that would eventually rank him among the most outstanding pilots ever.

On the ground, Mr. Wertz and his classmates stood waiting. His fellow cadets were all smiles and congratulatory. Mr. Wertz never really smiled; he just stopped frowning for a moment. As Bill managed to extricate himself from the cockpit, he and Mr. Wertz were ushered to the front of the plane by a base photographer, and there, joined by Cadet Weikal, a posed photograph was taken—Weikal, Wertz, and Witcomb—the three W's, stood before Old Number 70. This would be the last time they would ever be together—in fact, the last time they would ever see one another. Weikal went off to other flying duties. Wertz remained at Spartan Aerodrome under government contract, training flying officers for the duration of the war. Bill Witcomb was now a pilot. He was presented with his wings and a commission as a second lieutenant in the United States Army Air Force immediately. Gold bars now rested upon his shoulders, symbolizing the responsibility he would shoulder as an officer. He was a fledgling pilot, but he was destined to fly something more than that old metal trainer. His discipline and training had paid off. And he figured his prayer hadn't hurt either. It was a prayer that he would repeat on every future flight, and one that he would grow to rely upon— "Lord, make this a good flight."

Chapter 5

War Wounds

"I'm interested in your life after the war, Bill," explained Dr. Burns. "Tell me what happened right after the war."

"What's that got to do with it?" questioned Bill in an aggravated tone.

"Well, it may help explain some things," said the doctor.

Bill Witcomb reluctantly began to babble about his life immediately following World War II. More than two decades later, and seeing that the end of the war had been a time of great joy for him, he saw no point to the exercise. He was home alive, and in one solid piece, unlike so many of those who had gone with him to war. He had married while in the service and he and Ellie were raising a family then. He had a fine job with the Atkinson Lumber Company, as treasurer and chief financial officer. It had been a time of nationwide reconstruction. It was a time for getting back to work, doing a job, and living life as it had been before the war. But living that life was no longer possible. The world had changed. Bill had changed. And, like a pickle unable to revert back to being a cucumber, the changes were permanent and irreversible.

Tempering in the crucible that is war alters a man in one way or another. Like alloy steel formed in the extreme heat of a forge, war either consumes a man, or it produces the strongest-willed person imaginable. The latter was the case with Bill Witcomb. He returned from war more sharply focused than ever on the ideals and morals that had been ingrained within him as a child. He was more devout than ever in his spiritual Christianity, and he now possessed a more precise and clear definition of what was right and what was wrong. That strong internal compass was destined to be the controlling mechanism within him for the rest of his life. It was the reason for his strong sense of patriotism, his overwhelming sense of loyalty toward and concern for the people with whom he served, and for many of the troubles that would befall him in the post-war years. He never challenged the reading on that compass, never once compromised his ethics for ease or personal security. It made for a difficult road that was tough to follow in a world filled with imperfection.

– – –

Bill was married to Eleanor Atkinson during the war, and at war's end he returned to a new position at Atkinson Lumber, where he would sit at the right hand of Ellie's father. It was while he was in this position that their first child, Susan Kay, was born. A year later, Nancy Jean came along. Bill had always shown an aptitude for accepting and handling responsibility, and in fatherhood there was no divergence from this pattern. He was an attentive father, always relying on the sage advice he'd received so long ago at Jefferson Barracks. He raised his children with discipline and training, recognizing that it was his responsibility to prepare them for life. Ellie was a dutiful mother as well, providing the girls with all the tools and skills they would need to enter womanhood someday.

At work, Bill was not just the guy who had married the boss's daughter. His demanding work ethic had made him an indispensable cog in the mechanism that was Atkinson Lumber. He had completely reorganized the financial structure of the company, making it more profitable than ever. He had employed some of the methods of inventory control that he had observed in the AAF, which made product storage and distribution more efficient. Unlike so many of the stuffed shirts that lounged around the front office, Bill was unafraid to jump up on the loading dock and help out when there was a heavy load, a shortage of time, or when he saw that a fellow employee simply needed a helping hand. He wore a suit and tie, but he was the guy in the front office that everyone in the company could relate to and talk with. He not only sat at the right hand of Mr. Atkinson, he quickly became Willis Atkinson's right arm.

It was about this time that Ellie's father decided upon a new company initiative. Willis Atkinson entered into an unholy agreement with the proprietor of the Cashman Company—his only rival in the Newburyport area for the sale of coal and oil. The thrust of the agreement was that neither would undercut the other, thereby fixing the prices for coal and oil for that community. Most of the employees in the company were content with the notion that they would have to do very little work to compute or quote oil and coal prices to customers in order for the company to be competitive. They were in agreement that Mr. Atkinson had done well to strike such a bargain. But Bill Witcomb disagreed vehemently and vocally. He was not only opposed to the whole notion, he was irate at the way he learned of the affair—through a secretary who knew of the agreement before he did.

Bill challenged his father-in-law in front of the other company personnel and accused him of engaging in antitrust activities that would have rendered Standard Oil to oblivion had it been in similar cahoots with Gulf Oil. He demanded that the deal be abolished, and threatened to quit his job. Willis Atkinson did not relish the idea of losing his best and brightest employee, but neither did he find being publicly called what was tantamount to a thief very agreeable. He left the final decision to Bill, but Willis Atkinson refused to renege on the price-fixing treaty with his competitor. The deal was on, and there was nothing that Bill could do about it.

Disgusted with the lack of ethics displayed by Willis Atkinson, Bill went home to talk it over with Ellie. He explained that he had not fought a war against tyranny and world domination only to come home and stand idly by while domestic profiteers carved up the landscape for their greedy self interests. Willis Atkinson may have been Ellie's father, but he was a robber baron to Bill Witcomb's way of thinking, out to loot the neighborhood. Witcomb was adamant that he was not going to continue to associate with the Atkinson Lumber Company as long as such business practices were observed. Eleanor, ever her father's daughter, continued to remind Bill of his financial and family obligations. They had two children to raise, a substantial mortgage, and the costs of everyday living in a post-war economic slump. Jobs were not plentiful yet, and good jobs were even fewer. Leaving the Atkinson Lumber Company would hardly serve the financial demands or their immediate family interests, and Bill could hardly count upon landing something as lucrative as he stomped out the door. Ellie suggested a number of compromises. She even attempted to intercede with her father and broker a truce, trying to get him to back down from the profitable deal he had made with Cashman. Neither side would budge.

Bill left the Atkinson Lumber Company, refusing to compromise his ethics. It was a decision that had far-reaching and devastating effects. Bill was an industrious soul, never content to sit around and collect relief. He knew that if he needed a helping hand, he need look no further than the end of his own arm to find one. He spoke with his father at the Tolle Manufacturing Company on Merrimac Street and asked if there were any openings there. His father was elated. Finally, his son had determined to learn the trade of the silversmith. Bill started immediately in the "making room," where plates of silver were stamped into a variety of products with a die press.

It seemed clear to Bill, as he reminisced to Dr. Burns a score of years later, that it was the lack of financial security that had pushed Ellie over the top in their marriage. Things quickly unraveled after he left the lumber company. Had it not been for the reduced income, he speculated, everything would have been fine. But the truth is often a bitter pill to swallow. Bill had glossed over the litany of atrocities and abnormal behavior to which Ellie and the two youngsters had been exposed. His sudden outbursts of rage—episodic tirades that had thus far been confined within the family—and his moodiness and bouts of depression were more to blame than the lack of money. Ellie had exhausted her arsenal of weapons to combat the demons that stirred within her husband, but she had been fighting a two-front war of her own. On one side she had to contend with Bill and the natural aftermath of the war. On the other side she had two impressionable young girls to raise.

Ellie had tolerated the changed man that had come back from the war that stood in stark contrast to the one she had married. She put up with the bed sweats and the nightmares that ended in uncontrollable screaming in the middle of the night. She put up with the blank looks and the silence from Bill when he would stare into space and his mind was several miles up in the sky, re-flying and reliving combat missions that occurred years earlier. She even tolerated the mood swings—complacent one moment, enraged the next. Bill had become Jekyll and Hyde at the same time, his fits of rage bordering almost on the supernatural. She endured the constant roller coaster of emotions that he subjected himself and the family to, because she loved him. But Ellie was a dutiful mother, concerned and nurturing in every way. She had led a somewhat sheltered life, attending preparatory schools and colleges and never venturing too far from the protective wing of her family. Circumstances no longer allowed her the luxury of enjoying marriage and parenthood simultaneously. She was forced to make a choice. And on Christmas Eve, 1948, after yet-another inflammatory outburst from Bill in which physical threatening was imminent, Ellie bundled the two children out the door and left Bill forever. For the first time, Bill Witcomb felt actual pain from the internal and invisible wounds that he had sustained during the war.

– – –

"You had changed since the war, hadn't you?" asked Dr. Burns.

"I suppose I had, to some degree," replied Bill, fidgeting in his chair and shifting his robe to cover himself better. "But she had changed as well."

"You had nightmares?"

"So?"

"You had mood swings?"

"I suppose."

"How often?" inquired the clinician. Bill failed to respond. It was too difficult for him to answer. First of all, he didn't remember half the nightmares, and he seldom recognized the mood shifts. Only Ellie, or his second wife Fran, could have disclosed the severity and the actual frequency of either. Half the time, Bill put those things out of his mind and attributed them to everyday living. He supposed everyone had them to one degree or another and that his particular brand of somnambulant torture or his outlandish behavior during waking hours was merely the norm. For the first time, while talking to Dr. Burns, he came to realize that maybe his dreams and his bed sweats weren't average—that maybe his depressive moods and his volatile anger weren't normal—and that maybe other things were at play here.

"Let's go back and talk about your days in the Air Force, Bill," said Dr. Burns. Bill wrung his hands in his lap and continued his recollections of his time in the military. Those were not all pleasant memories for him.

Chapter 6

The Gift of Wife

During the early days in the Army Air Force, Bill Witcomb would travel from one base to another more often by train than by airplane, but like all pilots he endured his share of training in a variety of aircraft. The issuance of his wings after primary flight was a mere formality, a precursor of things to come; he was far from being the military pilot that the AAF had envisioned when he was sent to flight school. But then, the same was true for most of the young pilots who had just completed their primary and were ready to move on to more challenging pursuits. The second phase of training—basic flight—would place each new flyer into the cockpits of an array of airplanes in order to evaluate their particular set of flying skills. Each candidate would log a full seventy hours of flight time before moving on to his final phase of training. The trainees were merely lumps of raw material as they entered basic flight—hardly the polished combat experts that they would need to be in order to prosecute a modern and sophisticated air war. Some were destined to fly pursuit and fighter aircraft, sleek and fast. Others would fly transports, hauling the loads of mail, men, and materiel that a hungry army needed to fight on. Still others would take on the task of flying the big planes, the bombers—the medium-sized B-25 Mitchells, the giant B-24 Liberators, and the B-17 Flying Fortresses.

Unlike any other kind of flying, these big planes would require a special agility and patience, physical strength, and an attention to detail that other forms of flying did not necessarily require. Bomber pilots also had to learn to do something that other pilots never had to reply upon for actual survival—they had to learn to fly in formation. Although formation flying was used by most military branches as a means of getting from one place to another, bombers relied upon their formation for accuracy on the target as well as for survival from attackers. Their lives, the lives of their crews, and the very existence of their airplanes depended upon their ability to fly in tight protective formations. One of the fundamentals in aviation is to avoid close contact with other aircraft, as this invariably leads to major mishaps and air crashes. Most military air formations had a certain amount of leeway available. But then, most of those formations were not in the process of being strafed by enemy airplanes or barraged by artillery fire from below as they proceeded to their destination. In such cases, pilots were free to break formation and avoid the hazard.

But formation flying for bombers was essential for precision bombing and for maintaining the defensive integrity of the group. Therefore, bomber pilots were chosen for their ability to use gentle movements to persuade an airplane along rather than a penchant for bullying the stick or the yoke. Pilots who knew how to trim in order to acquire the desired result were the best for this. To hone this skill, they had to be seasoned pilots to start with. Bill Witcomb was far from a seasoned pilot in the fall of 1942. He was just another enlisted-man-turned-cadet, turned-pilot, with twelve whole hours to his credit and a pair of silver wings over his left breast pocket. Regardless, he beamed with delight as he saw those wings reflected in the coach window of the train while he glanced out at the night sky beyond.

Altus, Oklahoma was his next assignment. Here he would fly an assortment of airplanes, from a Fairchild Ranger, an open-cockpit two-seat monoplane made of a wooden frame and a canvas skin, to a North American Aviation BT-9, an under-powered all-metal plane that was less-than-stable in flight and fitted with a landing gear that was far too small to be practicable. He flew the AT-10, affectionately called the Bamboo Bomber by the pilots who flew them. This was his first foray into multi-engine aircraft. It was a wooden-framed, plywood-covered monster. There was also the BT-13, or Vultee Vibrator as the pilots identified them—so named because of the vibrations that were said to loosen the fillings from a man's teeth. And there was the A-9, a likeable airplane made of a metal skin; it had twin engines and a tricycle gear—something akin to driving a car on the ground. Bill checked out in all of them.

During all of the years of World War II, all of American society engaged in the war effort in as many different ways as there were people. Young women and girls from a wide area around military installations would find their way to a nearby U.S.O. and help entertain the boys. The young ladies enjoyed the male companionship and the ability to quickly get to know lots of men in a strictly controlled atmosphere. These girls always felt safe, protected by the crowd and the multitude of chaperones that were ever present. At many bases, dances were held right on the post itself. Though not strictly considered a southern state, Oklahoma nonetheless extended true southern hospitality. Posted in the recreation hall on the bulletin board was a list of area residents who would invite the soldiers to their homes for an evening of good food and informal socializing. Officers and airmen would sign up to be the guest of the families on a given night. Bill Witcomb signed up for such a night, and was met at the entrance of the recreation hall by a local Oklahoma farmer and his lovely daughter. The trio climbed into an aged pickup truck and the farmer drove them all back to their farm. The girl was nineteen and gorgeous. The best part of her seemed to be her cooking; it was as great as her looks. The three of them feasted on a delicious roast chicken dinner and Bill eagerly took seconds on everything, including the blueberry pie. After dinner, the farmer left the pair of younger people to the drawing room where Bill and the farmer's daughter listened to the radio and to phonograph records and spent the evening together. Even in his twilight years, Bill Witcomb never disclosed exactly what they did during their "socializing," but he was always quick to say, with a distinct twinkle in his eye and a sly grin, that she was one very special girl. But that was how it was during the war. Relationships between young men and women were staid and sophomoric by twenty-first century standards. They were also lightning-fast to develop, one of the many elements of the society that was necessitated by the existence of war. Friendships had to evolve quickly, or not at all. There simply wasn't time for all the time-honored formalities that heretofore had been observed.

In the early stages of his advanced flight training, Bill was flying one of the small, older monoplanes with an open cockpit. His instructor, for a change, took the rear seat and he was in the front. The old crate had an in-line motor, rather than one of the more conventional rotary configurations, where the pistons are situated around the propeller shaft and fire in a simple sequence that drives the propeller in a circle. The in-line engine was like the straight-line motors found in most automobiles, before the advent of the V-8 engine. Power was delivered to the propeller via an in-line shaft that was cranked via a camshaft within the motor. It made for an enormous waste of energy in an aviation application. But it was a simple trainer, and being overpowered was not the intention.

Bill and his overseer were cruising along at roughly three thousand feet when that simple in-line motor suddenly froze up solid for no apparent reason. The prop stopped dead, coming to rest straight up and down, and the instant the vibration of the motor had vanished it was replaced by a vibration in the stomachs of both occupants of the tiny airplane. Bill tried in vain to remember the emergency procedures for the aircraft, but nothing came to him. He quickly surveyed the countryside below him and spotted a freshly plowed field. The furrows were long and straight, and the field was flat and long. *If there was ever a place for an emergency landing, that's it*, thought Bill. He leaned the stick over slightly and gave it just a touch of rudder pedal, holding back from the temptation of pulling back on the stick right then. The nose was dropping at an alarming rate, but the beast soon leveled out a bit when it picked up airspeed. As the ground drew closer and closer, Bill pulled the flap lever and gave himself a little more altitude. The plane slowed somewhat, which was a primary purpose for using flaps. But to Bill, distance from the ground at that point was of chief importance. He still had a dirt road and a stand of trees to traverse before the newly plowed field was his. The instructor was resigned to sit and watch in the back seat. It was all that he could do. Bill had made the decision. They were going in for a classic dead-stick landing—if only he could clear those trees.

Bill pulled back ever-so-gently on the stick as the row of trees before him grew closer. The tiny airplane vaulted the branches with inches to spare, and slowed almost to the point of stall. He eased the stick forward again, and the nose dropped slightly. Just before they were about to touch down, he pulled back on the stick and gave her full flaps, creating a textbook flare at landing. The rickety little plane set down on the cornfield like a giant gull coming in for feeding. Bill had aligned the wheels of the plane perfectly with the straight furrows in the sod, and the plane rumbled slightly on contact, then came to a relatively short stop. She was upright on all three wheels, no damage to the airplane or ground structures of any kind, and absolutely no injuries to crew. It was a textbook emergency landing. At least it was to Bill's way of thinking.

Bill and his instructor managed to find their way to a nearby farmhouse where they called the base for rescue. A short time later, a salvage crew was on scene, going over the airplane. The only problem evident on board was that the motor didn't work, for some as-yet-unexplained reason. Everything else was fine. The plane was hauled back to the base on a flatbed truck, and Bill and his instructor were taken back for debriefing. The following day a review board was convened, and Bill Witcomb found himself more or less on trial. Any landing that falls outside the definition of a normal landing is considered a crash landing by AAF standards. It is investigated thoroughly, a report is filed, and a review by air officers and commanders is routine. There would be no exception in this case. Witcomb had crash-landed a plane. That crash had to be reviewed.

The review board entered the conference room, which was set up more like a courtroom than anything else. Bill was seated at a table with his instructor and questions were posed to both of them.

"What altitude were you at?" asked the presiding brigadier general.

"Approximately three thousand feet, sir," was Bill's reply.

"Were you wearing parachutes?" questioned the general.

"Yes, sir."

"Well, you had three thousand feet of airspace in which to jump, so why didn't you jump?" demanded the officer. "Regulations say you're supposed to jump under those circumstances."

"Well, sir," said Bill, groping for a reasonable explanation that would appease the board, "I've never parachuted out of a plane before."

"So?"

"Well, sir, I have landed a plane before. So I did what I knew how to do."

The panel sat back in their chairs, dumbfounded by the simplicity of the answer. Their initial astonishment gave way to some muttering between them for a few minutes, and then, an uneasy silence while the brigadier scribbled some notes on a piece of paper.

"Lieutenant Witcomb," said the general, nodding toward Bill that something official was about to unfold. Bill and his instructor came to their feet and stood at attention, awaiting their fate. "This review board finds that the cause of the forced landing that you executed was failure of the aircraft's power plant to function properly in flight. Although in the aftermath of this condition you did not adhere to recognized emergency procedures, the result of your decisions and subsequent actions was a swift and safe conclusion to the flight, causing neither injury to personnel nor further damage to military or civilian property. You are, therefore, excused from this proceeding, and ordered to return to your duties. You are dismissed. This review board is closed." With that, the brigadier ceremoniously closed the folder of papers on the table before him, squared the papers inside in a neat manner, and came to his feet. Bill Witcomb stood at ease for the first time that day.

As Bill walked toward the door, the presiding general came over to him and leaned in close for a quiet little conversation. He was a crusty older officer with his own set of silver wings and an array of ribbons over his left breast pocket that truly resembled what those in the military called *fruit salad.*

"Son," said the general, placing his arm over Bill's shoulder, "the next time you get into a fix like that, I want you to jump. That's what your parachute is for. Besides, between you and me," he said, with a glance to either side and in a conspirator's whisper, "we're trying to get rid of those old crates. We don't get any new ones until we've gotten rid of the old ones. So, next time, jump! Understand?" Bill nodded his understanding of the order and left the room.

– – –

If caution and presence of mind were with him the day of the dead-stick landing, they abandoned Witcomb and his student colleagues on other days. All the young pilots competed openly with each other for silly, often stupid, goals, none of which carried with it a prize greater than acknowledgment by their mates and the satisfaction in one's ability to say they had accomplished it. There was the predictable game of coming closest to landing on a specific stripe on the tarmac. Toward the end of each runway was an apron, and the aprons were painted with crosshatched lines for greater visibility. Each of the young pilots would do his best to plant the main landing gear of his airplane on the broad stripe that denoted the edge of the apron. One of Bill's fellow pilots felt he was coming in too high during such a competition. He suddenly cut the power and made radical changes in the trim at the same time, causing his plane to slam down hard onto the runway and driving the strut of the landing gear right through the wing. He came the closest to the mark and won the competition, but at a steep price—one previously serviceable training aircraft.

There was another occasion when the cadets all attempted to skip-land on the top of a steamroller that was operating at the end of the field, extending the length of one of the runways. The goal was to simply skip the plane's wheels off the top of the machine's large flat metal roof that was painted a bright yellow. This was right up there with the stunt fliers of the Twenties and Thirties that barnstormed all over America. In one New England town—not far from where Bill grew up—there was a local pilot who went out flying every Sunday morning before the war, about the time everyone was headed to church. He would buzz the center of town, coming closer and closer each time to the village green and the flagpole in the middle of the town square. It wasn't until the town had to restring the flagpole rope that they discovered an airplane tire mark atop the gold ball on top of the pole. The steamroller merely served as the young cadet pilots' flagpole, the difference being that flagpoles seldom move and steamrollers do.

Being reasonably close to the Mississippi River, it was inevitable that someone on a longer flight would attempt to land on one of the many barges that went up and down the big river. From the air, they looked like floating islands, big enough to plant a bomber on safely. Navy pilots did it all the time, on top of aircraft carriers. Of course, the youthful pilots discounted that Navy pilots also employed arresting cables and fairly sophisticated landing systems aboard aircraft carriers, and that these ships were inevitably longer and wider than the average river barge. Putting a trainer down on one of the barges would be a snap—all a pilot needed was a decent headwind for landing and takeoff. Of course, no one in the air figured that nice tan deck below to actually be an open load of grain. When the wheels of the unlucky cadet's airplane first made contact with the amber surface, they burrowed in like a tick on a hound dog's back. The nose of the plane was quickly pointing to the river bottom, and a frightened trainee was suspended by his seat belt harness, the tail of the airplane sticking straight up in the air to mark the exact point of the pilot's humiliation.

Lt. Bill Witcomb managed to persevere through the antics of primary and basic flight, and went on to more rigorous flying challenges in advanced flight training. Along the way, Bill was observed by his instructors and commanders with great scrutiny. All were impressed by his aptitude and his abilities. They saw him helping his fellow flight cadets with the difficulties of advanced flight—Bill displayed a natural ability to instruct. When he completed all the flight courses that had been offered to him, and he amassed a sufficient number of hours in the various aircraft available on the base, Bill Witcomb was reassigned to the station as a permanent flight instructor. He now wore a winged insignia at the end of his right uniform sleeve above the officer's embroidered roping denoting his instructor status. The Mount Rural graduate had indeed come a very long way. He had gone from cadet to cadre in a few short months, and his new assignment assured him a reasonably safe and sane alternative while serving in wartime. This resonated particularly well with his parents, who feared the premature demise of their eldest son at the hands of the Hun or those yellow devils in the Pacific. Bill would have preferred combat to the mundane assignment given him—instructing new pilots in tiny trainers.

– – –

Throughout the time that Bill was assigned to the bases in the South, he was also actively courting Ellie Atkinson romantically. He was able to steal some time here and there during his assignment to Randolph Field in Texas—long enough to propose marriage, acquire the permission and blessing of her father and, of course, his commander, and to marry her. Ellie joined Bill and energetically went about the tasks of a dutiful Army bride, setting up housekeeping in Texas. This was a daunting mission indeed for the young divinity major from Colby and Wellesley Colleges. She was far removed from the stereotypical military camp follower, and somewhat out of place in Texas. But Ellie made the best of it and did everything she could to make her husband's lot easier.

Bill still longed to fly the big planes. In 1943, the biggest things in the air were the bombers of the 8th and 9th Air Forces—the B-17 Flying Fortresses and the B-24 Liberators. These multi-engine giants were wresting control of the daytime skies over Europe away from Goering's Luftwaffe. They were complex Goliaths that required a wide array of skills to fly, and Bill Witcomb felt he was more than up to the challenge. He made no bones about this desire to his new bride when he was at home. He also made no mistake about his preference—he wanted the Boeing B-17 above anything else.

Ellie may have been a society girl from High Street in Newburyport, Massachusetts; she may have grown up on brick and cobblestone streets and resided in what could be called a mansion by almost anyone's standards; she may have gone to the proper finishing schools; but she seemed to know instinctively how to maneuver on a dusty military post. She did what every good military wife does in a similar situation: she assumed the rank and station of her husband—an officer and, by this time, a flight instructor on a training base. She became an integral part of the social structure of the field, attending teas and welcoming the wives of new officers to the group. Ellie became a force to be reckoned with among the officer's wives. Holding a position near the top of the junior officer's social order, she became close friends with the wife of the base personnel officer. It was this woman's husband who designated assignments of all personnel on the station, and pilot/instructors were no exception. Ellie methodically made certain that this lieutenant colonel's wife knew how much Bill wanted to fly bombers, and particularly B-17s.

Before he knew it, and before he could fully comprehend or appreciate how it came about, Lieutenant Witcomb found himself assigned as a trainee on B-17s and received orders to move immediately to Avon Park, Florida. Discipline and training had brought Bill a long way in the AAF by that time. The amalgam of his natural technical abilities combined with those characteristics imbued by the military had resulted in something very unusual. Now the tensile strength of that mixture would become essential for survival in a new, more complex, and more demanding arena. Once again, Bill was to be a student. Once again, he would have to bull into the task of learning as he had done so often before. Discipline and training had a lot to do with it. But what actually got him to Avon Park was Ellie's manipulation of the dark and convoluted military back channels. It was she that put him within arms' reach of his military dream. She had combined savvy and social grace to win that prize for him.

It was good for Bill to have help from someone else. Up to that point in his military career, he had relied almost exclusively upon his own initiatives; upon his own wits and performance. But now he was going to have to work with a crew of men in order to make things function properly, because no one flies a B-17 all by himself. In fact, one can't even start the engines on the B-17 alone—it invariably requires teamwork. Working as a team of two with his bride had managed to get him into bombers, but it also had helped prepare him for the rigors of flying a bomber. Marriage was merely a form of basic training for Bill—a dry run for the teamwork that would be required in order to put a giant bomber into the air and keep it there through countless combat missions.

Ellie had given Bill much thus far in their brief marriage. She would continue to be the giver of wonderful things in the future, including two beautiful daughters. But for now, Ellie had selflessly given him bombers through her own cunning, despite her knowledge that it meant Bill would eventually leave the safety and security of a training assignment and face the sword of war. She risked his being assigned overseas where bombing missions were just as real as the bullets and rockets that brought aircraft and airmen crashing back down to earth. It was the greatest gift that anyone could have given Bill Witcomb at that time in his life, and it was the unselfish gift from his loving and understanding wife.

Chapter 7

Parlez-Vous Français?

Avon Park was a paradise assignment, much the way Pearl Harbor had been prior to December 7th, 1941. It was a congenial climate, with amenities not available in other parts of the country. Ellie and Bill fit right in, especially Bill. It was at Avon Park that he first got his hands on a B-17. It was an early model, a B-17E training aircraft assigned to the base, used by many of the new pilots who were assigned to learn how to fly them. Compared to the trainers and fighters at Gunter Field that he had been flying, these were giants. Almost 75 feet from nose to tail, a wingspan of almost 104 feet, and a dry weight just under 30 tons, these behemoths were overwhelming the first time a new pilot looked upon them, much less climbed aboard. The cockpit was almost two full stories off the ground—truly an oddity in the 1940's.

Bill stood and gazed upon the olive-drab airplane sitting on the apron, devoid of markings other than the U.S. star and the five-digit tail number that began with one. He stared at the four Wright turbo-charged radial motors, each capable of delivering 1100 horsepower. He pondered what those engines would drink in order to sustain that horsepower rating, and questioned in his own mind where on earth an airplane could store such a volume of fuel. It would be a longer time still before he actually got a chance to handle the airplane. He had volumes of reading material to wade through before the Army would ever let him touch the controls. By 1943 and 1944, B-17s were at a premium. Every theater commander wanted as many as he could get his hands on. In Europe, the 8th Air Force was hitting the Germans where it really hurt—in the industrial heartland of their own country. The Navy was screaming for the heavy bombers, with their 3400-mile range, to patrol the North Atlantic in search of the submarine wolf packs, because they had the range to reach far across the ocean where coastal patrols could never venture. In the Pacific, the whole purpose of throwing thousands of young Marines, Navy, and Army personnel onto countless atolls and island chains was to establish bases from which long-range bombers could eventually reach the home islands of Japan. This part of the military mission would one day be satisfied by the B-29 that came late in the war. Most of the B-17s sent to the Pacific were being routed back for assignment in the States or in Europe. Even so, few, if any, would find their way back to the training bases. The training commands had their hands full as well, getting green pilots familiar with the giant bombers when aircraft were at such a premium. Hanging on to the existing aircraft in their charge was a full-time job for training commanders, and they weren't about to fritter away a single B-17 on some cocky rookie pilot who thought he was at the controls of some inexpensive trainer or reasonably priced fighter plane. Better to lose a plane in combat than see it squandered in a training mishap.

Young pilots had other ideas, though. They all knew how to fly. The principles of flight were the same no matter what type of airplane you flew—again, weight plus drag overcome by lift plus thrust. Why would the B-17 be any different? It would take months of arduous training before they learned the complexity of the answer to that question.

Again, Bill Witcomb burrowed into the books. Again, he scored well with the written applications he was given. Again, he was a leader because of his tenacious attention to detail and his devotion to preparing himself for the job at hand. Discipline and training; these had become the very essence of Second Lieutenant Bill Witcomb.

After what seemed like endless classes, lectures, and simulations, his turn finally came to take hold of that pale green metal yoke in the cockpit and test the control surfaces of the airplane. He pulled the yoke backward and then pushed it forward, cranking the black half-moon wheel first left, and then right. He looked out the window over his left shoulder to see if the ailerons were moving in sync with the yoke. He pushed the foot pedals with his feet, noticing their smoothness as the giant rudder at the back of the ship moved from one side to another. His hands reached down to feel the throttle controls, designed so that one hand could control all four engines simultaneously just by splaying the fingers apart. The mixture and the supercharger controls sat directly above and in front of the throttles, allowing the pilot to adjust and tune the engines easily for maximum efficiency and power. Below the throttles were the propeller controls, which allowed the pitch of each prop to be feathered in flight if an emergency made it necessary. And below those controls was mounted the autopilot transfer control panel that permitted the pilot to shift flying control of the airplane to the bombardier.

Bill surveyed the instrument panel knowing that, in flight, it was his lifeline. Those instruments alone could bring him home some day, if only he could properly interpret what they were telling him. He studied them carefully, as he had done countless times in the trainer. Each set of engines had their own set of gauges to tell Witcomb what they were doing. The altimeter was small but prominent and centrally located. The airspeed indicator was legible and convenient. The thermometer, although of little concern at low altitudes over Avon Park, would one day play a vital role in the survival of Bill Witcomb, his crew, and the airplane assigned to him. PDI stood for the Pilot's Directional Indicator, a gauge mounted on the left quadrant of the panel that was used by the bombardier to telegraph desired corrections while on the bomb run. Again, Avon Park was where pilots learned to fly the B-17, not where they learned how to fly the B-17 in combat. That would come later. This older model aircraft had the PDI in place, but later versions of the airplane (B-17Fs and B-17Gs) were devoid of this redundancy because the improved remote controls allowed for almost complete control of the airplane by the bombardier during the bomb run.

It was a marvelous machine, designed and built for combat. Although the thin metal skin would do little to defend the occupants against bullets and the shrapnel from German flak, it made for a sturdy and maneuverable fighting platform. Machine guns would protrude from every angle, offering intruding enemies a distasteful welcome. The bomb bay could house virtually every American- and British-made bomb of the day—sometimes several types simultaneously. Payloads could be as much as four-and-a-quarter tons of bombs.

Those huge engines that Bill had marveled over were now under his control. They would start and stop at his whim, and deliver their power upon his demand. He had studied their rate of consumption, and how to adjust high-octane fuels and air mixtures to deliver power under given weather and flight circumstances. He had studied how to feather a dead prop, to keep it from windmilling (simply turning with the passing wind, delivering no power and causing drag). Every pilot knew that windmilling was a double-edged sword. No power was being generated, true, and that loss of power was a significant enough handicap in itself under combat conditions. But there was an even deadlier problem that came from windmilling. If a propeller spun in the wind as the other engines pulled the airplane through the air, the turning shaft would generate vast amounts of heat from the friction of the propeller shaft inside the dead radial motor. Once the heat grew sufficient and was no longer able to be absorbed by the engine or dissipated into the air in flight, the metal shaft would literally melt down and the propeller would suddenly and unexpectedly fly off the engine—often, in the direction of the fuselage. If a spinning prop weighing several hundred pounds ripped into the thin metal fuselage, not only could major structural damage occur, compromising the flight of the airplane, but the buzz-saw action could easily sever the airplane control cables or cut a crewmember in half. Feathering the prop was the only way to avoid this, or so they had been taught. In time, Bill Witcomb would have to invent another, more taxing remedy for such a predicament.

There was something different about the B-17. Those big three-bladed propellers mounted on those 1100 horsepower motors could be controlled by the pilots like very few other flying power plants of the day. Feathering the propellers when they seized up was the primary method of reducing the risk of a troublesome engine. It was a matter of locking down the propeller shaft so that it wouldn't spin and adjusting the pitch of the propeller blades so they presented the least amount of profile to the oncoming air, thereby creating the least amount of resistance and drag. Bill Witcomb was to practice this emergency procedure many times before it would be necessary.

"Okay, Witcomb, let's go," said the instructor pilot in a gruff tone.

Lieutenant Witcomb reviewed the Form F that the ground crew had handed to him, to check weight and balance. He then completed Forms 1 and 1A and signed the release of the airplane. His walk around the airplane had been comprehensive, but he looked over the flight engineer's preflight inspection report to make certain that the chief concurred. The instructor pilot climbed into the cockpit and strapped himself into the right seat. He pulled out the clipboard, and he and Bill went over the preflight checklist to ensure that all the equipment and controls were in proper position and working order before attempting a takeoff. Once completed, he slipped the clipboard back down beside the seat and nodded to Bill. It was a relatively short checklist, considering the complexity of the airplane and the redundancy factor of four engines.

"Emergency ignition switch to 'on'," said Bill.

"Switch on," said the instructor.

Witcomb checked each of the batteries and tested them with the inverter to make sure the primary electrical system was functional.

"Master battery switch to 'on'," he announced. The instructor pilot again stated that the switch was in the "on" position. "Hydraulic pump switch to 'on'."

"Hydraulic switch on and reading 'auto'," said the instructor. Witcomb nodded his assent. He made certain that the landing gear and flap control switches were set to neutral, then told the instructor pilot in the copilot's seat to set the parking brake. The instructor reached down to the right of the panel and set the brake.

"Cabin heat, off," said Bill. "Set turbo controls to off. Open fuel shut-off valves. Throttles set to 1,000 RPM. Open carburetor air filters. Props set for high RPM. Magneto switch for number one set to 'both'."

In response to Bill's checklist commands, the copilot now began giving orders to the flight engineer, telling him to open the shut-off valves. He read the gauges telling him there was 800 pounds of hydraulic pressure and he ordered the shut-off valves closed. He opened the cowl flaps and set the valves in the locked position. The fuel transfer valves and pump switches were set to "off" and the fire extinguisher selector valve was set to engine number one. The intercooler was set to "cold," the carburetor air filters were placed on, and the mixture controls were moved to the "engine off" position. He started the number three fuel booster pump to establish primer pressure, and when it reached eight pounds he toggled the fuel booster pump for the number one engine. Everything was ready.

Bill then motioned to the ground crewman standing between the pair of engines holding the nozzle of a giant CO_2 fire extinguisher that was mounted on a trolley. The young airman moved behind the wing and out of sight of Bill as he aimed the nozzle toward the engine cowling and prepared for start up. Bill blurted out, "Turn on one," and the instructor threw the starter switch and pumped the fuel control pump as Bill spoke.

The giant propeller began to turn ever so slowly, with a labored whining noise, and then suddenly it exploded to life with a thunderous roar. Blue smoke billowed out of the cowling at first, but Bill adjusted the carburetor mixture slightly and brought the engine to a smooth purr in a matter of seconds. "Turn on two," he announced, holding up two fingers to another airman on the tarmac and repeated the process for the left inboard engine. The monster roared awake with billows of blue smoke at first, then settled right into a harmonious hum with number one.

The ground crewman now moved his extinguisher trolley to the other side of the plane and positioned himself between and behind numbers three and four. The inboard engine, number three, needed several attempts before it came alive in its cloud of smoke. Bill had to make a series of adjustments to the mixture before she'd catch, but it finally started up. Number four fired right up, making a quartet of roaring engines all turning at roughly the same rate. The sound around the airplane was thunderous, even in the cockpit. The ground crewman moved away from the front of the airplane now, taking his extinguisher with him. Bill played with the mixtures and the carburetor settings until he could see that all four engines were turning at the same RPM. The airplane vibrated like an angry dragon straining at a chain leash. It seemed as though it wanted to fly; more than any other plane that Bill had ever piloted, the B-17 wanted to fly. He could feel it in the yoke. He could feel the ship straining against the locked and chocked wheels to get free. Witcomb motioned with his thumbs apart to the man outside, and the young airman pulled the rope attached to the wheel chocks and dragged them free. He jogged under the nose of the airplane and turned to his left to run parallel along the left wing where the pilot could easily see him. The only thing holding that giant airplane in place on the ground now was the force of gravity and the parking brake. This would soon be overcome by a release of the brake and the application of a little throttle.

Bill cleared the flight with the Avon Park tower and was granted permission to taxi. The radio aboard was set to a single frequency for training flights, so no radio operator was required. The pilot instructor nodded to him to roll, and Bill reached down, for the first time, and spread his fingers over the throttle controls. Instinctively, the instructor reached down to back up the young pilot—a technique that copilots always employed to ensure that all four engines were all fired up equally and together. Bill checked to make certain the tail wheel was unlocked and free, and then nudged the controls forward slightly. The mammoth olive-drab bird began to roll from her parking spot on the apron.

On any given day, Avon Park was a beehive of flying activity, with training flights in and out of the pattern constantly. Darkness was the only peaceful time, because this was within the coastal area and could be viewed by offshore enemy ships. Blackout conditions were strictly maintained, thus limiting training flights to daylight operations. B-17s were not the only aircraft that flew in and out of the base, and many of the smaller airplanes were difficult to see from the cockpit of the Fortress, especially those on the ground. Bill peered through the windshield and out the side windows to survey the path before him. To a great extent, he had to rely upon the alertness of the tower personnel who oversaw both ground and air operations on the base. He had to have faith that the controller knew his job and was performing it properly. It was his faith in Ellie that allowed Bill to begin having faith in other people. He was grudgingly learning to rely upon the competence and commitment of others. He discovered that the air traffic controller was merely a more visible member of a very large team that supported Bill and other pilots in the air and on the ground. Bill was gradually learning that he was now truly a member of a very large team. Pilots relied upon mechanics to make certain their aircraft was in top condition. Mechanics relied upon supply personnel to get them the parts and materials they needed for their jobs. The Army Air Force was no different than the Army when it came to traveling on its stomach. Cooks provided the fuel for the human element. Medical personnel kept people in good health, caring for their cuts, bruises, and more serious maladies. Clerical personnel kept the paperwork straight, accounting for everything from paperclips to an entire airplane. Field maintenance personnel were the public works department on any station, cutting the grass, keeping the fresh water supply flowing, plowing snow where it fell, and changing light bulbs in street lights and landing systems. Military police were responsible for keeping the entire station secure from anyone who would disrupt the mission. It was a big team, and everyone was essential to the mission. But in the end the mission was to keep them flying, and Bill Witcomb was just one of the many flyers.

The big green airplane rolled up to the end of the runway, and Bill Witcomb applied the brakes with the tops of the rudder pedals. The plane lumbered to a stop, and Bill and his instructor went over a final checklist to make certain that all was in order. Bill did the *run up*—a test of the engines while the airplane was locked into place. Bill made sure that all three wheels were on concrete, and that no one was parked behind him so the prop wash from the run up would not buffet another aircraft. All four engines were cranked up all the way, cowl flaps open to vent them properly and to keep heat from exceeding the proper limits. Satisfied that all was well, Bill reduced power to idle, closed the cowl flaps and the carburetor filters and prepared for takeoff. He quietly said his prayer, *"Lord, make this a good flight,"* then he released the foot pedals and steered the airplane onto the active runway. As she turned her nose down the centerline of the airstrip, the instructor noted the time and Bill started walking the throttles forward slowly. Simply jamming the levers forward all at once would have stalled the motors out completely, or it would have caused enough vibration to shake the motors right off their mounts. Walking the throttles up was the only way. Slowly, the big bird gained momentum. She was racing along, increasing her speed with each second, while Bill pushed the throttles almost all the way up, pouring fuel to each of those thirsty power plants. The purr of the motors was replaced by a deafening roar, and the vibrations throughout the ship were enough to shake the very marrow of a person's bones.

Suddenly, the tail of the plane began to lift itself off the runway, and the fuselage began to level out slightly with the ground. The pilot instructor reminded Bill that this wasn't a conventional tail dragger. The attack angle of the B-17's wing was already at the appropriate angle when all three wheels were in contact with the ground. Allowing the tail to lift off the ground before takeoff actually reduced the lifting capacity of the wing. Bill adjusted the trim and brought the tail down gently. Instantly, the giant airplane began to feel lighter. The instructor, who had constantly been watching the airspeed indicator, barked out the familiar phrase, "Vee One!" V1, or Velocity One, was a common aeronautical term meaning the aircraft had reached minimum flying speed. Once it was reached, upon the pilot's initiative a change in the control surfaces of the airplane would propel it into the air. "Rotate," announced the instructor.

Bill pulled back ever so slightly on the yoke, rotating the ailerons and the horizontal stabilizers upward. He resisted the urge to pull back the yoke sharply and deeply, knowing that this would only stall the giant bird. The plane responded immediately, lifting itself into the air with a perfect three-point takeoff. Bill Witcomb had come a long way in a short time from his days in primary flight training. Had it not been for broken ribs and adhesive tape restraining him during his final check flight, he probably wouldn't have even become a pilot. But now he was in control of America's largest and most powerful airplane, and executing a textbook takeoff. Bill had indeed come a long way.

As the giant balloon tires of the main gear left the ground, Bill's first instinct was to raise them to reduce the drag. But the instructor was quick to correct him and have him lock the wheels first. Stopping the spinning of the tires would not only eliminate drag, it would reduce the gyroscopic effect caused by the spinning wheels. The instructor reminded Bill that getting the gear up quickly after takeoff was a good idea. Better to belly-land than to chance a short landing on the remainder of the runway. Once the B-17 was aloft, the airspeed could drop off suddenly, depending on how much rotation a young pilot had exacted upon it, or if any sudden downdrafts caused by thermal inversions occurred. The airplane could drop back down onto the runway without warning for any variety of reasons. If the wheels were retracted when this happened, the props would be forced into the ground and Bill Witcomb would have yet another air crash to his credit. But that wasn't going to happen today.

Bill banked the airplane at the far end of the runway and gained some altitude. The wheels were neatly retracted into the engine housings of the two inboard engines, and he could really feel the airspeed pick up. The flight engineer, a staff sergeant, made his way to the tail of the plane where he retracted the tail gear. This had to be done manually on this particular model of B-17, and a canvas seal was then zipped up after the wheel was safely retracted. That canvas seal was the only thing between the air outside and the air inside. Once again, this meant very little in the warmth of the Florida sunshine. But it would mean plenty flying between five and six miles up in the winter air over Germany.

The instructor let Bill get the feel of the controls, as he had done when their seating was reversed. Bill banked to each side and turned the plane now and then. They simply cruised. It was leisurely flying; the kind of flying that is truly enjoyable. There was no destination, no schedule to be maintained, and no worry about getting a cargo or a passenger manifest to a given location at a given time. It was flying for the sake of flying. It was simply getting to know an airplane. Bill Witcomb loved it. He loved the B-17 above all other airplanes he had ever flown. She was complex and demanding, she was large and cumbersome, and he loved her.

Bill's discipline and training were paying off with big profits. He was soon the master of the enormous airplane, understanding the intricacies and its innermost secrets. He knew precisely when it would stall in flight, when it would spoil in a bank, and when it would wither in a yaw. He could tell by the vibration of the aircraft what it was about to do. It was a wondrous machine to him, and his love for Ellie was almost eclipsed by his love for that airplane.

This love affair would soon grant him yet another new job—that of teaching young pilots in a short space of time everything that he'd learned about the B-17. It was a job that would boost his self-esteem, and one that would give him the perfect opportunity to impart unto others what he had been taught: that discipline and training are the only things that would get them through the war. But first, he would have to overcome yet another hurdle.

– – –

Most soldiers and sailors believe that military personnel assignments rarely pay deference to an assignee's pre-military training or capabilities. Recruits were often taken aback that their past experience was not taken into consideration when assigning them to permanent duties after basic training. Men who worked as short-order cooks in civilian life were suddenly assigned to the motor pool, and grease monkeys who spent the pre-war years turning wrenches were suddenly put in charge of the Army's chow lines. Soda jerks were transformed into medical technicians, and skilled construction workers became tank drivers. A radio repairman was turned into an infantryman, and a police officer was assigned to drive some general around Washington for the duration of the war. There seemed to be no end to the ways that assignments ignored a recruit's most basic capabilities. Some of this was due to the military's insistence that everyone be brought to the same level, both physically and emotionally, before training them the military way. Severing of the apron strings from mom was a big factor—expunging anything from a recruit that smacked of home and the life he had left behind. But mostly it had to do with a lack of common sense.

In Bill Witcomb's case, at least, his next assignment would take on a level of absurdity that even military personnel experts would have difficulty defending or rationalizing in later years.

Young Lt. Witcomb was assigned the task of training new pilot candidates with their basic and primary flying at Gunter Field in Montgomery, Alabama. The candidates were volunteers to a man, all young and eager to serve, like Bill. But unlike Bill, they were all Free French forces sent over to America, the famed Arsenal of Democracy, to learn from the newly emerging experts in the endeavors of aerial warfare. An unknown wizard in the Army Air Force personnel office was sifting through records and discovered that Bill Witcomb was born in Montreal. Montreal is a bilingual city whose inhabitants speak both French and English. Having a working familiarity with both languages is essential for doing business in that city. Therefore, surmised the personnel official, Bill Witcomb was the perfect flight instructor to train the Free French troops who themselves spoke no English—he was a capable instructor pilot and he was from Montreal. The only problem with the logic employed by the personnel official was that it failed to discover that Bill Witcomb left Montreal around his fifth birthday, never having spent a day in school in Canada. His parents were both English immigrants who themselves spoke only English, and Bill was raised on nothing but his father's mother tongue. Regardless of his inability to understand or speak French, as with any other military assignment, Bill was expected to carry out his mission.

Lt. Witcomb, with barely two years of high school French to his credit, was thrown into a crash course of aviation French. Words like *parachute* and *aileron* came easily to Bill, and to his pupils as well. But phrases that would snap a French-speaking flight student back to reality on final approach came a tad slower—dangerously slower. He did his best, climbing into the front seat of those canvas coffins and praying each time that the young Frenchman behind him had either a clue as to how to fly, the luck of a leprechaun holding a four-leaf clover, or an ability to instantly read Bill's mind in midflight. "*Lord, make this a good flight*," became his most-uttered phrase at the outset of each day, spoken almost as a mantra. Ground loops, awkward takeoffs and landings, and stalls were commonplace. The wheel struts of the tiny trainers were pushed to the limits, requiring servicing from the mechanics after almost every flight. Wingtips were scarred on the underside where they had touched the ground after a student improperly leveled the aircraft on a takeoff or landing, forcing Bill to wrest the controls from them and trim the airplane himself at the very last moment. It was a frightful time for him, more harrowing than he'd ever imagined. He never knew when he boarded an airplane whether or not it was destined to be his last flight.

On the ground, Ellie Witcomb bit her lower lip every morning, as Bill would head out to the airfield for his daily dose of "French dressing." Like the wife of every AAF pilot, she was prepared to hear that her husband was injured or killed in a flight gone awry or lost in the line of duty during a combat mission. With the war raging the world over, she was even somewhat prepared for the telegram that would say her husband was killed or missing in action. But it was too much to contemplate that she would have to face such a bitter reality as losing her spouse at the hands of an ally who was incapable of comprehending an order spoken in aviation French or shouted out in desperation in very guttural English. Like the limited number of B-17s available to training command, better to lose Bill in combat than in some foolish training mishap—especially a mishap that was the result of a simple language barrier.

Bill struggled along with his French flying cadets. He acquired familiarity with their language at the same rate they acquired the ability to fly—it was a slow process at best, and neither side made much progress. The French Foreign Legion was where most of the cadets had come from, and many were now anxiously willing to return to the inevitable discomforts and risks of being an infantryman in combat pitted against the formidable German Afrika Korps, rather than risk their lives trying to assimilate flying instructions from an ally whom they could barely understand. They were volunteers to a man for the Legion, but they had been ordered to learn to fly, and none were effervescent at the idea of continuing with such risks. Bill was not the least bit offended when one of the students stated, without reservation, his complaints about flying. He said he'd just as soon die in the obscurity of a foxhole, or be blown to small pieces by bombs from above, than to continue to risk his life every day in those canvas kites that he was being forced to fly. Many of that man's fellow cadets agreed that facing the Nazis on the ground was preferable to flight training, and they pulled the plugs on their flying careers as well. Better to be shot by the enemy and die a hero in the trenches than to crash and burn in obscurity in Alabama. The program was ultimately doomed as a result.

The only real perquisite of the Free French training assignment was that Bill had his own airplane at his disposal. It wasn't one of the spare trainers with an in-line engine with no amenities. Instead, it was an AT-9—a twin-engine, aluminum-skinned beauty with enclosed cockpit, instruments, and advanced navigational gear. He spent his regular duty time with the French cadets in the canvas trainers, but his free time was spent in his own airplane. Those were the good hours for Bill Witcomb—hours spent in acquiring information rather than disseminating it. He was honing multiengine techniques that would serve him well when he returned to his beloved B-17.

It was during this time as a basic flight instructor that Bill learned that his younger brother Ken, now eighteen years old and fresh out of high school, had volunteered for the U.S. Army. Ken was already through his basic training and undergoing advanced infantry training when Bill was able to steal some time and fly to his base to see him. It fit in with Bill's professional agenda because he had to occasionally make routine cross-country flights of 500 or 1,000 miles in a hop in order to maintain his flying proficiency and qualify for his flight instructor's pay. Ken's first instinct, being so fresh out of basic training, was to salute the handsome lieutenant that he saw standing before him on the tarmac. But, upon closer scrutiny, he saw the unmistakable countenance of his big brother and quickly broke his stance to embrace Bill in a brotherly hug. They talked for several hours, the two Witcomb boys—Ken marveling at Bill's shiny new airplane, and Bill cross-examining Ken on the condition of their mother and father. Both found it hard to believe that they were doing their respective jobs. Bill had always been the consummate organizer and expeditor: presumably more suited to the demands of the quartermaster corps or some engineering pursuit. Ken had always had a fascination with airplanes, and would have been right at home in the cockpit of any Army Air Force airplane. But war has a unique way of redefining lives in ways that are often hard to envision—like having to instruct French students—and the individual capacities and motivations that each Witcomb boy brought to the war determined where each would serve. Ken had been an accomplished Boy Scout, and was about to put the skills he had acquired earning merit badges to good use in the field as an infantry soldier, just as Bill had parlayed his mathematical and organizational skills into his present position.

Before they parted in the twilight of that waning afternoon, Bill and Ken prayed together. Unlike Bill's prayer before each flight, they asked God to watch over each other and keep them from harm, and to keep their parents safe and secure in their home in Newburyport. They embraced as brothers do—hard and long, firmly patting each other's back—and said their goodbyes. Bill then climbed into his cockpit, spun up the engines, and took off to get back to his French foreign legionnaires. It was the best time the two had ever spent together as brothers. As Bill moved the throttles forward and the plane began to turn, he glanced out the window on the left side and saw Ken at full attention, holding a crisp military salute. Bill backed the throttles down gently, sat erect in his seat and returned the salute with pride. Bill smiled, and then waved as he moved the aircraft away from the operations building to the taxiway. Ken returned the wave to Bill in the dusk from the tarmac, waited for his plane to vanish from sight, and then walked back to his barracks. Each brother was in his place—Bill in the clouds in his silver bird, Ken consigned to the ground with his M-1 rifle and field pack. It was from these positions that these two young men would now fight the war.

Of course, Bill's "hands-across-the-sea" training program was destined for dismantling anyway. On June 6, 1944, the Allied invasion of Europe began in full force. The largest armada ever known, consisting of thousands of ships and boats, embarked from hundreds of English ports to deliver their cargoes of men and materiel to the Normandy beachhead. Thousands of airplanes delivered bombs, paratroopers, and supplies onto the French peninsula during the coordinated pre-dawn attack. Hundreds of thousands of men were deposited on the beaches along the French coast in the early-morning hours of that day. Thousands would never see noon. The need for the Allied military to create pilots from infantrymen was no longer critical. Maintaining the beachhead and the toehold on the continent of Europe was the essential objective now. Ken was completing his training on the longest day. Destiny dictated replacement duty for the invasion force in store for him.

Among the stories that have become legendary in American history, the story of D-Day ranks among the top in the annals of military heroism and valor. The wall of concrete, steel, and fire that greeted the American, British, Canadian, and French troops from the ridges of the Normandy coast was nothing less than extraordinary. The venomous sting from the hedgerows, where German sniper rifles and artillery batteries lay in wait, was devastating. The ground exploding beneath their feet from millions of German mines, planted like so many potatoes, cost the average foot soldier plenty. "Fortress Europe" would be breached that day in June, but at a stiff price for the Allied forces. Millions of men would soon pour into Europe and slug their way slowly toward Berlin. There was now a new focus for warfare, and it was on the ground.

Hitler's great Atlantic Wall had been penetrated, and in grand style. His psychic intuition told him to keep his crack Panzer units in the north in reserve to counter the invasion that was certain to come at the Pas de Calais; the narrowest part of the English Channel. When the anticipated invasion course wasn't followed, Hitler refused to be dissuaded from his fervent belief that the real Allied blow would come in the north, despite overwhelming fighting in the south near Cherbourg.

With the new Supreme Headquarters Allied Expeditionary Force (SHAEF) emphasis on supporting the ground invasion of France, Allied air power moved from tactical considerations to strategic ones, concentrating efforts on the precision bombing of Germany. The air mission was less concerned now with the point of the German javelin, and more focused instead upon the hand that wielded it. Although tactical aerial support of ground operations was still an enormous part of the Allied air mission, striking the factories, bridges, marshaling yards, and overall infrastructure of the Third Reich—waging total war against all the German people for their support of the Nazi regime—was the new focus.

There was a feeling of jubilation in the days and weeks after the Normandy invasion. There was an optimistic belief that it would all be over soon. Hitler's forces were retreating for the first time, and many outside, and even inside, the U.S. military believed the war all but won. Many military training programs were discontinued as a result, sending thousands of trainees off to combat assignments. With the reduction in the number of trainees in the various programs, the demand for qualified instructors was reduced greatly, and instructors in all fields were being melded back into regular units for combat assignments. In the case of the heavy bombers, aircrews were hastily being assembled from the ranks of instructors and former trainees alike. Bill Witcomb would hurriedly be assigned to train B-17 pilots for a short period, but he would also eventually receive his orders to prepare for an assignment overseas, and he would meet his newly assigned crew in due course. Everything was in place now for a wrap-up of the world war.

But the resolve of the Third Reich was great, its resistance fierce, and there was much more fighting to be endured by both sides before the curtain would be drawn on the ultimate finale. Before the war would end, military strategists would be faced with grave second thoughts about their discontinuance of training programs when they were faced with an all-out winter offensive launched by a German war machine that they presumed was dysfunctional. There were more battles to be waged, and Bill Witcomb was determined he and his crew would be ready. But first, they had to get to know each other.

Chapter 8

The Civil Rights Movement of 1945

"You mentioned something about being in charge of some Negro soldiers, Bill. Was that during the war?" asked the doctor.

"No," answered Bill matter-of-factly, "that was just after the war."

"You had some troubles with that?"

"The only troubles I had were with the white soldiers. The black kids were alright."

"What kind of trouble did the white soldiers give you?"

Bill explained that he had been assigned as a staff officer assisting the commanding officer of Gunter Field upon his return from Europe. He told of his perilous trip back from England aboard the refitted luxury liner, which was re-contoured to accommodate roughly three times the number of passengers it had been originally designed to carry. It made for cramped, uncomfortable conditions, even for young officers, and resulted in the ship being slightly top-heavy. Fortunately, the threat of U-boats along the Atlantic corridor no longer existed, and the seas in the north Atlantic in late spring and early summer were relatively calm, save the occasional iceberg that stumbled into the path of the steamer.

Bill Witcomb may have fulfilled his flying obligation with the 35 missions he flew, but he still lacked the number of points needed to muster out of the military. He had acquired more points than most soldiers, but his failure to write himself up for medals that he truly deserved while at Station 111 left him a bit short.

Upon reporting for duty at Gunter Field, now-Captain Witcomb assumed an adjutant's position to the CO, handling a variety of troublesome administrative chores that cropped up. Gunter Field was an integrated base on paper, but blacks and whites were segregated within the station by design. The commander had lost his ranking officer, who was squadron commander of the Negro soldiers, to the points system, and he was hard-pressed to find a suitable replacement. It was then that he turned to Bill Witcomb.

"I need a man I can trust in there, Witcomb, and a man who can get the job done," explained the colonel. "We've got a problem with morale there. Can you handle it? Can you straighten this out for me?" Bill was startled at the question. *Bill Witcomb to take charge of an all-black unit*? Witcomb was not only as white as the sheet on a Klansman's head; he was a Yankee from Massachusetts—from north of Boston to boot. How was this going to help with the Negro morale problem? But Bill Witcomb was not one to shrink from a tough assignment. He was a seasoned combat veteran who had earned plenty of service medals to prove it, despite those medals having never been awarded. He didn't shrink from the enemy under fire, and he wasn't going to shrink from his responsibilities now.

"I can handle it, sir," was his reply. In no time, he was standing before a crisp formation of black soldiers, assembled on the parade ground to meet their new immediate commander. Many were combat veterans themselves; some served in support units, and others were recruits that had only been in long enough to endure training. Regardless, they were all proud to be serving, and all convinced that this was just another lily-white officer sent by command to sit on the lid of the garbage can and keep the refuse inside. Bill Witcomb didn't see that as his job. He was their C.O., nothing more, nothing less. They were his soldiers, nothing more, nothing less. As long as they acted like soldiers, they'd be treated like soldiers.

They marched like no other squadron on the base. There was a rhythm and style in their marching that was lacking in the white companies. There was a harmony of sound in their singing, and a symphony of step as they moved like a machine from one part of the station to another. Bill would watch them drill and marvel at what they displayed on the drill field. Precision movement, that was their way—an entire squadron of men moving as though they had become a single living organism—a true metaphor for teamwork. Those who would stereotype would say that it was something innate, something tribal—something black. But Bill chose instead to believe that it was a collective attitude about themselves, feelings brought forth deep from within the well of pride that was inside each man. It wasn't black so much as it was American. He admired them for serving a country that still didn't regard them equally with the white man.

Bill remained a pilot throughout his post-war years. To do so, he had to maintain a certain number of flight hours, and had to complete certain minimum requirements of flight. One such requirement was the cross-country requirement. This basically involved flying a thousand miles or more in any number of increments. He could take off from Gunter Field, fly to Florida, and then hop to Mississippi and back to Alabama. As long as he logged the requisite number of air miles, the necessary number of takeoffs and landings, he met the qualification.

He scheduled himself for just such a cross-country, planning a trip that included a brief pit stop at Jacksonville NAS (Naval Air Station). Most Army Air Force pilots tried to show a little more posh and precision on naval air stations because of the inter-agency rivalry that existed. For that matter, when an AAF plane touched down on a NAS, Navy personnel were much more observant and much more critical of the maneuvers executed by the pilot, simply because he wasn't Navy.

Captain Witcomb asked the sergeant major of the squadron if he would care to accompany him on the flight. He planned on landing near the sergeant's home in Mississippi and spending the night with friends there. This would give the sergeant an evening with his family. The sergeant major accepted with gratitude. The pair climbed into the two-seater and Bill spun up the engine for takeoff.

Within a few hours, they were cleared for landing and refueling at Jacksonville. Bill sat the bird down with precision onto the field and moved to the far end of the runway, near the junction of another active runway. He glanced toward the tower and saw two controllers there staring at his plane with binoculars. This was not unusual, in and of itself, given that Bill was in an Army Air Force airplane on a Naval Air Station runway. He radioed for taxi instructions and there was no reply. He tried it again—still no reply. And then it dawned on him—the sergeant major in the front seat of the airplane was black. *Those bastards*, thought Bill. The sergeant major was a decorated veteran from the European theater of operations. He had been in his second year of medical school when the war broke out, and he volunteered for active duty immediately. He was a patriot! But he was black.

"Did that make you mad?" asked the doctor.

"It made me damn mad," said Bill defiantly.

"And what did you do about it?" questioned the clinician.

Realizing that this was just another sterling example of race prejudice, Bill decided to push his position and the issue to the limit.

"Okay, boys," he said calmly into the microphone, "if you want to play that game … " Bill pushed the throttle forward just a little and moved the airplane right smack into the middle of the intersection of two active runways. Federal Aviation Administration rules, even in the 1940's were explicit: as long as any airplane occupied one inch of an active runway, no other airplane could use that runway. Air Force Captain Witcomb, his black sergeant major, and their little two-seater airplane had ostensibly shut down all air traffic into and out of Jacksonville NAS. They wouldn't have to wait long now for their instructions to taxi. In short order, they came, and

Bill rogered the instructions and moved off the runway to the tarmac near the refueling area. The plane was gassed up and back in the air in minutes.

Bill had endeared himself to the sergeant major not only by his display of bravado at Jacksonville NAS, but also in his demeanor around the station. Capt. Witcomb had endured considerable harangue from his fellow white officers. When eating in the officer's open mess one day, a spiteful young captain remarked that the black troops were unsuitable for military life because of their lack of moral code and because of their overwhelming number of sexual indiscretions.

"They got more syphilis then you can shake a stick at," commented the bigoted young officer. Bill took this very personally and immediately marched himself to the base hospital where he spoke with the chief medical officer. He wanted to know if this accusation was true. Did the black troops have more venereal disease? After researching the records, the chief medical officer rendered a report back to Bill that was astonishing. Not only did the Negro troops have no reported syphilis, the highest incident rate of all venereal diseases on base was concentrated in the white junior officer corps. Bill Witcomb got on his soapbox armed with the truth and put the young captain to shame in a public display at the open mess.

"It was just like the price-fixing thing with your father-in-law, wasn't it Bill?" asked the doctor.

"What?" asked his patient.

"You were trying to right a wrong, correct?"

"I never thought of it that way," said Bill. "I just knew that I couldn't be party to what they were saying about those men. They were good men. They did a good job. And it wasn't right for people to belittle them simply because they were black."

"So, you were correcting an injustice?"

"I was doing exactly the same thing we all did during the war."

"Like I said, you were correcting an injustice," said the doctor.

"Have it your way," replied Bill.

Throughout his therapy, Bill Witcomb was confronted with incontrovertible facts about himself. The war that America had waged with the Axis had been replaced by a war being waged inside Bill's mind. There were a host of unresolved conflicts from the war at odds with each other in there, and more were being added all the time. Under normal circumstances, the conflicts associated with race or greed would not manifest themselves into a debilitating psychosis. But the open wounds that were left behind after his combat experience were just too much for him to deal with. Bill finally began to see this. He began to realize that a good portion of his anxiety was the result of the questions that remained in his head from the war. He started to see that none of the conflicts that had been instrumental in his breakdown were really all that monumental. The underlying troubles were located deep within his subconscious—and this was the key to everything. Getting the demons out of there and onto the table where he could deal with them was essential. Realizing this was the first step toward his recovery.

Bill remembered out loud another side of his experience with the black squadron—a not-so-good experience. He was in his office one day when one of the black soldiers came rushing in, screaming about two men trying to kill each other. The sergeant major and Bill scrambled out the door and followed the hysterical young soldier to a nearby barracks. There, in the squad bay, Bill found two Negro soldiers squared off against each other. Each wielded a knife, and each would lunge at the other, swiping at his opponent with the weapon. The men in the barracks had been cheering them on, until they realized their commander was present. Many of them snapped to attention. Others continued to jeer. The combatants were inhibited in no way by the presence of an officer, much less their commander. They each meant to kill the other man, or at least defend their own life. Neither would back down.

The sergeant major yelled at them, to no avail. This pair meant to see this duel through to the death, one way or another.

Bill was compelled to do something radical. He reached down on the floor and retrieved an empty Coca Cola® bottle. He held the bottle by its neck and smashed the base of it against a metal bedpost. The glass shattered, breaking some of the tension in the room. The chorus of onlookers was silent for the first time, realizing that a new and powerful element had been introduced to the fight. The fighters were distracted only slightly at first; then, gradually, even they had to pay close attention to the officer who was edging his way between them.

"Okay," said Bill firmly, as he brandished the jagged bottle glass toward each of them in turn, "You wanna kill somebody, you gotta come through me first!" The sergeant major was overwhelmed. He couldn't believe that any officer would risk himself in the middle of a knife fight between a couple of coloreds, and a white officer was just out of the question. Yet, there he was, bottle in hand, ready for their next move. Bill poked the glass at each of them one more time, and slowly, in turn, they dropped their knives to the floor where the sergeant major was quick to pick them up.

"Both of you, to the orderly room," demanded the senior enlisted man. "NOW!" The pair of soldiers moved grudgingly across the squadron compound to the office where Bill and his top kick had been. They entered the office and awaited their fate.

Back in the barracks, Bill pointed to the broken glass on the floor and asked one of the men to clean it up before anyone cut himself. The soldier nodded his assent, amazed at the cool and collected way the captain spoke. It was as though nothing at all had just happened. There was no anger, no fuss, and no fumes. Nothing! It was just another business day for the squadron commander.

Bill strolled back across the compound to his office at a leisurely pace and wandered in slowly. He poured himself a cup of coffee and sat down.

"Sir, the men are ready for punishment," said the sergeant major. "I've told them about the UCMJ (Uniform Code of

Military Justice) and Article Fifteen. They're willing to accept commander's punishment for their actions." Article Fifteen was a provision in military law that was tantamount to a plea bargain in civilian courts. It basically meant that you pled guilty to your commander and subjected yourself to his punishment rather than face a general or special court martial—the higher up the commander, the greater the punishment that could be imposed. For an infraction of the rules of this magnitude, Bill had it within his power to send both of them to the stockade for months. He could assign them additional duty, or even refuse to punish them and force them to stand court martial. The risk of a court martial was a dishonorable discharge plus jail time with hard labor in a military prison. The pair of young soldiers knew they were in deep and troubled waters.

Bill sat back in his chair and sipped his coffee in contemplation. "What started the fight?" he asked. Neither soldier was able to recall what started things, or they simply chose not to tell. "Men, there are hundreds of people right here on this base who think you are nothing but animals. They think there should be a barbed wire fence strung up all around this squadron area and a lock put on the gate. There's probably a Klan meeting going on in town right now, as we speak. On top of all that, you've got to finish your training in order to move on to your next assignment. Now, with all that to fight against, don't you think it's pretty stupid to be fighting with each other? Look at each other," said the captain, and the pair complied. "That's not the enemy you're looking at. That's your ally—your buddy. That's the guy who's going to save your life in combat. But to do that, he's got to be alive himself, and killing him off before you get out of training isn't going to help your chances in combat. It won't do much for your social life either, spending the rest of your life pounding rocks at Leavenworth."

"First," said Bill, "I don't ever want to hear of an episode like this again. That display you put on in the barracks was pitiful. Second, shake hands with each other." The pair of soldiers slowly faced each other again and shook hands reservedly. "Like you *mean* it," demanded the commander. They shook hands again, but this time both cracked a small grin for the corners of their mouths. "Now, get out of my orderly room. The sergeant major and I have real work to do. And airmen," said Bill as the pair turned in unison and marched for the door, "Don't let me hear about any more trouble in the future. If I do, I won't hesitate to drop the roof on you. This is your only break. Use it wisely." The men came to attention facing their commander and raised their hands to the eyebrows in salute to him. Bill stood and squared himself behind his desk and returned their salute in crisp military fashion. The airmen held their salute, even after Bill began to lower his hand to his side. It was a rarity—enlisted airmen prided themselves in getting their hand to their sides a split second after the saluted officer acknowledged their salute by raising his hand. Holding their salute until Bill's hand was at his side was their way of saying "thank you" for being unexpectedly understanding.

"So, you tip at windmills and you're Santa Claus too," observed the doctor.

"What's that supposed to mean?" asked Bill sharply.

"What would any other officer have done in that situation? Wouldn't he have punished the men for the fight?"

"I have no idea what anyone else would do. I only know that I did what I had to do to keep that squadron running at peak efficiency."

"Were there any more incidents like the knife fight?"

"No. That was all the excitement for that squadron, for as long as I was there anyway."

That statement was far from the truth. True, there were no more outbreaks of violence between black soldiers in that squadron while Bill was commander. But there were hundreds of cases of race prejudice being foisted upon the black airmen under his command all the time. In town, if a white man approached a black man on the sidewalk, the black man was obliged to cross the street in order to clear the way for the white. This was expected more of the black airmen because, after all, they were in the service of the white man. On the station, the "coloreds" were thought to be slow and dim-witted, and white soldiers never missed an opportunity to express this to them. They were jeered and insulted with venomous language wherever they went. They were the butt of hideous pranks that amused only the smallest minds on the planet.

Maybe the doctor was right. Maybe Bill had been tipping at windmills. Maybe he *was* trying to be Santa Claus. Maybe he was just trying to right an ancient wrong somehow. But if that were true, what was so wrong in that? After all, wasn't that what the entire war was about? For some time, Bill's post-hospitalization treatment sessions were among the most difficult hours of his life. He was expected to fragment his entire life, place the pieces on the table in front of him, then reassemble the whole thing in a completely different configuration and have it all make sense. It would be a long road to recovery.

CHAPTER 9

A Cohesive Mob

At Avon Park, Bill Witcomb's fate was about to change. He had been content training pilots—even French Foreign Legion cadets—during the previous two years for the Army Air Force. He was pleased that he had been making his contribution to the war effort, even though the contribution seemed somewhat passive in nature. His mother and father were elated that he was out of harm's way and in a safe stateside assignment that was likely to keep him out of combat. But Elsie and Bill senior had little way of knowing that their eldest son was destined to fly combat missions all too soon.

Bill had been instructing pilots in the subtleties of handling one of the largest airplanes ever built. He not only showed them the standard methods of flying a B-17, he demanded of them the ability to demonstrate practically that they had learned the lessons he had taught them. His air exams were among the toughest in the air force, pitting a young pilot's skill achieved over a few short weeks of multi-engine training against the rigid standards of both the United States Army Air Force and Second Lieutenant Bill Witcomb. They were a tough pair to come up against.

During his months as a flight instructor for the B-17, Bill used to spend as much time as he could inside the Link C-3 Trainer, an early flight simulator. Aside from the serious business of learning how to fly using nothing but instruments, Bill enjoyed as many hours as possible inside that tiny machine, because it was one of the few rooms on the entire base that was air-conditioned. In fact, air conditioning wasn't even the appropriate term in 1943 and 1944—the proper word was *refrigeration*. The trainer was a fairly sophisticated piece of equipment for its day, and it was necessary, due to the abundance of heat that it generated, to keep it cool. To do this properly, the room in which it sat had to be refrigerated to compensate for the massive heat production. Summertime at Avon Park was hot and humid, and Bill relished every minute he spent inside the chilled simulator. In the end, not only was he refreshed by the respite from the local weather, he was also gaining valuable experience with the instruments that were similar to those on the B-17, which would prove invaluable to him in the future.

But the war in Europe, where the majority of the B-17's true capabilities were being tested to the limit each day, was perceived to be winding down. Germany—although far from being defeated by either the Allied forces in the west or the Russian army in the east—was still producing vast quantities of munitions and arms, still marshalling huge stores of supplies, and still mobilizing large numbers of men to throw against the rest of the world. The two remaining Axis powers were still very much intact and very much allied, even though neither was any longer in a position to come to the fighting aid of the other in their opposite corner of the world. Both the Germans and the Japanese were well-occupied in their respective theaters of operations and could spare nothing to assist their ally. As a result, Allied military planners could finally foresee the end in Europe. The D-Day invasion on June 6, 1944 had given SHAEF the foothold it needed to move swiftly up the continent. Losses for the Japanese in the Pacific were setting the stage for an Asian demise as well. It was now only a matter of time, men, and materiel. Or so it was believed.

The USAAF reasoned that it could now move some of its primary flight instructors into actual combat assignments because the volume of trainees that they were preparing would soon be significantly diminished. The kind of flying that Bill was teaching—formation flying—was not used extensively in the Pacific war. When B-17s were used, their primary function was not necessarily bombing. Because of their long range, they were spread over a much wider geographic area of island bases in order to cover more square miles of ocean with more individualized aerial reconnaissance patrols. But almost all of the Fortresses had been recalled from the Pacific for duty elsewhere. By late 1944, they were also gradually being replaced by the larger, longer-range, and more formidable B-29 Superfortresses. Furthermore, the Japanese air umbrella that had once been impenetrable, was now reduced to more of a nuisance to American air power provided by the Army, Army Air Force, Navy, and Marines. After the "Marianas Turkey Shoot," where dozens upon dozens of enemy airplanes were vanquished from the skies by naval gunfire, Japanese air attacks consisted mostly of desperation flights, stemming from the new policy that saw the rebirth of an ancient warrior sect, the *Kamikaze* (Divine Wind). These suicide pilots were responsible for the destruction of many Allied ships, but they sacrificed themselves and their airplanes for their cause, thus further reducing the number of trained pilots and aircraft available for combat. They could only die once for their Emperor, no matter how devoutly loyal they were. This meant that Japan would have to bring up yet another generation of soldiers to replace those lost in battle, and this would take at least a decade and a half. The problem both Axis powers faced was that they needed that next generation of fighters now.

In the Pacific theater of operations, the U.S. Army handled moving men and supplies, the Army Air Force bombed or provided reconnaissance, the Navy strafed and torpedoed, and Marine pilots provided close air support to invading amphibious Marine units that began moving up the island chain toward Tokyo. It was a ballet of aerial warriors, all focused on a single motivated and tenacious enemy.

Europe was the same ... but different. Navy and Marine pilots played virtually no first-line role in the primary air war over Europe—they had their hands full in the Pacific where they were fighting a Navy war. After the Normandy invasion, Army cargo aircraft were used primarily for reconnaissance, cargo, and re-supply of Operation Overlord (the Normandy Invasion) forces, and the airlifting of thousands of troops during the subsequent Operation Market Garden (the Allied invasion of Holland and Belgium). British Bomber Command continued to attack strategic targets with carpet bombing during night missions over Germany and tactical locations all over Europe. This left the task of precision daylight strategic bombardment to the USAAF.

Unlike the Japanese, who steadfastly believed that their divine leader, Emperor Hirohito, would, with some Godlike gesture, turn the tide of battle into victory, in Hitler, many Germans no longer saw spiritual greatness or military genius. Fighting toward an honorable peace would have pleased the general staff—just surviving the war would have pleased pretty much everyone else. Europe had been reduced to a cinder in far too many places. But the madman Hitler still retained his evil reign over Germany through his totalitarian grip on the people, and the Fatherland would fight on, despite the internal dissension and the recognized futility of such a struggle. This meant stepping up the air campaign for both 8th and 9th Air Forces—the 8th based primarily in England, hitting western European targets, and the 9th, based primarily in North Africa, hitting targets all over the Mediterranean and eastern Europe. It meant reaching into the industrial heartland of Germany and attacking the source of production of Hitler's war machine. It ultimately meant bringing all of the horrors of war to all of the German people, not just those exposed to the conflict on the front lines.

By the middle of June 1944, the Allied army was moving across France toward Belgium and the Netherlands, and threatening the industrial heart of Germany itself. By July, the

8th Air Force and Bomber Command of the RAF (Royal Air Force) had set Hamburg ablaze, killing 50,000 in a firestorm that reached 1800 degrees. By August, the 9th Air Force had flown from Libya to the Ploesti oil fields in Romania with 178 B-24 Liberators. On that raid, the airplanes flew roughly 50 feet above both sea and ground levels from Africa to Ploesti in order to evade enemy radar. Fifty-four airplanes were lost during the mission—540 airmen—a loss of over 30%. But the raid did cut into Hitler's primary source of oil, and forced the German Army, from that time forward, to forage for fuel wherever it went.

In 1944, the Norden bombsight had been thoroughly integrated with the autopilot in B-17s, resulting in dramatically increased bombing accuracy. This change allowed the bombardier to fly the airplane completely over the bomb run from his seat in the nose of the aircraft. Prior to this, bombardiers had to telegraph instructions to the pilot and copilot to alter headings—a laborious chore that created a significant lag time that left much to be desired.

Also, the airplanes in a given squadron were linked electronically by this time. It fell to the bombardier in the lead aircraft to set up the bomb run and toggle the bombs at the appropriate time. The tight formations flown by squadrons ensured a narrow spread of bombs if all aircraft dropped their bombs simultaneously. So the lead plane would toggle its bombs, which automatically toggled all the bombs in the trailing aircraft.

As a result of these changes, bombing accuracy rates went from 20% to 76%, based upon a standard of dropping bombs anywhere within 1000 feet of a target. With five-hundred-pound contact bombs, this standard was usually sufficient to knock out a target, given that each plane carried at least nine bombs, and there were usually, at minimum, twenty planes in a squadron or group. Given that many planes, this put at least one hundred and eighty bombs—or forty-five tons of high-explosive ordnance—within proximity of a target, thereby eliminating it from existence in many cases. The vibrations from impact alone were often enough to topple targets that were left unscathed by direct hits. Still other airplanes carried incendiary bombs that set flammable structures ablaze. This firebombing demanded very little precision on the bomb run. The result was usually a firestorm that subsequently consumed the targeted objective, along with the remainder of the adjacent countryside. It created an inferno that devoured everyone and everything; sucking all the air so no one could breathe. Collateral damage was no longer calculated separately; it was now just another part of the equation and the objective.

Stateside, air crews were being assembled to train together quickly and rotate over to Europe for their turn at combat. A year earlier, the famed "Memphis Belle" and her "lucky" crew of ten had completed the then-standard twenty-five-mission requirement and had come home to a hero's welcome. Like all of the air crews in the war, the combat crews of the 8th Air Force were comprised primarily of young men from a variety of places, all of whom were only interested in getting the war over and getting back home to their families and their lives. Most had volunteered, knowing the risk and the cost. Yet they continued to bravely step forward by the thousands and say no to tyranny, fully aware that the odds that they would survive the war were only marginally in their favor. The combat crews of the 8th Air Force were not to have such good odds, losing more men in one day than all the Marines killed during the month-long battle for Iwo Jima. In fact, of all the American combat losses during World War II, aircrews of the mighty 8th Air Force accounted for over ten percent of those killed in action. The B-24 Liberator and the B-17 Flying Fortress were among the most survivable combat aircraft ever put into service by the United States. But the staggering number of casualties suffered by this one combat unit is stark testimony to what those crews continued to face each day. The German war machine was a considerable and immeasurable distance from defeat in 1944.

It stood to reason that the more training a crew had, the better its chances of survival in combat. In this respect, Bill

Witcomb was truly lucky. He personally had the benefit of over two years of intensive flying experience before he was ordered overseas. He had amassed an impressive number of hours in the Link C-3 trainer. He had flown a wide array of aircraft during that time and logged countless hours of four-engine time with the B-17. He knew the inner workings of the airplane, how it was assembled, and how it was maintained. He understood what was required at every crew station, from the bombardier to the tail gunner. He would need to know these jobs intimately in order to keep the crewmen assigned to him properly trained in their respective jobs. The primary job of the pilot was flying the airplane, but his secondary job was training his crew. Bill's own knowledge and experience would prove invaluable, but not nearly as valuable to the missions at hand as the knowledge and experience that his crewmembers brought with them. With the exception of his waist gunner, every man assigned to Bill's crew had been an instructor in his respective field. Each brought a level of expertise and experience that was unmatched in other crews. This volume of experience would often mean the narrow margin of difference between survival and total disaster. But before they could function as a team, they would have to get to know each other.

– – –

Of the three officers assigned to him, Bill Witcomb first encountered his bombardier, Bob Wilson, and his navigator, Wyatt Gillaspie, on the same day. Both were Texans; Wilson seldom made a point of the fact, Gillaspie always did. Both were young, handsome, and swarthy, both ready for action of all kinds, and both highly trained and capable of handling their jobs. But the most significant fact that had to be faced by the young pilot was that both his subordinates were first lieutenants, while Bill Witcomb remained only a second lieutenant. This made for an instant uneasiness between the three men. The pilot of the airplane, the commander, was outranked by two of his key crewmembers. They were Texans and Bill was just another damn Yankee. This alone was sufficient cause for friction. But there would be more.

Gillaspie, or "Gill" as he soon became known, was a lean, tall Lone Star boy from Belvoir, Texas who loved liquor. He had been to college, where presumably he had developed his acuity for drinking, and had been faithfully training navigators for some time when his call to combat came. He was eager for the assignment. He had done his job as he had been ordered, but he didn't much relish the idea of sitting the war out in some training command, teaching youngsters how to navigate airplanes. He was anxious for some action, something other than the ordinary. Regardless of his burning curiosity and anxiety for getting into combat, he didn't much favor the idea of going into battle led by someone whom he outranked. He surmised, appropriately, that there was a reason for this apparent military foul-up. It was simple: Bill Witcomb was a skilled pilot who had not yet been elevated through promotion beyond his initial commissioned rank. Stateside advancement took a back seat to theater promotions, and Bill had been out of the limelight for some time, buried in a quagmire of training commands where promotions were rare, if not nonexistent. Being assigned to train the French flying cadets alone might have sealed his fate, had the program not been eliminated. Gill and Bob Wilson were the exception rather than the rule when it came to promotions, or else they, too, would have been relegated to mere *butter bars* on their shoulders.[1]

Bob Wilson was a bright-faced young man with a warm smile, a keen eye, and a ravenous appetite for the ladies. His precision and expertise with the Norden bombsight were considered exceptional even among bombardiers, and he managed to somehow clone this ability in those whom he instructed. Like

---

[1] *Butter bars* refers to the single gold bar that was the emblem of rank of a second lieutenant. A single silver bar represented a first lieutenant

Gill, Wilson was not inclined to be ordered about by an underling. But then, this was wartime, and orders were orders. Witcomb was the airplane commander, and that was that. The alternative was a court martial. Both Wilson and Gillaspie grumbled often and loudly about being placed under someone who was their junior, but both did their jobs to Witcomb's satisfaction, and that's all that any airplane commander could have asked of them. If they griped and complained while doing those jobs, it was of little consequence, because such utterances were considered—even among officers—a soldier's right. They got the job done.

Both of the Texans routinely wore cowboy boots, despite screaming directives from command for flying personnel to stick strictly to what was issued in both equipment and clothing. Witcomb had no problem with what the pair wore on or off duty, and feared only that one of their pointy boots would accidentally poke a hole in the skin of their airplane. Bill forbade the wearing of cowboy boots while airborne and both the Texas cowboys reluctantly complied. It meant little at the low altitudes at which they were flying, basking in the warmth of the Florida weather. But the altitudes and the weather would be markedly different in Europe.

Witcomb was assigned a fresh new copilot in Frederick Norris Hales, a South Carolina native who had been university trained before joining the Air Force. Hales was a good second pilot, instinctive in his reactions to given circumstances, and capable, in Bill Witcomb's estimation, of taking over the airplane at any time. Like Bill, Hales had been a flight instructor before being assigned to the crew, albeit not with B-17s.

The skies over England were not nearly as hospitable as those over Avon Park, and the winter air over Germany was even less inviting. The weather anomaly made the cumulative benefit of climatic training minimal relative to the environment that crews would face under actual combat conditions. Flying practice missions stateside was no big deal. The climate was warm, the weather good, and the missions were short and unopposed by an aggressive enemy that was out to destroy them. But soon this group of officers would all learn the value of teamwork, because practicing for combat and flying combat were worlds apart. It was important that they function as a well-oiled machine. This would come in time. But first—like long-lost brothers reuniting after an extended absence—they had to get to know how each of the others reacted while flying missions.

Practice bombing missions were flown regularly—almost every day—and additional formation flying was practiced as well. Small groups of B-17s would take off, assemble in a specific formation at a given altitude and location, fly a predetermined route for navigational exercises, and then return to base. Most of these were dry runs, with no payloads of any kind. The gunners were not assigned at first, so the back halves of the airplanes were virtually empty. Occasionally, an observer would climb aboard and fly in the waist area of the fuselage. In the beginning, the only enlisted man aboard was the flight engineer and top turret gunner, Eli Nelson.

Nelson was a small-town boy from northern Alabama, fresh out of the rural south, and now well-versed in the maintenance and in-flight repair of the B-17. He was also an expert gunnery instructor. His combat station made him the only enlisted man on the crew who flew ahead of the bomb bay, in "officer's country." It made him privy to a great deal. But Eli Nelson was up to the task; he was what all four of the officers considered the consummate southern gentleman. In fact, the whole crew, including the ground echelon, revered Eli for his knowledge, his understanding, and his tolerance. The officers never thought about his rank one way or the other. He was the flight engineer, and their best hope for an in-flight patch-up of a disabled airplane. The enlisted men all looked up to him because he was the first man assigned to the airplane after the pilot, making him the elder statesman, so to speak. There was a great view in the top turret, looking out over the top of the airplane. Eli enjoyed that view, even though it was a very confined space in which he had to stand throughout the majority of a flight.

Gill would plot the course, Bob Wilson would align, calibrate, and sight the Norden, and Bill and Hales would steer the airplane within the formation. It was exactly the same as any other military training. In most of the armed forces, it was believed that *practice makes perfect*. But this crew instead followed the USAAF tenet that *perfect practice makes perfect*. Adhering to this philosophy would soon serve them well.

The remainder of the crew—the rest of the enlisted men—joined the team a short time later. Due to cutbacks in crew assignments and the need to stretch the available manpower the AAF had at its disposal, Bill Witcomb was assigned only one waist gunner. During the early stages of the air war, when the missions required two gunners in the waist to stave off fighters, manpower was allocated accordingly. Formation flying at that time had not yet been perfected and German fighters were at their zenith. But in the latter months of 1944, the grand German Luftwaffe had been battered considerably by Allied air power—only a handful of fighters were mustered to face the greatest beachhead in history: Normandy. American bombers came together in formation in what was now called the *bomber stream*. It was in the stream that tight cohesive groups of airplanes flew in close proximity to each other, giving each other the protection of one another's guns. As a result, fewer gunners were needed to battle the dwindling number of German fighters. Consequently, fewer gunners were placed at risk. German antiaircraft artillery (AA) called *fliegerabwehnkanon*—also known as flak—was now of primary concern to Allied crews on bombing runs over Europe, and having a second gunner at risk in the waist of a B-17 would do nothing to bolster an aircraft's chances against it. Flak was random and arbitrary, and the only sure defense against it was to avoid it at all costs. Bill assigned to the waist position the youngest member of the crew, Francis C. Dusenberry (nicknamed "the Kid") of Hampton, Virginia. Dusenberry was a bright, blonde kid right out of high school. He did what he was told to do, and had no problems with Bill being in charge of the airplane. In fact, he preferred it when it counted the most, and he wasn't afraid to say so.

Louis F. Dorenbush was a farm boy from Minnesota who enlisted in the signal corps prior to his being drafted. He had studied radio and telephone at the Dunwoody Institute until the fall of 1943, when he was put on active duty and tested for placement in the Army Air Force. He was accepted to flight school as a pilot trainee and sent to Fort Hayes, Kansas, but the flight training program there ended before he could complete it. From there, he'd been sent along to train as a gunner, and eventually an aerial gunnery instructor. He was the quietest member of the crew. That made him a natural for the loneliness and solitude of the tail. When Witcomb's crew was in the lead, Louis would be the one to see the carnage in the aftermath of a bombing run. He would see the death and destruction on the ground below him as the bombs they had dropped wreaked havoc. He was the first to see airplanes from both their squadron and group being hit by flak. He'd see them exploding into small pieces in midair, or damaged so badly that they couldn't keep up with the group. The wounded war birds would drop from formation and attempt to limp home, usually falling prey to the carnivorous German fighters that prowled the skies in the wake of the bomber stream, like jackals trailing a herd of antelope. Still other airplanes would simply spin downward, spiraling out of sight—the centrifugal force inside the fuselage pinning their doomed crews against the inside of the fuselage and trapping them there until the giant metal coffins drilled themselves into the ground. Had he not been stoical to begin with, Dorenbush would have become so in the wake of all that he witnessed in the tail. He seldom talked on the command set, and then only to call out the location and direction of enemy fighters.

Raymond Dinger, a hard-bitten spark plug from the Bronx, was assigned to the ball turret. He was the shortest of the gunners, which made him physically a more likely candidate for the ball to begin with. But he also had a feisty personality, matching what would become the hallmark of ball turret gunners in the

8th Air Force. He was quick to snarl at anything that displeased him, and Bill Witcomb's landings, at first, were target number one. In the beginning of their association, Dinger would render a demonstrative and disgusted thumbs-down to Lieutenant Witcomb on every landing. From his position in the ball, Dinger could see the trim and position of the airplane with respect to the ground, more so than either the pilot or copilot. His proximity to the ground at landing was far too close for him to tolerate a lot of bouncing at initial touchdown. Traveling at one hundred and twenty-five miles an hour was perilous enough in the ball without being bounced up and down on landing by an insensitive or cavalier pilot. Dinger would crawl out of the aluminum hatch at the top of the ball and into the fuselage, then out the crew door on the starboard side of the airplane. He'd pull a cigarette from the crumpled pack in his leather flight jacket and pull an unhealthy drag into his lungs as he'd walk forward toward the nose. There, the officers and Eli Nelson would swing themselves down through the tiny square hatch on the port side of the nose. He'd wait to catch Lt. Witcomb's eye, then extend his right arm to his side and make the gesture. Stateside, Dinger never gave a thumbs-up. Some pilots might have considered this insubordination. Bill Witcomb deemed it Dinger's right. After all, the risks associated with the ball turret were the highest on the airplane—indeed, among the highest risks in all the military—and odds were that Dinger would never survive a tour of duty without being killed, wounded badly, or literally frozen to death during a mission. There was also a challenge for Bill in Dinger's evaluation, and Bill Witcomb never winced from an honest challenge. Bill never made mention of the fact that riding in the ball during a takeoff or a landing was strictly prohibited by orders.

Gregory Ringwald rounded out the crew. He was the radio operator and would have manned the overhead fifty-caliber gun that was just behind the bomb bay, had one been installed. Instead, when the need arose, he would move aft of the radio room, stumble over the ball turret, and man one of the two waist guns. He too had been an instructor in both radio school and in gunnery, and was well-suited for this assignment. But, for some unknown reason, Greg Ringwald and Bill Witcomb never really hit it off. Ringwald quickly became the pet whipping boy on the crew for the airplane commander.

So now they were assembled, the nine warriors, and now they would train together before going off to war. The weeks and months ahead would bring the adjustment of their lives. In order to demonstrate his leadership of the crew and his command of the aircraft, Second Lieutenant Bill Witcomb made the crew stand formal inspection before every flight. The entire crew, officers included, was required to stand at attention in crisp military formation below the nose of their airplane, where Bill would inspect their uniforms and equipment and point out any and all discrepancies and deficiencies. Other crews would file past in awe of the butter-bar martinet who made his crew jump through such hoops. The pre-flight formations and inspection became the talk of the station, as well as a ritual for his crew. Before their training phase together was completed, they would stand inspection and Lt. Bill Witcomb would be unable to find any flaws. This was the underlying purpose, to Bill's way of thinking—to make certain that these men were ready for combat. But reinforcing the notion that he was the boss was always in the forefront of his mind.

But despite all the cohesive aspects of this initial training phase, and all the positive behavior that it imparted on the crew, there remained one crewmember yet to sign on—the airplane itself. The biggest and most important member of this crew was their airplane, for they were nothing without her. To fight the war and to protect this crew, it would need to be a very special airplane. And, indeed, she was.

CHAPTER 10

43-38711

In 1944, the flag of the United States of America consisted of seven red stripes, six white stripes, and a field of blue with six rows of eight stars each. It was a symmetrical flag indeed. The United States of America consisted of just the forty-eight contiguous states on the continent of North America. Alaska and Hawaii were only U.S. possessions, each containing military installations that were vital to the defense of the United States, to be sure, but still just possessions. The country, as a nation, had not yet expanded its thinking beyond the shores of the continent. Manifest Destiny had been fulfilled in the minds of most people when the southwestern states joined the Union in 1912. America fought in World War I primarily to support the concept of freedom in the western European democracies. But America's involvement in that conflict was partially undertaken to keep the fighting offshore. It meant exporting troops, but, at the same time, it was believed that this ensured the safety of the American democracy in the Western Hemisphere. In 1918 this was, for the most part, true.

By 1944, many things had changed. Advancements in technology had brought the world's divergent interests much closer together, geographically speaking. Since Charles Lindbergh's historic adventure, transoceanic flights were now a reality, even though they were usually accomplished in a hopscotch fashion. Transoceanic crossings by ship were faster than ever before. These two combined capabilities catapulted invasion of the United States by a hostile power for the first time to something far beyond a theoretical possibility. This did not escape the notice of American military leaders who, even in 1944, feared that an invasion by its clearly defined enemies was both probable and imminent. This explains, to some degree, the reason the burgeoning new military machine still maintained a vast Army, Navy, and Air Force contingent well within the confines of the 48 states. True, many of these troops were still in training. But a substantial standing military lay in readiness, ready to counterstrike if the need arose. Justification was simple: the Germans had been prolific in their conquest of other nations up until then, even though they had yet to venture across the Channel to England, and the Japanese were vicious in their capture and occupation of China and hundreds of islands and tiny nations throughout the Pacific. The fear of invasion, given the foe that America was fighting, had become a legitimate one, and worthy of a sound homeland defense strategy.

Despite the vastness of this standing army in the early 1940s, the emphasis of the people on the home front was actually the fighting front. In every walk of life, Americans pitched in and helped the war effort. Many of the norms that had been in place for decades were suddenly and irrevocably set aside. Everything that could be used toward the war effort was collected and forged into weapons or equipment for the fighting men abroad. Children willingly donated their steel toys to the cause. All Americans were subjected to the strict rationing of food, fuel, and other commodities that had previously been taken for granted. Scrap metal drives and rubber drives provided a wealth of raw materials for military use. Bond drives raised the needed cash capital with which to finance the war. Blood drives were constant and provided a chance at life for those wounded in combat.

People at home went without meat, without sugar, and without butter in order to save them for the soldiers fighting abroad. Even prison inmates at the New Hampshire state prison in Concord maintained their own victory garden to support the boys overseas, vowing that their incarceration was not going to be an added burden upon their government in wartime. They ate what they produced and shared what was left with the poor people of the city of Concord. The clergy across the land sold war bonds and advocated a philosophy that justified—even sanctified—the waging of war against the powers of evil in Berlin and Tokyo, though this was in direct conflict with everything they had preached prior to the war. Women quickly entered the workforce and picked up where the men had left off in industrial America. Females of all ages were handling heavy equipment, doing precision machining, and welding together the hulls of ships and the frames of airplanes in factories and assembly plants across the country. Their men were facing the Axis forces firsthand, and they wanted to ensure that those men had the very best equipment with which to wage the war. Toward this aim, the women of America's new workforce put forth every effort to learn their jobs and do them well throughout the various defense plants in which they worked.

One such defense plant was the Boeing Aircraft plant in Seattle, Washington. There, countless skilled workers—men and women alike—were assembling the airplanes that would carry American bombs to their targets around the globe. It was at the heavily camouflaged Boeing plant, the largest manufacturing structure in the world at that time, that the Boeing-built B-17G numbered 43-38711 was constructed. Like the other 4,034 B-17Gs built by Boeing, a special care accompanied every rivet and weld. There was a certain integrity and strength to the airframe that transcended that of most airplanes. The design was undoubtedly the critical factor, since the Douglas and Lockheed-Vega plants helped turn out the 8,680 B-17Gs constructed for the war, all of which had a special something built into them. Multi-engine pilots and combat crews from all theaters had raved about the airworthiness and survivability of all the B-17 models during the preceding two years of aerial combat. But the

B-17G, with its new twin fifty-caliber chin gun turret, was the one they'd all been waiting for.

The "Flying Fortress"—the moniker given the B-17 by the press when it first rolled onto the tarmac in the mid-1930s—was a fitting name. Like a porcupine, there were prickly protrusions sticking out from the fuselage in almost all directions. For the most part, no matter which way you approached a B-17 in flight, you were staring into at least two fifty-caliber machine guns. Within a matter of a few seconds, a pilot flying a pursuit or a fighter aircraft attacking a Fortress could encounter as many as ten guns firing down his throat. It was a formidable defensive platform from which to fight an air war.

Among the biggest problems to be faced with earlier versions of the B-17 was the vulnerability of the front of the airplane. Although there were guns facing somewhat forward, they didn't constitute a cohesive defensive pattern of fire from frontal, or nose-to-nose, attacks. German pilots were quick to learn that there was a soft spot on the B-17 if they flew nose-to-nose, and fired long bursts until closure forced them to veer off. The pilot and copilot on the flight deck were defenseless from such attacks, and they, in fact, eventually became the primary targets of the Luftwaffe. The Germans reasoned that killing off the pilot and copilot would render the airplane dead. More often than not, they were right.

Both the bombardier and the navigator had but a single thirty-caliber each with which to attempt to counter an attacker, and the nose of the airplane was a very cramped place—too cramped for two grown men to effectively maneuver weapons in an emergency. The ball turret had little or no hope of hitting such a frontal attacker because of the depressed angle of his guns and the external equipment of the airplane that hung between him and the enemy. The top turret had a shot at intruders, but that gunner was almost invariably preoccupied with other fighters coming in from above and from the sides. The designers went to work to overcome this shortcoming, and added a set of mechanically-operated chin guns that were remotely controlled by the bombardier. This left the two nose guns to be operated by the navigator. These guns handled attacking aircraft coming in angularly toward the front sides of the airplane. The result of all these changes was the new and improved B-17G. As for head-on attackers, the bombardier now had a clear shot with the new chin guns. These guns were fifty-caliber machine guns instead of the smaller thirty-caliber, and the results were devastating to the Luftwaffe. The twin fifty-caliber was formidable. It operated from a primitive joystick that would swing out of the way and to the right of the bombsight. When aerial combat was necessary, the bombardier swung the gun controls into place and operated the machine guns from the comfort of his regular aiming seat. He aimed the system with a set of fixed optics mounted in the overhead just aft of the bubble. This vantage point placed him slightly back from the bubble in the nose. This resulted in the navigator's vision being focused forward and his peripheral vision precluded by the metal fuselage of the airplane. Unlike the ball and top turrets, with their 360-degree visual capability, the chin gunner was concerned with roughly a 45-degree area that lay just ahead of the airplane. This cone of concern had been responsible for the loss of countless early B-17 models in the past when the airplane's defenses were less formidable. With the introduction of the G models, it had become the dead zone for German airplanes instead of vice versa.

It took very little time for the powerful Luftwaffe to learn the meaning of the new enhancements to the firepower of the Flying Fortress. Third Reich aerial tactics that had once called for frontal assaults on Fortresses had to be reconsidered in light of their losses from the twin chins. The Luftwaffe actually planned suicide missions—like Kamikazes—with fighter pilots aiming their aircraft like flying bombs at the approaching forts. It was a strategy of desperation, seemingly the last gasp of a nearly defeated enemy that could not surmount or even keep abreast of the Allied juggernaut that had been hurled against it.

During this same period of time, USAAF formation flying had evolved into the equivalent of a fine art. Flying the "combat box" involved bombers flying in a tight formation that consisted of the lead plane at a given altitude with another two planes trailing slightly behind and at the same level on each wing, plus a duplicate group of three planes trailing behind and slightly below or above the first. Each portion of the box required that airplanes in the group play follow-the-leader with the lead plane—banking and turning when it banked and turned, dropping their bombs when the lead plane dropped its bombs. The closer together these planes flew, the smaller the target they presented to the enemy, and the more concentrated their firepower was at an attacker. Instead of a German fighter facing four or five fifty-caliber machine guns, it was greeted by a firestorm from between twenty-four and thirty guns at any given angle. This greatly increased the chances of knocking down the enemy fighters before they could get their licks in against the bombers, and dramatically lessened the chances of battle damage and casualties from enemy fire.

Formations of bombers flying in these boxes would depart from fields all over England and join the main body of bombers headed to a given target in what was now called the "bomber stream." The stream was the equivalent of a river of airplanes in the sky and, like a river, it had small tributaries that fed into it from a variety of places and directions. When these groups and squadrons would meet at the confluence of these tributaries—a spot in the sky designated as the "rally point"—they would form the major artery that would flood its way to the target. Sometimes segments of the stream would break away from the main group to hit alternate targets, or to approach the primary target from a different direction. This was done for a variety of reasons, the most important being to confound the antiaircraft artillery batteries below. Regardless of the destination or the size of the striking force, from the rally point forward, successful formations of Fortresses were close and tight, presenting an attacking fighter force with the smallest target mass available, and offering a wall of fire and steel from the combined and concentrated firepower. The tighter the formation, the less likely the German pilots were to even attempt a penetration with strafing fire.

A simple line chart of bomber losses during the three-and-a-half years of America's air war reveals that U.S. losses to fighter aircraft declined significantly from the beginning of the war in Europe to the end, while a corresponding increase in losses due to flak occurred over the same period of time. A host of reasons were responsible. First, for America, the Luftwaffe was strongest in 1942 when American bombers first entered the war. RAF fighters had done an amazing job of whipping Hermann Goering's air forces to a standstill over England, and the British Bomber Command was doing a good job hitting the German ground forces on the continent with night raiders. But the Germans maintained a formidable air operation that was responsible for heavy British and American losses in 1942 and 1943, and their combat tactics exploited every observed weakness that could be found. Blind spots on bombers, like the nose-to-nose problem with the B-17, and sloppy or loose formation flying, were all keyholes for penetration by skilled German fighter pilots.

Second, German antiaircraft artillery, from the outset of American air operations in Europe, was steadily improving in capability, size, and performance. The famed 88-millimeter guns that were used by the Germans everywhere were a menacing threat from the beginning of the war. Coupled later with radar guidance systems and highly accurate altitude and range-finding instruments, these cannon could deliver a wide array of ordnance at almost any altitude. In addition, the German armament industry produced thousands of these guns during the period that America was involved in the war, accounting for the increased frequency of use against aerial targets. 88's were configured as separate artillery pieces, as self-propelled field pieces, and the primary weapon on many German tank models. The result was deadly accuracy and a significant loss of Allied aircraft and personnel to flak.

As the war raged on, the German 105-millimeter guns were introduced and brought on line, reaching even higher altitudes with ever larger and more deadly bursts of shrapnel in the air. The big guns were maintained in emplacements around the Germans' most important targets, making those prime targets an Allied bomber crew's worst nightmare. Cities like Frankfort, Hamburg, and Berlin were ringed with antiaircraft artillery emplacements that were linked to listening posts and radar systems that could pinpoint a single airplane in the sky or spot a group of aircraft from great distances. These systems were coupled with searchlights to help fight off the night bombings conducted by the RAF. Gun batteries linked to radar by day and searchlights by night often made short work of attacking bombers. The shrapnel alone from a barrage of 105-millimeter guns at the right altitude was often enough to wreak havoc because of the extended reach of the larger explosive shell.

But the skill and courage of the young Allied pilots, the perseverance of the Allied forces, coupled with well-built aircraft, weather, and a bit of luck, constituted a strong opposition for the German high command. The bomber stream in itself was a tactic that often overwhelmed the gunners on the ground—they simply couldn't reload and fire fast enough to knock down all of the airplanes overhead.

On the ground, the irresistible force of the invading army had met the immovable object of the Third Reich head-on and managed to move it back in the direction from which it had come. The Germans were on the run in August of 1944, and every soldier, sailor, and airman in the United States knew it. The war seemed to be grinding slowly to a halt, and many military volunteers felt as though they'd never see action. The eight men of Bill Witcomb's crew were among them. They were happy at this prospect, naturally. Their lives were apparently to be spared. But they were saddened by it as well. Sitting the war out in training assignments was not what any of these men had signed up for. They wanted to contribute actively, not passively.

The adage that "they also serve who sit and wait" did not appeal to their youthful exuberance, nor did it fit their definition of patriotism. They wanted more.

The day that these men would meet their new airplane came, and the crew assembled on the tarmac in flight gear, as Bill had ordered them to. Each had his equipment with him, including a parachute to hook up in case of emergency. They carried the chute packs under their arms, for they were far too bulky to wear inside the airplane. The whole crew was wearing their flying suits and their parachute harnesses except Gill. He was wearing his Class A dress uniform and his pointy-toed cowboy boots. Bill had spoken with him about that before, but Gill was determined to wear his boots. Being a Texan apparently superseded being a soldier.

Their new airplane wheeled up to where they were standing. It was powered only by the outboard engines, the inboards being shut down completely. The nine men of Bill's crew stood by and watched as those aboard got out. The pilot, copilot, and crew chief were all women—all members of the WASPs (Women's Airforce Service Pilots). These dedicated aviatrixes flew eighty percent of the combat aircraft delivered from factories to destinations throughout the United States. This freed up their male counterparts for combat duties. The crew chief handed Bill Witcomb a clipboard with forms on it that Bill and his crew chief, Eli Nelson, signed, accepting the airplane. Bill's entire crew stared with mouths open at the curvy young women clad in coverall flight suits. They were beautiful. But they were women, and they had just landed and taxied their new combat-worthy airplane—it was an incongruity that many servicemen would never resolve. Bill Witcomb had encountered the feminine flyers on many occasions over the previous two years, so they were nothing new to him.

"What's the matter?" he asked of his crew. "You've never seen pilots wearing lipstick before?"

The airplane was then turned over for shakedown and training with the permanently assigned crew. It was bright shiny silver from nose to tail, unlike the olive-drab green camouflage covering that previous editions had been given. The Army Air Force had found that the painted versions of the B-17 were slowed somewhat by the paint job (not only because of the added weight of the paint, but also because of the drag upon the airfoil). It was also determined that the camouflage paint jobs did little to hide a B-17 in the sky since radar easily found them no matter what color they were. As for hiding them on the ground, the Luftwaffe made fewer and fewer strafing raids on English bases, making camouflage somewhat superfluous. So, the later models were left bare polished metal. This increased their airspeed by five miles per hour, and added to the amount of fuel they could carry by weight.

"Hey, Lieutenant," cried Dorenbush, the tail gunner. "Look at that. This is one lucky airplane."

"How do you figure that?" questioned Dinger in his Bronx disgust.

"The tail numbers … Seven, eleven," instructed Dorenbush. "Get it, seven come eleven. You know, dice?" Dorenbush was right—the last three digits in the tail number were 711. The numbers painted boldly on the tail were 338711; her complete identification number being 43-38711.

"I get it, I get it," insisted the ball turret gunner.

The men climbed aboard the airplane for the first time and familiarized themselves with their stations while Bill and Hales did a walk around the airplane, checking everything. They checked the amount of polished metal showing on each of the main landing gear struts to make sure the shock absorbers were functioning properly. They checked the superchargers on each engine to make certain the intakes were free of dust and debris. Bill chinned himself on each engine cowling and peered inside, making certain that everything was in order. The pair of second lieutenants moved each of the control surfaces on both sides of the wing as far as they could to ensure that each was free to rotate to the maximum extension in each direction. Bill checked the many antennae that hung down from the airplane or were strung between points along the fuselage, making sure they were all in place. Hales moved the horizontal stabilizers on the tail of the plane and climbed up on the tail to move the rudder, inspecting the hinge points for debris. The young pilot and copilot then climbed aboard themselves for their first look at the interior of their new ship.

The guns weren't aboard at this point, and only some of the mounts were installed—these would be checked out before each mission by the gunners. The same was true for the football—the upper portion of the Norden bombsight that housed the computing device used for targeting the bombs. This too would be obtained at the outset of each mission, usually under armed guard to and from the equipment shack where it was maintained. Each crewman was at his station as Witcomb and Hales walked forward through the airplane from the fuselage door near the tail. They both inspected the craft, making sure emergency equipment such as fire extinguishers were in place, checking to see that each man had his parachute close by, and checking all the control cables that ran overhead. They inspected the bomb bay doors to see they were fastened tightly, and that the landing gear cranks were in place in the event that they were needed to manually lower the gear. Bill paused near the top turret position and glanced down to the lower deck where Gill and Wilson were checking out the navigational and bombing equipment.

Bill Witcomb climbed into the cockpit for the first time. He had flown countless hours in B-17s, but none of them were actually assigned to him. This one was. This beautiful silver bird was his, and the cockpit was his new office. The panel before him was an array of gauges, dials, switches, levers, and controls like no other aircraft ever built, and he knew the function of each and every one of them. The yoke was a half-wheel of green-and-black metal with the classic art-deco logo of the manufacturer at the hub—the black-and-silver emblem of Boeing, a set of wings to either side with the letters spelling Boeing starting at the top and projecting downward. It looked like a medical caduceus. How appropriate, given the number of lives that this aircraft was likely to save.

The throttles and engine switches were arranged between the pilot and copilot for easy reach. The windshield and side windows were short and narrow, but allowed for extremely good visibility, up to a 270° range from one side to the other.

Hales crawled into the second seat and plopped his parachute down as a cushion before sitting. He strapped himself in and grabbed the small clipboard at his right for the checklist. Bill was turning the wheel and pushing the foot pedals to make sure the control surfaces were smooth. They were sleek and refined in their movement—more so than other Fortresses he had flown. Before starting the checklist, Hales called on the intercom to each of the crew stations to make sure they were on the command set and ready for flight. In turn, each one responded: bombardier, navigator, top turret, radio operator, waist gunner, ball turret, and tail gunner.

Bill and Norris Hales completed their checklist, and Corporal Ringwald on the radio cleared their takeoff with the tower. Bill gave the word to start the engines, and after several clouds of blue smoke whisked away into the air, 43-38711 was ready for her maiden voyage with her new crew. Bill drove the silver airplane along the taxiway with pride—it gleamed in the morning sunlight. The crew assembled at their stations for takeoff, checking what little equipment there was, but mostly getting used to the view from their positions. After the run up, he got a light signal from the tower. Bill and Hales moved the throttles forward on cue, running the motors up slowly as the giant metal bird began to lumber down the runway. It would be an easy run today, a simple run, a short run. Bill had flying power and Hales called out "V1" in what seemed like no time at all. But then, there was no bomb load, no guns, and no ammunition on board. It was like flying a kite in a strong wind. Nothing could hold this airplane on the ground.

Even though this inaugural flight was destined to be a short trip, it would be a memorable one for Gill. Military airplanes in 1944 were Spartan environments, lacking anything that wasn't strictly necessary for the mission. A lavatory was a luxury that was consigned to the base from which you flew, not an item of necessity on a combat mission. The alternative was a simple metal pail with a canvas cover over it that was kept below the flight deck for all crewmembers to use. Several of them did just that during the flight. In time, the warmth of human urine, combined with the warm Caribbean air, produced a pungent odor that wafted down to the navigator's position and drove Gill to distress. He voiced his extreme displeasure at having to fly seated next to a makeshift toilet, and he told Bill that he was dumping the bucket overboard.

"I wouldn't do that right now, Gill," warned Bill sternly. *What does he know? He's only a second lieutenant*, thought Gill. *I'm a first lieutenant, and I'm tired of smelling everyone else's piss.*

"I'm dumping it, Bill," he snapped over the intercom.

"Gill, I'm telling ya, you don't want to do that right now," repeated Bill.

Wyatt "Gill" Gillaspie didn't listen. He retrieved the pail from under the flight deck and moved through the bomb bay and radio room of the airplane to the hatch opening where the waist gun mounts were. The Kid was sitting there, watching the ground from the starboard side hatch as Gill moved to the port side with the pail. Dusenberry quickly moved forward to the radio room with Ringwald, knowing full well what was coming. Gill swung the bucket backward, heaving the contents out the portal into the air outside. He was confident that it would most likely evaporate completely before reaching the earth. He was wrong. The prop wash from those two 1200-horsepower motors on the port side blew everything back into his face. His head and the upper half of his body were covered. Gill's Class A dress uniform was soaked with the leavings of his crewmates. Dusenberry came back through the bulkhead and let Gill pass as he made his way forward to the navigator's table. Ringwald held his nose as the lieutenant passed the radio table, and Eli Nelson, grinning ever-so-slightly, stood aside as the navigator found his seat in the forward compartment. Humiliated, Gill resumed his position at his desk, while his fellow Texan, Bob Wilson, smirked broadly as he reclined against the inside of the bubble-window in the nose of the plane.

It was an uneventful flight, other than Gill's humiliation. From that episode, he gained a new respect for the junior lieutenant in charge of the airplane. Bill Witcomb had not ordered him not to do something, thereby foisting his authority and position as the airplane commander. Witcomb could have lorded it over Gill, but he hadn't. Instead, Bill merely suggested that Gill didn't want to do something, leaving the decision up to him. What Bill hadn't done was explain himself to a member of his crew, because, he reasoned, he shouldn't have to. After all, he was in charge. He wouldn't be able to explain every order he gave when they were in combat, so why should he explain himself now? Bill reasoned (and rightly so) that the best way to win Gill and Bob over to his authority was for them to learn for themselves—firsthand—why he was the boss of this airplane. Gill had just had his first lesson. Another would soon follow.

Chapter 11

Navigating and Nancy

Bill Witcomb gazed out the window of the office, knowing that Fran was waiting for him in the reception area. He'd been coming to these sessions for years—sometimes reluctantly, other times ... So far, the doctors he'd been seeing for more than two decades had agreed that Bill still harbored many internal problems, but none had found the key that unlatched the door to them. He had been given an assortment of drugs in attempts to moderate his radical and often violent mood swings, but nothing truly moderated them. There was still depression, still doubt, still fear. There was anger present, and it was difficult for any of the doctors to get a real handle on its source, until the day a key word was introduced into the dialogue.

"You said it was tough keeping the crew together," repeated the doctor, as Bill Witcomb shuffled in his chair.

"Yes," came the quiet reply.

"Why?"

"They were all so … so experienced in their fields. They were used to doing things their own way. They were used to teaching, not being taught."

"What's wrong with that?" questioned the doctor.

"You don't build teamwork by being an individual. There had to be one leader—one boss."

"And you were it? Because you were the pilot, you were it?"

"Hey, I didn't ask to have a crew full of instructors. The Air Force assigned those men to me. It was my job to bring them together as a crew—to make them fly like a team."

"And just how did you go about doing that?" questioned the doctor.

"There was no way I could be friends with any of them. Gill and Wilson both outranked me on the ground. The rest of them were either too new or too experienced as instructors to be my friends. My job was to lead them."

"How did you do that?"

"I kept them training, all the time."

"Training?" queried the therapist.

"Training! When I was at Jefferson Barracks, my drill instructor told me time and time again that the only two things that were going to get me through that war were discipline and training. I was a second lieutenant. My bombardier and navigator both outranked me. I couldn't call them to jump to attention or have the whole crew do close order drill. The only thing I could do was set the training schedule and keep them on it. If we were training, I was in charge, and both Gill and Bob Wilson knew that. They may have outranked me on the ground, but in and around the airplane, I was the boss."

"So you kept them in the air all the time?"

"Just about," said Bill with a quick smile, thinking back to that summer and fall in 1944. It had been a hot summer in the south, and the fall had been warm as well. Flying weather had been CAVU (clear and visibility unlimited) most of the time, leaving few opportunities to cancel training missions. Witcomb had his crew up in the air at every opportunity. When they weren't flying, they were studying emergency procedures on the ground. Hales was drilled on dealing with a dead engine or a windmilling prop. Bill drilled him on dead-stick procedures, and on the choices between bailing out or ditching the airplane. If there was no hope of salvage, everyone was to bail out. If there was even a remote chance that you could land the airplane, he drilled the young college grad on how to select a hard and level spot to put down the heavy bomber, loaded or unloaded.

There were quizzes for the pair of first lieutenants as well. With the pilot and copilot confined to the flight deck in order to deal with an unforeseen emergency, it fell to them to shepherd the enlisted men to safety—either braced properly in the fuselage for an emergency or crash landing, or suited up and ready to bail out and get clear of the airframe upon the sounding of the warning bell. Both Gillaspie and Wilson were charged with making sure the life rafts stored in compartments on top of the airplane were always ready for a water landing. There had been malfunctions of this equipment on other airplanes, and Bill was determined that this wasn't going to be the case with his ship.

Bob was given a set of instrument readings by Bill, and he was expected to come up with a bombing solution in a matter of a few seconds based on a stated airspeed, crosswind variable, and list of conditions over the target. Gill was repeatedly told to come up with a new course heading and speed while in midflight in order to avoid and circumnavigate a given landmark. Once the new course was established, Bill would demand a new heading to bring them back to the original base course. It seemed like needless mathematics to both Gillaspie and Wilson, but, in time, it would prove its worth.

Bill Witcomb went through a dozen fire extinguishers on the base, giving each man a chance to actually extinguish a real fire in a smudge pot with a single bottle extinguisher. The brass cylinders mounted all over the airplane were small, with a pump handle on the top and the words *Fyr Fyter*® embossed on a metal plate on the side of the extinguisher. The whole crew knew where each one was located, and they learned where to point the nozzle to get the most out of the little extinguishers.

The gunners were drilled and drilled again on clearing jams in their guns. They were taken to the gunnery range and drilled with shotguns and skeet while standing in the back of a moving pickup truck. It was among the most useful training they were ever given, because it was as close to aerial gunning as they could get on the ground. They were moving, the platform upon which they stood was moving, and the target was moving at very high speed. It was the same in aerial combat.

Every man on the crew was familiar with cranking down either landing gear, with lowering and locking down the tail wheel by hand, with the emergency bomb release, the emergency fuel transfer hand pump, the electrical grid, and the hydraulic system. They all knew how to secure the bomb bay doors, and to avoid walking on them. The bomb bay doors and the fuselage openings were designed to open with the exertion of a man's body weight. This was an emergency feature that provided a measure of safety for the men in the event the airplane went into a spin. The centrifugal force may have pinned them to the outer skin of the airplane, but if they could get to any of the openings, their body weight against the doors during a spin would be sufficient to open the door in flight, thus allowing them to escape. Each man was trained in how to crank around the ball turret and rescue the ball gunner, and how to attach a parachute to their safety harness blindfolded.

"So what you're saying is that these men, with whom you were about to go to war, weren't like *brothers* to you?" These were no longer questions—this was an interrogation.

"No, they weren't *brothers* to me. My brother is dead!" exclaimed Bill.

"Tell me about your brother, Bill," said the doctor softly, trying to tap into the pain and anger that suddenly welled up inside the former bomber pilot. It took some time for Bill to regain his composure, remembering the last time he and Ken saw one another.

"What's to tell?" he asked, holding back a sniffle.

"You loved your brother, didn't you Bill?"

"That's a stupid question to ask! Of course I loved my brother."

"Then tell me about him. What was his name?"

"Ken," said Bill, with glassy eyes that were staring at a spot on the carpet halfway between the toe of his shoe and the desk.

"What was Ken like?"

"He was a good kid … a Boy Scout," said Bill, still focused on the floor. "He was a good soldier." Bill started to recount the last time he saw Ken. Ken had joined the Army and was just completing his basic training a few hundred miles away when Bill flew up to see him during that quiet weekend. They talked and laughed together as brothers do, about mom and dad and Bundles for Britain that were constantly being sent to the relatives abroad that neither of the boys had ever met. Ken told Bill about his training as an infantryman, with a specialty in heavy weapons like bazookas and heavy machine guns. Even though he was so young, he was an anchorman for the rifle company that he would be assigned to when he left for Europe a few days later. Barely out of high school and hardly old enough to have seen much of anything outside of Newburyport, Massachusetts, Ken was being assigned to a combat unit that was destined to join General Patton's newly-mobilized Third Army. Bill knew enough about Patton from his exploits in Africa and Italy to know that where he went, many men were wounded, and many others died. True, the enemy suffered greatly at the hands of the military machine placed in Patton's charge. But many young American men paid what Abraham Lincoln called "the last full measure of devotion" for those victories. Bill felt uneasy about this pending assignment for his little brother, but didn't show it, for fear of tainting Ken's morale. He was the last person who'd want to hex a mission for anyone, much less his brother.

The hour had grown late, and Bill had to take off and return to his own base before nightfall. Bill recalled Ken escorting him to the field and marveling at his brother's shiny airplane. Ken had been the brother who played with model planes as a kid, and here Bill was the one flying the real thing. The paradox still mystified Bill.

"Happy landings," Ken had said.

"Good hunting," said Bill. Bill recalled crawling into his cockpit, running up the engines, and motioning for the ground crew to pull the chocks. He remembered fondly glancing out the window one last time and seeing Ken standing at attention, saluting him from the edge of the apron. Bill unconsciously brought his right hand to his eyebrow as he spoke to the doctor, returning that salute so many years later. It was the last time he ever saw Ken, but certainly not the last time he ever thought of him.

"So, what happened to Ken?" asked the doctor.

"He was killed in action, in France."

"When?"

"September 27, 1944. He was in a town called Nancy. He was killed in a battle near there." The doctor paused a moment, then flipped through Bill's patient record for a bit.

"According to your chart, Bill, you have a daughter named Nancy."

"Well, we couldn't very well name her Ken now, could we?"

"Do you feel some kind of responsibility for your brother's death, Bill?"

"That's absurd."

"You felt no responsibility for Ken's death at all?" Bill pondered the question. He continued to deny any feelings of responsibility, but there was an ember burning deep inside him that didn't come to light for many more sessions. He *did* feel somewhat responsible for Ken. He was the older brother, and he had raced out and joined the military the moment the war started. He was older and he led the way. Had he not joined up so fast, maybe Ken wouldn't have been so eager to jump in harm's way the moment he was old enough. Maybe Ken would have remained the young carefree kid that he'd always been. Maybe Bill's sacrifice would have been the extent of the Witcomb family's direct contribution to the war effort. That damn Boy Scout ethic of Ken's! If only he'd stayed out of it.

It was a crisp fall morning in northern France when the armored division moved up the gap into the industrial region around Nancy, only a few short miles from the German border. The rifle squad to which Ken Witcomb was assigned was an advance vanguard that would probe to find the enemy. Caught in a murderous crossfire in which a hail of lead engulfed the riflemen, the sergeant ordered them back. Private First Class Arthur K. Witcomb helped cover the withdrawal with his B.A.R. (Browning automatic rifle), returning fire at the German infantry that was dug in along the roads and well-entrenched in the buildings on the outskirts of the city. The continuous bark of the MG-42's announced the enemy positions, but the Germans laid down a base of fire that was impossible to overcome. No offensive or defensive tactic ever devised could compensate fully for the arbitrary round of ammunition that found a solid target. Ken Witcomb's Browning fell silent. So too did Bill, as he sat before the clinician with his head bowed in silence.

Bill Witcomb went back in his mind to all the training films that the military had flashed before him. The famous movie director Frank Capra had been enlisted by the government to make films that would motivate the American troops to fight. Among the series of films made for troop consumption was a set of films entitled simply *Why We Fight*. They were perfect examples of the propaganda techniques that had been employed so successfully in Nazi Germany. American soldiers, sailors, and airmen would emerge from a film eager to take on the enemy single-handed. But Bill Witcomb needed no such inducement to convince him of the course he would follow. He now had Ken.

– – –

"Tell me more about training and discipline," said the doctor after a reasonable pause. Throughout the session, Bill's mood would swing first up, then down. At one point he was enraged with the things around him and he reacted almost violently to questions being posed to him. Without warning, his mood would then shift to one of solemn depression, where he appeared almost catatonic for periods. Just as suddenly, Bill would become cheerful and cooperative. The doctor was puzzled. Could the memory of a lost brother or the horrors of war alone be the reason for these radical shifts in behavior? The clinician perused the chart to see if there had been some foul-up in medications prescribed.

Bill fidgeted in his chair as the doctor had him recall more and more about the training and discipline regime that he levied upon his crew. The psychiatrist dug deep into Bill's psyche with his questions, probing depths of his subconscious mind that Bill had long ago covered over with a bandage of impenetrable silence. Bill was just beginning to touch upon emotions that he had blocked with a veil for decades. It was like peeling back the scab of a wound, gingerly making sure that the bleeding had stopped. He sparred with his past like a prizefighter in the clutches of an opponent. The sessions with the doctor became more and more taxing on him physically, with the emotional upheaval causing his mind to wander. The doctor had posed questions about his relationship with his deceased brother; questions that Bill had trouble facing. As a result, a reservoir of guilt began to well up inside of him, altering his outward behavior. Had Bill been a good older brother to his younger sibling? Had he shown him the wrong way by hastily joining the service? Had he been tolerant enough of Ken when they were kids? Suddenly, all the times that Bill had been mean to his kid brother, all the squabbles and fights between them, all the pranks played and all the harsh words that crossed his lips; suddenly, these were the only memories that Bill could conjure of Ken Witcomb. Those sessions were among the most demanding for Bill Witcomb. They made him come face-to-face with himself and with the emotions that possessed him both then and now, and he didn't much like what he saw.

Throughout his time in combat, the years that followed the war, even through the Korean Conflict in which he served and the years leading up to his treatment, Bill Witcomb had been a devout practicing Christian. He prayed and attended church regularly. He maintained a pious, almost evangelical composure, living his life by the tenets of his religion and the underlying theme offered in the Golden Rule—a difficult task indeed, given the dichotomy of being a Christian and a citizen soldier caught in the clutches of war.

But now he was faced with a new demon: himself. He was being compelled to analyze all the things he had done in his life, all the demands he had placed upon others, all the orders he had given during his time as an airplane commander. He began to question his motives. When it came to his crew, had he given those orders to make them a better crew, thereby increasing their chances of survival? Or were his motives self-adulation and self-aggrandizement? Were they only a way of proving to those around him that he was worthy of command—worthy of respect? Bill began to really reach back in his memory …

- - -

The newly formed crew assembled on the tarmac near the bomber. Grounds crewmen were still tending to the airplane, topping off fuel tanks and cleaning the windshields and nose bubble. The whining of the fuel pump motor made talking in a normal voice impossible. Coupled with the normal din of the flight line, Bill Witcomb was compelled to use hand gestures to convey orders to his crew. He did a quick head count and came up one short. Gill? Where was Gill? He asked the question generally of the crew and received shrugged shoulders from most of them. He then stared directly at Bob Wilson, who only nodded in the general direction of the dormitory building where the officers lived. Bill ordered everyone to standby while he marched toward the dorm to retrieve his navigator. He went straight to the room that Gill and Bob Wilson shared and found no one there. He then went to the "day room" —the air force name for the lounge area in a barracks or dormitory. There he found Gill, sitting at a large round table. Many evenings Bill had sat at the same table playing cards with other officers. Whenever there was a celebration of some kind, or a send-off party for a crew being rotated overseas, the oversized table was the center of activity. Now, a lone lieutenant sat there. Wyatt Gillaspie sat in a stupor, the table ringed with empty beer bottles all around the edge. Gill was silly in his drunkenness, singing "Home on the Range" and slurping beer from a fresh brown bottle.

"Gill," barked Witcomb, "we've got a mission to fly."

"Mission?" questioned the drunken Texan.

"We've got a night navigational exercise. It was on the schedule."

"Piece a cake," retorted Gill, attempting to snap his fingers, but failing miserably.

"Gill, it's a *navigational* exercise," emphasized the airplane commander. "You're the navigator!"

"It's simple, Bill. We're supposed to fly the peninsula, right?"

"Right."

"All ya have to do is look out the damn window. You can see the whole damn state of Florida in the moonlight. You'd have to be blind stinkin' drunk not to be able to navigate this one."

"And look at you. What do you call your condition?"

"I'm just stinkin' drunk," replied Gill with a snicker and a short laugh. "I ain't *blind* stinkin' drunk … yet."

"You're grounded, Mister," barked the junior lieutenant.

"You can't ground me. You don't have the rank."

"Watch me," announced Witcomb, as he turned sharply toward the door and marched back out to the flight line. Gill stumbled to his feet and made a feeble attempt to keep up with the angry pilot. Bill reached the airplane first and ordered the rest of the crew to their stations. The enlisted men, minus Nelson and Dorenbush, climbed in through the access door on the starboard side of the airplane. The two officers and the flight engineer slung themselves up into the nose hatch like circus acrobats, and the tail gunner got in through a tiny compartment door in the starboard tail. One moment they were standing on the ground; the next, they had disappeared into the skin of the airplane, as though they were swallowed up whole by some giant silver monster. As Bill tossed his parachute up into the hatch where Eli stood braced to catch it, Gill staggered up to the airplane.

"I'm all set, Bill," he mumbled. "I can fly the mission."

"You're drunk, Gill, and you're staying here," ordered the second lieutenant.

"I can fly this one, Bill. It's a milk run."

"You're grounded, Gill. I won't carry you. And the rest of the crew won't fly with you."

"Whatta ya …?"

"You're a good navigator, Gill. You're good at your job, when you're sober. But when you're like this, you're worthless."

"But you'll need a navigator," Gillaspie said in a whimper.

"We'll do without," said Lieutenant Witcomb curtly. "It's better to have no navigator at all than to have to rely on a drunk!"

"But, Lieutenant," pleaded the navigator.

"But nothing! You're grounded, mister! Now clear the tarmac, we're taking off." Bill Witcomb motioned to the ground crew to escort the intoxicated officer to an area clear of the airplane. Bill then swung himself up into the hatch, secured it, and began the procedures for takeoff. Gill stood at the edge of the tarmac in his disheveled Class A uniform. His tie was loosened and askew to one side, and the top three buttons of his shirt were undone. His "dress blouse" (uniform coat) was completely open, revealing that the left shirttail was untucked and his web belt buckle sat off-center. His hat was nowhere to be found. Gill chuckled at his first thought of being left behind. *They'll get lost as hell*, he thought to himself.

As the Cyclone motors sprang to life, Gill paced nervously near the side of the airplane. He glanced up to see Bob Wilson looking at him from the navigator's portside window. Gill shrugged his arms to his side in a pleading gesture to his fellow Texan, but Wilson only shook his head in disgust, then disappeared into the nose of the airplane. As the chocks were pulled away by the ground people, Gill rocked forward and backward on his heels, hoping that Bill Witcomb would somehow change his mind and let him aboard at the last second. As the airplane began to roll slowly forward and make headway toward the taxi lane, Gill began to whimper and whine at the thought of his crew leaving him behind. What if something happened on the flight? What if they couldn't find their way in the dark? What if Air Force 43-38711 was swallowed up by the Florida night sky? It wouldn't be the first training flight that never returned after a night operation, especially when flying so close to the dreaded Bermuda Triangle.

Aboard the airplane, word of the condition of the navigator spread throughout the ship like wildfire. Every member of the crew now knew that Gill was drunk and Witcomb refused to carry him. They were all sympathetic to some degree over the harsh way that Witcomb had of conveying orders. They knew that he most likely had blasted Gill for his condition. But their sympathy stopped short when Gill crossed the drunkenness line. No crewman wanted to entrust his life to the hands of a perpetual drunk, least of all a drunk who was inebriated at the time of a mission. In this, Wyatt Gillaspie's crew was in total harmony.

Gill paced the floor of the operations building, waiting and waiting for his plane to return. He smoked cigarette after cigarette. A major entered the operations area, and Gill came to a shaking attention. The field grade officer looked the first lieutenant over and shook his head in disgust at his appearance. Gill adjourned to the men's room where he rearranged his uniform and combed his wavy brown hair. He was still well under the influence of all the alcohol he had consumed in the day room, but he was now standing erect for the most part. He was sobering up quickly. Sweating out a mission on the ground was among the most nerve-racking chores for any member of the Army Air Force.

It was even tougher for those who were supposed to be on the mission, like Gill. Whether a man was wounded and restricted by his medical condition, or merely sidelined by being granted a day off, waiting for his crew on the ground was nothing less than a torturous ordeal. But for an airman who was grounded for insubordination, or failure to meet the standards of the airplane commander—like being drunk—the wait was interminable. This was destined to be the longest night of Gill's life.

Witcomb and his crew lumbered along with the mission as best they could. Since it was a night navigational exercise, there was no formation flying. The mission called for each airplane to fly from their field to the Florida Keys, then northerly up the windward coast to roughly the state line, then westerly back to their base. The last part was the only tricky spot. Gill had been right—all Witcomb had to do to keep her on course was to look out the cockpit window to his left and see the Florida peninsula distinctly outlined in the moonlight. The lack of civilian blackout enforcement made the body of land easily distinguishable; a stark contrast to the black water directly below them. Bill simply flew a heading of 165 degrees for a given length of time, he then turned due east for 20 minutes, then due north. He had laid out a course while sitting on the taxiway as they waited their turn for run up and takeoff. Hales had checked his figures and agreed. Neither considered the extremely light winds that prevailed that night a significant factor. In the end, they didn't need to. They weren't trying to plot a specific target or hit a precise spot. Their orders were merely to fly to the Keys, acknowledge they had reached the Keys via a radio transmission to some ground station in the area, turn and head up the Atlantic coast to Georgia, then return to base.

It was hours of flying for Bill Witcomb and Norris Hales. The success or failure of the mission rested squarely on their shoulders. In the recesses of his mind, Bill knew that it was easy to get lost without navigational expertise aboard. He knew the risk he was taking, flying a navigational mission at nighttime without a navigator. But Gill, in his present condition, would have been a gross liability, not an asset. Besides, Gill needed to be taught a lesson about his drinking, and excluding him from the crew, making him the odd-man-out, was just what the doctor ordered. If Gill was going to assume his rightful place as a member of the team, he was going to do it at Witcomb's pleasure, not his own. He was going to have to become a true team player, not just some aloof specialist who had nothing in common with the others. It was vital that he come to understand that every member of the crew was interdependent. The pilot and copilot needed the navigator to plot a straight and safe course, the bombardier relied upon the pilot and copilot to fly their airplane to within close proximity of the target, and the gunners were there to protect all the others. It was a symbiotic relationship that was the essence of teamwork.

On the ground, Gill was sick with worry as he watched the other planes in the training squadron land safely, one after the other. The crews from those planes all disembarked their airplanes and bantered back and forth about the mission. They were all happy to be on the ground safely, happy that they were headed to their bunks for a good night's sleep. Gill listened intently to them for any indication that his plane had been seen or heard from. Since part of the exercise required maintaining radio silence except for the checkpoints, it was unlikely that any of those crews would have heard from Bill Witcomb and his crew. He heard things from the crews he'd rather not have heard: *it was as dark out there as three feet up a bull's ass; you couldn't tell the land from the water; the moon obscured some of the better constellations so celestial navigation was near impossible*. All of this heightened Gill's anticipation and anxiety. If these other crews found it a difficult mission with their navigators along, how was his crew going to fare without theirs? He resumed his pacing back and forth in front of the large glass windows of the operations building. Above him in the tower, the ground controllers searched the night skies with binoculars for the one remaining B-17 flight that had not returned home. There was nothing but empty sky.

More than an hour after the last airplane had touched down on the field and been secured for the night, Hales nudged Bill Witcomb's elbow and pointed out the windshield on the copilot's side.

"See that?" asked Hales with a grin.

"I haven't used dead reckoning since I was flying those open cockpit kites in training," said Bill, relieved that the primitive navigation that he and his copilot had utilized had brought them full circle back to their base. They could now see the outline of the field, the illuminated runway, and the lighted control tower that stood erect in the darkness at the edge of the field. It was a welcome sight. Had something gone wrong, had the plane been forced to land at another field, or, worse, crash landed somewhere, Gill would have been court marshaled for certain. But Bill Witcomb would have faced a similar fate, given that it was his decision to takeoff on a navigational exercise without a navigator. Bill was just as relieved to see the field as Gill would have been to hear the distant engines of 43-38711, and Bill happily accepted landing instructions and clearance from the controller in the tower.

Gill continued to pace the floor until suddenly he saw the glimmer of landing lights from a large airplane inbound to the field. He raced out of the operations building and ran down the tarmac to the parking spot assigned to Bill Witcomb's airplane. Sure enough, the silver giant lumbered up the taxi ramp with only the outboard engines turning and was waved into position by a ground crewman with flashlights. Bill hit the mark assigned to him, then cut the throttles, shutting off the outboards. No sooner did the props stop turning than the hatch door in the nose popped open and Bob Wilson swung down to the ground. As he gathered his parachute and started walking toward operations, Gill rushed up to him. Bob

Wilson said nothing. He merely shook his head from side to side and kept walking. Gill's heart sank to his knees. Then the rest of the crewmen departed the airplane from the fuselage door and began to follow Wilson. As each passed the young Texan, they stared at him, but said nothing. Gill asked each how the flight had gone, but silence was the only reply. The Kid—who normally bantered with the officer—also gave the lieutenant the silent treatment. Eli Nelson—the most forgiving and understanding man aboard—said nothing to the officer as he walked toward the debriefing room. He barely looked at Gill as they passed one another. Gill now knew how much trouble he was in. He wasn't concerned that Bill Witcomb was going to do anything official. He'd been wrong and he would willingly take his official lumps for it. He was in trouble with his crew; the men who were supposed to rely upon him, and upon whom he was to rely. Hales was the next one out of the nose hatch where Gill was now standing. He cocked his head slightly to one side, and opened his mouth as though to speak. He said nothing, just like the others. He closed his mouth, collected his kit and walked off in the direction of the debriefing. The only crewmember to remain aboard was Bill Witcomb; Second Lieutenant Bill Witcomb; airplane commander Bill Witcomb. This was a reckoning to which Gill did not look forward.

The legs of the young pilot finally dangled from the hatch opening, and moments later Bill Witcomb was standing directly in front of Gill. First Lieutenant Wyatt Gillaspie snapped to full attention and saluted Bill for the first time ever. Bill came to attention and returned the salute slowly. Lt. Witcomb stared at the Texan before him a bit before addressing him.

"Lieutenant," said Bill with an authoritative voice, "I won't have drunks on my crew."

"Yes, sir," replied Gill.

"If you want to be part of this crew, you've got to quit this."

"Yes, sir."

"Stand easy, Gill," instructed the airplane commander. Gill relaxed somewhat, but remained at almost a full attention. "I can't have this on my airplane, Gill. You're too good a person for this. You're too good a navigator."

"Sir, I'm sorry. It'll never happen again."

"That's not good enough, Gill. Getting drunk and missing a mission can't be washed away with an apology and an empty promise. We're in a war—a shooting war—and the other side's using live ammo. My job is to get the bombs on the target, and then get this crew home safe each time. I can't do that with people I can't rely on."

"What can I do?"

"Your job, Gill. You can do your job."

"I don't …"

"Your job is to plot our course and to take your orders from me," said Witcomb sternly. "Ever since you were assigned to me, you and Bob have been bucking my authority all the way. I'm the commander of this aircraft, Gill, and that's the way it is. Make up your mind right now. If you want to go on being part of this crew, you have to accept this. If you'd rather go elsewhere, I'll endorse your transfer request right now."

A chill ran down Gill's spine at the word *transfer*. For the first time he was faced with the possibility of being tossed from the crew. This didn't sit well with him. He liked the crew. He even liked Bill Witcomb in some respects. In the final analysis, he knew he didn't want to go to another airplane.

"I want to stay with you, sir," said Gill firmly.

"If you stay, Gill, you play by the rules—my rules—right?" cross-examined Bill.

"Yes, sir."

"And the drinking before missions stops right now!"

"The drinking stops, sir."

"You'll have to make your own peace with the rest of the crew. They're pretty sore right now, Gill," said Bill Witcomb as he placed a hand on Gill's shoulder and motioned him toward the operations building.

"How can I make it up to them?" asked the sobering navigator remorsefully.

"By doing your job Gill, just like you were trained … just like you've trained so many others to do."

The pair of lieutenants walked to the operations building where they would meet the rest of the crew. Gill never again questioned Bill Witcomb's authority as the airplane commander, and never again got drunk before a mission. He quickly became the consummate team player, doing his job expertly and willingly pitching in to assist others when he was needed. Wyatt Gillaspie could handle anything—anything but being shunned by his crewmates. The episode was closed, according to Bill Witcomb. No more was ever spoken about it between the two. Gill got some well-deserved ribbing for a few days from Bob Wilson about the bender in the day room. The rest of the crew took their cue from Bill Witcomb. If Lieutenant Witcomb was satisfied that this guy could handle the job after the perilous position that Gill had put the entire crew in, then they'd accept that. Witcomb knew what he was doing, and he was enough of a tyrant that they all knew he wouldn't hesitate to dump any crewmember who truly endangered the airplane.

As a result of the episode with Gill, the ornery pilot was given a nickname that stuck. No one remembered who came up with the name first, but from then on, Bill Witcomb was known as "Iron Ass" by all eight men. At first, it was a derogatory title, meant to disparage the second lieutenant behind his back. In time, though, it grew to be an explanation by the men as to why they were training when other crews were enjoying free time. Still later in their relationship, Iron Ass became a way of praising a man that they admired, and a way of demonstrating what they had all endured together. In their subconscious, if they managed to survive working under Iron Ass, they were somehow bigger, better, and stronger than the average airman. But this evolution of attitude would take time.

It wasn't long after the episode with Gill and the night navigation exercise that Bill Witcomb learned of the death of his younger sibling in the town of Nancy, France. Like most people, Bill was enraged by the news. He wanted to fight and defeat the Axis powers more than ever. But he contained his anger and focused instead upon the crew that had been assigned to him. He was the pilot, and it was his job to drive this crew to war and bring them safely home again afterwards. That became his sole mission, his reason for existence. Witcomb's internal compass pointed the way and he merely followed, and his crew in turn followed him. Ken had written to him several times about how comforting it was to hear the groan of the motors from American bombers as they made their way over Nancy on their way to Germany. He related how welcome a sound it was for an infantryman, because it meant that the deadly German 88-mm guns were trained upward instead of zeroed in on his position. From the summer of 1944 until the end of the war, American navigators—including Wyatt Gillaspie—would use the town of Nancy, France as a navigational checkpoint on the skyward path to Germany. Nancy …

Chapter 12

Scotland or Bust!

During the fall months of 1944, Bill Witcomb's crew had their hands full learning the art of formation flying, with practice bombing missions and training sessions on the ground, and learning all about their airplane. They more-or-less came together as a crew, each recognizing the value and contribution of the others. Gill was respectful now of Bill's authority, and more outwardly supportive of him around the others. But he still wore his cowboy boots whenever the situation permitted, and he still flew missions in his Class A uniform—a luxury that he was permitted while in the warmth of the Florida sunshine.

It was during these few weeks of final preparation that Bill and his crew began to talk seriously about what they would do in given circumstances in combat. Although no man can predict how he will react in combat, and no crew can make a perfect plan, Bill Witcomb was determined that his crew would be prepared for whatever was to confront them. Not only did he continually drill them on emergency procedures with the aircraft, he had them physically prepare for the worst: having to bail out over enemy terrain. Each man maintained his own "escape kit," as they were called. The kit contained a recent small black-and-white photograph of the man in civilian clothing. In the event that they had to abandon their uniforms and come up with a photo for identification papers, they had one ready-made. Most importantly, the photo would show them in clothing other than that they would be wearing if they were captured—a dead giveaway to Gestapo agents looking for escaped prisoners and downed flyers. Each man had escape boots that would attach to their parachute harness with a clip and a strap. The boots were the rugged combat boots used by infantrymen, not the soft-soled fleece-lined shams that kept the feet of airmen warm at high altitude. They had detailed silk maps of Europe tucked neatly in between the inner and outer layers of their jackets, accessed by pulling open the seam in the shoulder or under the armpit. On close inspection upon capture, the enemy would only feel fabric—nothing unusual, just more insulation. The silk material would blend in and seem like part of the coat. Each kit contained a compass, some matches, a pocketknife, a tin of hardtack, and some French and German currency. Each man routinely checked his escape kit, along with his parachute and the equipment he would use on the airplane. It became second nature for each of the crew members to know where his kit was and to have it ready in the event that they had to bail out.

Aside from preparing their equipment for the eventuality of escape, Bill felt that it was important to prepare their minds as well. It was democratically decided that no one on the crew would voluntarily surrender. If they were shot down, each man vowed that he would do his level best to get back to his home base by whatever means he had available to him. It was the first of only two votes to be made by the crew, and it was a unanimous one, reflecting not only the attitude of their never-say-die generation but also a point of cohesion upon which they could build a mutual respect for each other.

During the first week of September, the entire crew reported to Hunter Field in Georgia for bombing training. The first thing they did on Monday was to stand for a photograph. Nine bright smiling faces gleamed before the camera. Nine Class A uniforms with nine sets of shining wings cloaked nine young American airmen who felt they could easily conquer the world. Those were the easy days, before they were to go to war. Those pristine expressions would turn somber and gray in a very short stretch of time.

In early October, word of Ken's death reached the elder Witcomb and he was whisked home to Newburyport to attend a memorial service for his younger brother. It was a surreal experience for Bill—a funeral without the deceased. Like many of the soldiers killed in World War II, Ken was buried close to where he fell—in the military cemetery at Lorraine, France. The gathering of family and friends at the little church just up the street from the Tyng Street home of the Witcombs was a quiet but fitting tribute to the younger Witcomb. Bill maintained a rigid veneer, believing that it was his place to be strong for his grieving mother and father. He played the part of the battle-hardened veteran, even though he was yet to see combat. He accepted praise and the adulation for being a volunteer in wartime, but the accolades being heaped upon him were really for Ken's sacrifice, and Bill knew it. His outward countenance was that of steel, but the memorial service had ignited an ember within that had turned his insides into a molten gelatin. It would take months before that ember would erupt into an inferno that would captivate his soul and push Bill and his crew toward the edge that was the crucible of combat.

After a tearful farewell, Bill returned to his borrowed airplane, which was parked at a nearby airfield. He hedgehopped his way back to his duty station and resumed his duties as an airplane commander. The feelings he had about Ken's death were put on the back burner, and his outward appearance was back to normal—Iron Ass. Nothing was going to get in his way of being a good pilot, and nothing was going to keep him from eventually avenging his dead sibling.

Shortly after his return to the base, both Bill and Norris Hales were called out of bed in the middle of the night to bail Dinger out of the stockade. Dinger had been in the airman's club shooting pool. None of the enlisted men assigned to Bill

Witcomb had yet been promoted to the rank of buck sergeant (three stripes), even though each man had acquired his wings. In fact, all but one was a corporal at that point. The rule was a simple one—the Army Air Force couldn't make you fly combat unless you were at least a sergeant. This was how the military got the enlisted men to volunteer for combat: the prestige of rank and the corresponding pay increase that came with it. Each man on Bill's crew would be elevated in rank, just as soon as orders were cut for the crew to rotate to Europe. Meanwhile, they were merely four corporals and one private amid a sea of corporals and privates on the base.

While Dinger and his chums were shooting pool, an oversized staff sergeant swaggered into the club boasting about his exploits in combat. The man bragged about the number of Japanese that he had encountered in the Aleutian Islands. He didn't claim to have killed or captured any enemy soldiers himself, merely that he had "encountered them." He then offered sentiments to the effect that people who had remained stateside up to that point in the war were tantamount to cowards, and Dinger, with his fiery Bronx temper, was quick to pick a fight with any man who would thus impugn his character. Of course, the braggart was twice Dinger's size and he was able to make short work of the diminutive ball turret gunner. Dinger took his lumps from the giant and got carted off to jail by the military police (MPs) as well. It was here that Bill Witcomb and Norris Hales found their gunner. Curled up on a hard oak bench in a cell and smarting from the blows he had sustained, some at the hands of the braggart but most from his captors when he resisted their arrest. Dinger was a sight. Hales shook his head in disbelief at the condition of the airman and told him that not even a general could get him off the hook for this fight. Dinger was used to getting into trouble as the result of fighting with people. He was a New Yorker and used to street fighting. It seemed to come naturally to him, like perfect pitch to some people or an innate ability to spell with others. But the

This photo was taken when the crew was first assembled in August 1944. Note that the enlisted men have not yet been promoted beyond two stripes, and Bill Witcomb is wearing his instructor's insignia on his right sleeve.

Front Row: Bob Wilson, Fred Hales, Bill Witcomb, Wyatt Gillaspie
Back Row: Francis Dusenberry, Louis Dorenbush, Eli Nelson, Gregory Ringwald, Raymond Dinger

This photo was taken after the crew had flown several missions together (circa February/March 1945). Note the changed expressions from the crew photo taken in August 1944. Also note that the enlisted men are all wearing sergeant stripes except Raymond Dinger (front row center).

368th Bomb Squadron headquarters

Tail number for *Lassie Come Home*

Old Dobbins

Bombs away

Cadet Witcomb

The three W's: Wenkl, Wertz and Witcomb, and *Old Number 70*

Lassie Come Home in for repairs

368th Bomb Squadron forming up for a mission – *Lassie Come Home* is the lead airplane

13 Year Old Ken Witcomb

The wingman is hit

11 Tyng Street Newburyport, MA

Bill Witcomb's escape photograph taken in civilian clothing while stateside

Two Texans: Wyatt Gillaspie and Bob Wilson outside their quarters

Memorial plaque located at the front entrance of the
Wright Museum, Wolfeboro, NH

Formation flying of the 368th Bomb Squadron – photo taken from the cockpit of *Lassie Come Home* by Bill Witcomb

CHARLES WITCOMB

"Nothing endures but personal quality."

"Give me a chicken farm any day." Big Bill Witcomb of local tennis fame thinks that he could do much worse than raise chickens the rest of his life. If he can sell eggs as well as he can sell ads, the chicken business will hold a bright future for Bill.

Bill Witcomb's high school year book photo.

Charles William Henry Witcomb – August 2002

military frowned upon intramural fighting, and Dinger seemed to specialize in fights with fellow servicemen.

Lieutenant Witcomb pleaded with the captain in charge at the detention center. The captain wasn't inclined to do any butter bar a favor, especially a pair of them that had wings on their chests. He was yet another washout from flight school, relegated to administrative chores and consigned to the ground. Eventually, though, he capitulated and agreed that the only charges pending against Dinger were those lodged by the MPs for the fight. The other combatant wasn't pushing the issue—he'd gotten his pound of flesh during the fight. So, after a lengthy stint of offering logic, apologies, and assurances that such a thing would never happen on this base again, Dinger was released to the custody of his airplane commander and the charges—this time—were dropped. Bill Witcomb was fit to be tied. Dinger was a scrapper with a two-millimeter fuse, which made him a natural for the ball turret. He was feisty and fearless and incorrigible. All these traits in the air were deemed ideal for his position in the airplane. On the ground, Dinger was part of a select group of servicemen who were revered even among infantrymen. Most combat veterans knew that the ball turret was probably the most dangerous place to be in a firefight, and few would volunteer to be there. As much trouble as Raymond Dinger was to Bill Witcomb, he was essential to the team and integral to the defense of the airplane. Scrapper or not, Dinger was necessary to the success of the mission, and Bill would do almost anything he could to get him off the hook with the local MPs. Bill Witcomb also used this to his advantage. He had something on Dinger now, something to hold over his head. Or so he thought.

– – –

By the end of October, Bill's crew and airplane were ordered to Grenier Field in Manchester, New Hampshire. This was where their plane was to receive her final adjustments and her complement of guns and armaments. While traveling to the Granite State, Bill and Norris Hales plotted a course that took them directly over Hales' hometown. When they reached an open field near his home, they saw a crowd of people standing in a small cluster holding bedsheets spread out to form the word "HELLO." Bill banked the airplane sharply to starboard and circled the clearing several times. This gave Hales an unobstructed view of his family, friends, and his fiancée who stood in the open field, waving frantically at the bomber as it flew over them. Hales waved back through the open cockpit window on his side of the airplane. He'd said his formal goodbyes weeks before during an all-too-brief furlough, but he couldn't resist just one more send-off. He managed a phone call home to set things up the day before, and he was astonished that everyone in his hometown seemed to be there to see him off. He could hardly believe the entire town was able to crowd onto that open patch of ground.

The orders to New Hampshire put Bill in his own back yard before the anticipated trek to England. He utilized the little time available to him to see family and friends in Newburyport, but—unlike the all-too-obvious flyover of Hales' family in the Carolinas—he kept his visits brief so as not to flaunt his good geographic fortune in front of his crew.

There was a substantive reason for Bill to spend most of his time on Grenier Field, aside from crew morale. The airplane modifications and the weapons systems being installed on his airplane were the most advanced and sophisticated the air force had to offer. Since he was flying a B-17G model, the nose of the airplane was heavy with machine guns. The twin chin fifty-caliber guns were augmented by two additional fifty calibers mounted in the fuselage just behind the nose bubble. The airplane modifications in Manchester did not include the cheek mount modification for the port and starboard fifties that many of the G models subsequently received; 43-38711 would receive that modification after she reached England. But the tail gunner now controlled a brace of "Ma Deuces" instead of the single fifty-caliber assigned to earlier models, which doubled the weight of guns and ammo in the tail. Some of the new airplanes were being fitted with Cheyenne Turrets—a remote-controlled set of guns that turned in azimuth, much like the chin guns—but Louis Dorenbush would continue to use just the tandem fifties without all the gizmos. The waist gunner still had a single side-mounted fifty on each side of the fuselage, and the ball and top turret gunners still had their twin fifties, separated by the space where the gunner stood or sat. The radio operator's rear-mounted single gun was gone now, deemed redundant with improvements made to the top turret. Ringwald would move from the radio room to the waist area and handle the open gun when things heated up.

Attaching all the mounting hardware to the airplane was no easy task. The mechanical crew at Grenier had their hands full setting up the heavy bombers with the defensive shields they would need in battles to come. Installing the mounting stands for the waist guns was a relatively easy job, because the waist area of the fuselage offered wide openings where the equipment and hardware could be passed into the airplane. But the nose and tail presented another set of challenges. Neither area was accessible from the outside of the airplane, which meant snaking the mounting hardware through narrow portions of the airplane in order to put it into the appropriate spot. Although the B-17G was the biggest thing in the air at the time, the inside of the airplane was a very confined environment. Within the main fuselage, a man of average height could stand, without crouching, in the center of the airplane. But toward the sides of the waist, where the gunners had to stand, the arc of the airframe had a very low overhead with an arcing space below. There was nowhere to stand. The same was true in the nose. A man could almost stand upright, but only in the very center of the airplane. Everywhere else the space was just too short. To get to the tail gunners' position was like crawling through a sewer pipe. The tail gunner had a private door just under the horizontal stabilizer, but inside that door it was cramped quarters—a crawl space at best. The ball turret was the worst of all. It was well-named. It consisted of a ball of aluminum and glass that was suspended from the belly of the airplane. It could rotate around completely and pivoted 180 degrees on its axis. A man of any height had to literally curl himself up into a little ball to fit inside the tiny metal and glass pod. The gunner had foot pedals that electrically controlled the movement of the ball, and his feet rested on the pedals like the stirrups on a very short sulky. There were handheld controls that also held the firing triggers for the machine guns. These flanked the ball turret gunner. When the guns were engaged, the noise was deafening because the pair of fifty-caliber machine guns were positioned on both sides of, and right next to, the gunner's head.

Like all of the B-17G models, 43-38711 was fitted with the now-famous "Tokyo tanks" —bladder-like fuel cells located inside the wing tips that provided much-needed fuel for long missions. These expandable and contractible gas tanks had the added feature of being self-sealing in the event they were punctured by gunfire. The vulcanized material would simply seal itself up after a bullet or piece of shrapnel ripped through it, preserving the fuel for use and preventing explosions. It made for a safer airplane that could travel much greater distances.

Just before Thanksgiving, Bill picked up the orders for him and his crew to report to England for duty, assigned to the 8th Air Force. This is why this crew had trained together for months, and individually for years. Bill read over the orders again. Each of the enlisted men on the crew was promoted to the rank of sergeant. Nelson and Ringwald were assigned the rank of staff sergeant—four stripes—due to their assignments on the crew. All of the crew was given a short leave to spend at home. They would miss being home for Christmas, having to return to the base before the holiday, but they could enjoy the spirit of the season together with their families before they would have to report back for duty. For some of them, the majority of their leave was spent on trains, going to and coming from home. Norris Hales accompanied Bill to the Witcomb home in Newburyport for Thanksgiving, while Gill and Bob Wilson managed to wangle a hop to Texas aboard an air transport. The enlisted men all managed to find their way home for the brief respite. All of them sported sergeant stripes upon their uniform sleeves denoting their advancement in rank. The entire crew wore wings over their left breast pockets, and most wore ribbons below the wings that denoted their service in wartime. The wings alone were distinctive and a source of pride for all of them.

After the few short weeks in New Hampshire, which had seemed like only minutes to Bill and his men, the B-17G number 43-38711 was ready for war. So was the crew. Nine young American men ranging in age from eighteen to twenty-three reassembled on the tarmac in Manchester. They stood at attention in the now-familiar crew formation while Bill Witcomb put them through their final check. Across the field was the town of Londonderry. Soon, these young men would be in close proximity to the namesakes of both these towns in England. But first, they had to traverse the Atlantic Ocean. Even by 1944, despite the range of this particular airplane and the incorporation of the Tokyo tanks, such a trip was still done in stages. It had been a mere seventeen years since Charles Lindbergh crossed the Atlantic for the first time, and that was with a specially equipped aircraft that had ample fuel reserves.

Bill Witcomb, Norris Hales, and Wyatt Gillaspie together plotted a course to Goose Bay, Labrador, their first stop. From there, they would fly to a remote field in Scotland, and then make a final short hop to their assigned base at Thurleigh, Bedfordshire. It was Christmas Eve morning when the four Wright Cyclone engines came to life and the airplane lifted off the north end of the runway, arcing over south Manchester, then Candia, then on to Portsmouth. Each man aboard had all his military belongings with him—his uniforms and his equipment. They each carried photos of loved ones and a few other personal items. The guns were all mounted, giving the appearance that this fighting machine was ready for action of any kind. But truth be known, there wasn't a single round of ammunition aboard aside from the spent fifty-caliber shell that Dinger kept in his breast pocket as a good luck charm. The added weight of the ammunition would have robbed them of the precious fuel they'd need as they traversed the north Atlantic toward Goose Bay. The fact that no weapons were loaded did not stop Bill Witcomb from demanding that each gunner man his station during the trip. German U-boats still prowled the waters below, and German submariners could still engage low-altitude aircraft with light and heavy hand weapons and their versatile deck guns. Manning their stations and keeping their guns moving—especially the top turret, ball turret, and the chin guns—meant this would not look like just another B-17 being ferried to England for service and thus appetizing prey for Wolf Pack submariners. Flying in the warm air below 10,000 feet meant they didn't have to carry the heavy oxygen tanks for life support, and their flight would look like an aggressive North Atlantic coastal patrol seeking out U-boats and trying to sink them. It meant a long arduous flight for the crew, stuck at their combat stations rather than gathered together in the waist or nose as most traversing crews had done. But then, this was Bill Witcomb's crew, and this was just the beginning of the many extraordinary demands that he would place upon his men.

Goose Bay was hardly a tourist haven in December 1944. But for an airplane low on fuel, or a tired air crew, it was truly an oasis. It had only been a few hours since they left Manchester, but weather had made the journey that much longer, that much harder, and that much more dangerous. Bill and his crew encountered the trailing edge of a storm that had wreaked havoc in New Hampshire a day or two before, and they were stuck in a holding pattern around the field waiting for landing instructions. Goose Bay pilots were used to the soup, but Bill and Norris Hales were not. Visually, it was like trying to fly inside a light bulb. But Bill Witcomb's hours in that simulator, working out landing problems just like this one with the instruments, had not been in vain. This became just another tactical exercise, reading the instruments, passing the information to Gill to verify course, speed, and altitude, and then making the necessary adjustments. Bob Wilson peered through the nose bubble, hoping to see lights or landmarks that indicated terrain underneath the bomber. But all he saw was gray. Gill tried shooting the sun through the astrodome situated on top of the plane between the nose bubble and the pilot's window, but the cloud layers above were far too thick. Dinger pivoted the ball turret so it was facing forward—something he rarely did during regular flight because of the cold air that would stream in around the gun ports. He, too, strained his eyes to pick out anything that would give the pilot a reference point for the ground, but … nothing … just gray-white bleak and barren sky. The altimeter showed they were at eight hundred feet and still there was no visual sighting of land. This could only mean that they were no longer dealing with just the low ceiling that had been forecast; they were confronted with a huge fog bank as well that had engulfed the field. Bill and Hales throttled up a bit, to maintain airspeed on what they believed was going to be their final approach, and to lower the giant bird a single foot at a time. The heading was right, their course perfect—this had to be it. Foot by foot, the Goliath descended toward what both Bill and Wyatt Gillaspie fervently believed was the airfield. It seemed like hours of breathless anticipation. Lower and lower Bill ventured with the aircraft, and still nothing in sight.

Suddenly, Dinger yelled out, "I SEE IT!"

"See what? Be specific!" demanded Witcomb.

"The field—we're right over it!" said the astonished gunner.

"I see it, too," announced Bob Wilson on the command set. "You're right over the end of the apron!"

Suddenly the fog dissolved around the airplane's flight deck, and Bill and Hales could see the field as well. Their navigation by instruments had been perfect. The airplane was aligned perfectly with the runway. They were a tad high, maybe one hundred feet or so above what would be a normal glide slope, but there was plenty of room on the strip to adjust for a landing.

The pilot backed the throttles down a little and nudged the yoke forward, then back to create a flare. Lt. Witcomb, the airplane commander, said, “Nice job, Gill. We’re dead on target. We couldn’t have been closer to the mark if we’d been in bright sunshine with CAVU.”

Gill sat back in his tiny seat and watched as Bill landed the airplane. The touchdown was relatively smooth, considering the rapid descent that was required at the very end of the flight, but Dinger still gave a thumbs-down when they exited the airplane. Bill and Eli Nelson saw to the refueling of the airplane, and to the maintenance list that Eli presented to the ground chief at the field. It was a short list, thankfully. A handful of men then approached the airplane with tools and scaffolds and began preparing it for the next leg of the flight. Norris Hales and the two first lieutenants made their way to the operations building where they arranged for billeting for the crew. The enlisted men were assigned to a transit barracks not far from the operations shack, and the officers were given an empty Quonset hut just off the flight line. Both locations were cold and damp, but they offered shelter from the weather and a place to sleep. Bob Wilson scrounged around the installation for food and found that the only mess hall catered to both officers and enlisted men alike. Gill checked in with operations to get the weather for the next day and to check navigational matters. He’d plotted a perfect course to get them to their destination that day, and he wanted to do the same on the next flight. It was he who first learned that Bill Witcomb’s crew was destined to spend more than one night in Labrador. The weather front that had caused them such difficulty at landing was stalled over them, and threatened to remain for several days. The problem was that the low-pressure area was being fed by warm moist air from the south coastal region of the

United States, and this caused the front to grow until it covered an enormous portion of the ocean and the Labrador coast. Not only was Labrador socked in, but Greenland, Iceland, and the northern and western portions of the British Isles were socked in as well—a herald of the weather they were destined to face over Europe for months to come. The airfield in Scotland to which they were destined wasn't like Goose Bay. It offered no radio navigation beacons, and no other technical systems that would allow for proper instrument landings. It didn't even have a conventional light beacon. It was only a flat piece of ground with smudge pot barrels at each end of the clearing to mark the beginning and end of a makeshift grass runway, like most 1940's airstrips in Britain. Any approach there would have to be in clear weather. They would need a clear view of the sun, the stars, and the field in order to find their way.

After a good night's sleep, Bill and his crew awoke to a dismal low overcast and drizzle. There was patchy snow on the ground around the airfield, which eroded rapidly as the ground fog that had formed mixed with the snow and the light rain. After breakfast, it was quickly understood that the flight was grounded. Bill wasn't happy about the unforeseen delay, but there was no choice. The weather east of their position was as thick as it got, even though the ceiling immediately around Goose Bay had lifted somewhat. Bill Witcomb and his crew were faced with an entire day in Labrador with nothing to do. To top it off, it was Christmas morning.

During breakfast, there was a somewhat festive mood in the open mess. The Canadian waitresses sang Christmas carols to the servicemen during their meal, and a number of airmen from other grounded flights made a leisurely meal of it. There was no rush to eat the powdered eggs, the SOS (shit on a shingle, or creamed chipped beef on toast), or the heavily salted bacon that lay on the plate before them. Dusenberry was the first to learn from one of the cooks that a number of moose had been sighted that morning not far from the base. He relayed this news to his crew and it took little for the men and officers to convince Bill that it would be good sport to go moose hunting. So, just for sport, not knowing the countryside around them, having no inkling as to the regulations governing hunting in Labrador, and armed only with Model 1911 Colt 45-caliber automatic pistols, the aircrew of nine men trudged off into the snow and the woods and hunted the mighty Labrador moose. They saw tracks everywhere and followed them for hours. They crossed streams, climbed stone walls, and ambled along open pastures tracking the giant creatures, but saw none. It was a Christmas day none of them would ever forget … a holiday from flying and a day off for rest and relaxation before they faced the air war in Europe together. It was a time for them to get to know each other a little bit better on a personal level. They were in a strange place, universally cut off from family and friends, bound for a combat assignment together. For the first time in their lives they clung close to each other as a result. Dusenberry or Ringwald would make a comment about something and Dinger would make fun of them as usual—some things were perpetual. Gill and Bob Wilson took the lead and paced the group, their cowboy boots leaving strange footprints that were easy to follow in the Newfoundland snow. Bill Witcomb and Norris Hales were accompanied most of the way by Eli Nelson, and carried on a light conversation. Dorenbush trailed the rest in the drag position, alone and quiet. It was as though they were aboard the airplane, each in their respective position and each in the appropriate place to carry out his job. Yet they weren't on a mission, they were on the ground … on Christmas Day … in Labrador … hunting moose … with pistols. Fortunately no moose were ever spotted.

The following morning, the weather lifted and they were cleared for takeoff. Operations advised that only marginal conditions were reported at their destination field, and Bill was given the option of remaining another day at Goose Bay in the hopes of getting better conditions in Scotland. After weighing all the pros and cons and discussing the options with Norris and Gill, Witcomb firmly nodded his head and ordered the crew aboard the airplane. With that, the eight men of Bill's crew entered their airplane and nestled in for the longest leg of the flight. The weather they would face on this trip was unknown, and the positions of enemy ships and planes were a mystery, but it was certain that they would now be within the operational area of the German naval and air forces. What was also known was that they had enough fuel to get them to their assigned field in Scotland, and very little surplus, and still no ammo. Gill feverishly worked the numbers at his plot table, checking the air charts and ensuring that every calculation was precise. Whenever the sun shone brightly, Gill was in the astrodome taking a sight to ensure their exact location. Bill and Norris watched the instruments closely throughout the flight, and did their utmost to keep the fuel consumption to a minimum. Maintaining the stabilizer trim and working the carburetor heaters to ensure that every molecule of the 97-octane gasoline was combusted efficiently fully occupied their time. Eli Nelson handled the fuel transfer valve, moving the precious fuel from one tank to another in order to keep the ship balanced and the engines running smoothly. The course was a long one, calling for heading adjustments regularly to compensate for wind speed and heading changes. It was anyone's guess whether or not they were going to make it.

Chapter 13

Thurleigh

A lookout stood within an artillery emplacement along the craggy coast, surrounded by a kneewall of sandbags and wearing the flat metal helmet of the British Army. He had his gas mask canister slung over his shoulder hanging down around his buttocks, and an aged double-barreled shotgun leaning against the sandbags, ready for use. He was an older man, in his late fifties, hardly the sentry that one would expect at a coastal gun emplacement in wartime. But then, most of the young men in England, Scotland, and Wales were engaged elsewhere, battling the Germans on the continent of Europe, leaving the home guard to be augmented by all manner of retirees and local volunteers who were considered too old for induction into the regular Royal Army, Navy or Marines. These farmers and shopkeepers and lawyers and dentists would stand their watch like any soldier, and then return to their homes and their professions to carry on the British way of life. They contributed regularly to the war effort in this special way, freeing up hundreds of regular troops who could be better and more effectively utilized elsewhere. After the Normandy landings and the subsequent commitment of airborne troops and ground forces to the regions around Holland and Belgium during Operation Market Garden, British Regular Army troops at home were a rarity and home guard volunteers had become essential.

Peering through a large set of binoculars, the sentry—wearing a brown tweed suit and a tattersall vest, and only his helmet to distinguish him from his fellow civilians—scoured the late-afternoon sky for signs of airplanes. The field had been put on alert that another American bomber was due in, but no one had a clue as to when it would arrive. If it came in after dark, it would more than likely crash from the lack of visibility around the rugged mountainous area. The western coast of Great Britain was no place to be flying heavy bombers after dark, especially just above sea level, where this particular field was located. The approach corridor from the convergence of the North Atlantic and the Irish Sea was extremely narrow with mountains along the windward side, presenting formidable obstacles, and the hills at the end of the field were treacherous even under the best of conditions. That afternoon was particularly dangerous, given the low ceiling, the accumulation of ground fog, the bone-chilling temperatures, and the powerful updrafts that were coming off the water at the southwestern end of the field. The smudge pot barrels were ignited by the ground crew as the first vestiges of dusk were evident, acting as visual beacons to any plane in the area. The fires in the barrels could be seen from great distances, provided that the flickering of their flames was not obscured by clouds or the thick fog that would routinely settle in. As the afternoon wore on, and day began to erode into evening, the weather began to enshroud the tiny field even more. Diligently, the man in the tweed suit paced his post, looking out to sea for any signs of airplanes. None were seen.

– – –

Aboard the American bomber 43-38711, Bill Witcomb and Wyatt Gillaspie labored to make sure they were in the proper place in that great gray sky. It had been the longest uninterrupted flight for both of them and the only one where they couldn't check reference points by looking at the sun, the stars, or the ground below them. They had to trust their mathematics, their estimates of the wind speed and direction, and they had to trust their instruments. They must be in the right place—they just must be.

The rest of the crew fidgeted at their stations, painfully aware of the circumstances they would face if Gill was just a little bit off in his navigation, or if Bill was just a little bit off in his flying. All they could see out the windows of the ship was a dismal gray. It was disconcerting. It was disorienting. Bill reduced his air speed a bit and dropped a little altitude in the hopes of being able to get under the ceiling. The crew could see water several hundred feet below them, but the fog still completely obscured the rocky Scottish coast. As they all strained to find any sign of land, the radio crackled with the voice of an older man possessing a deep highland brogue, who announced that their intended landing field was now completely socked in by weather. Gill quickly plotted another course for a secondary landing site which was further south. He obtained a radio plot from a navigational beacon inland, and used the direction from which the voice transmission had come to fix his position. It was dead reckoning at best, but it was all that he had.

Another 45 minutes of flying southwesterly brought another three quarters of an hour of fingernail biting aboard. They were on the right bearing; both Bill and Gill knew it. The only question was: how far were they off the coast—how much of an error had they not compensated for? The bomber now continued along a mostly easterly heading, the crew hopeful they would sight land soon, and just as hopeful that they wouldn't sight it by slamming into it. Even if they weren't in the right spot, just seeing land at that point would suffice. Everyone aboard winced to peer through the murky air—Wilson in the nose, Dinger in the ball, Eli Nelson in the top turret, and the others at their various stations. This time it was Norris Hales who saw land first.

"There it is!" he cried, as though he were Columbus discovering the new world.

"Hey, Gill," said Bill Witcomb over the command set, "Look at that. Not only is it land, it's the right land!" Witcomb was right. Their heading was bringing them right up to the secondary landing field assigned to them. Bill only had to adjust slightly to the left to align the bomber with the runway. "Perfect navigation, Gill," he said into the interphone so every man on the crew would hear him. It was indeed an example of perfect modern navigation. Wyatt Gillaspie had done a superb job, and Bill was truly appreciative of having a great navigator on the crew.

Bill and Hales scurried through the checklist and prepared for landing. The wheels were lowered, the flaps extended, the trim adjusted, and power to the engines cut back almost to a stall. The giant silver bird swooped in over the artillery emplacement where the older Welsh sentry in the tattersall vest and the gun crew stood watching. As it roared by, the men on the ground swiveled their heads about to watch it land. It was only a few feet above them. It had to be. This was an extremely short piece of ground, and the pilot and copilot had all they could do to get the mammoth airplane in safely. They'd need every inch of ground available to them; hence, the low pass over the western approach of the field. Touchdown was smooth, but very wet. The clouds and fog had deposited an ample supply of rain and mist over the grassy and muddy field during the day, resulting in huge puddles here and there. Dinger was the one most affected by them. The wheels on touchdown kicked up an enormous volume of spray, and the ball turret gunner was drenched through the narrow gun ports that were facing forward, contrary to policy or common sense. Dinger had positioned the ball so he could look for land, and the abrupt landing gave him no time to return the ball to the usual landing position or for him to exit into the fuselage. He saw this landing looking forward from inside the ball. Had it not been for all the cold water hitting him in the face, he might even have enjoyed it.

Bill taxied to a makeshift operations building—it looked more like an old tool shed—and he and Norris Hales shut down the airplane. The crew disembarked and Dinger walked beyond the nose of the plane and stood just off to the side where Bill could see him from the cockpit. Bill waited for Dinger's now-familiar gesture, anticipating a nasty thumbs-down. Instead, Dinger pasted a cracked smile on his face and gave Bill a half-hearted thumbs-up. Witcomb's face showed his astonishment. Dinger had never before given him his blessings on a landing. As Bill's face began to change from an astonished expression to a smile, Dinger flattened his hand out slightly and began to rock the palm slightly, implying that the landing was so-so. Bill nodded an acknowledgment to the stubby gunner and continued on with his tasks.

The crew assembled near the operations hut and milled around in the fog while Bill and Norris went inside to get their orders. Their airplane was being refueled from an aged tank truck that barely made it across the muddy field from the fuel tanks that were built into the side of a nearby hill. A short elderly man sporting a scruffy white beard, his head covered by a dingy sort of tam-o'-shanter, was asked by the operations officer to show the crew to their quarters. He clasped an oil lantern in his rugged hand and motioned to the pair of lieutenants the way to the door. They followed.

The old man led the crew along a narrow stone pathway for what seemed at the time like miles. Upon reaching a clearing, the men could make out a large, dark gray structure carved into the side of the hill. It was three stories of austere stonework, capped with a rustic wooden roof of timbers and covered with a fray of tarpaper. There was an amber glow coming from within the monolithic structure through one of the many large windows on the lower level. As the bomber crew found its way into the building, each man quickly realized that they were standing inside the walls of an old prison. The elderly Welshman held an arm out, extending the lamp in the direction he wanted them to walk and pointed to the "rooms" where they would spend the night. The rooms were nothing more than former cells with the bars removed from them. Inside some were military cots. Others had wooden frame beds with rope springs and straw tick mattresses. These were humble accommodations to be sure, but dry. In the main reception room, where they had entered, there was a large standing hearth with a roaring fire blazing. The airmen paused to warm themselves a little—especially the half-soaked ball-turret gunner—then moved down the corridor to their rooms. Dinger and Dorenbush grabbed a pair of the cots, while the other enlisted men flopped themselves down on the tick bedding. The officers were shown to separate quarters, presumably in keeping with their station as officers but in reality, nothing better than the enlisted men were given. The quarters were separate, but truly equal.

The old man and his thick Gaelic accent disappeared into the dark walls, leaving Bill and his crew to fend for themselves. Bill, Hales, and Gill were all exhausted from their flying adventure, while the others were merely fatigued from doing much of nothing. Despite the cold damp air outside, the stale and musty environment inside, the lack of a decent hot meal, and the complete absence of a soothing hot shower before going to bed for the night, every man on the crew slept like a rock.

– – –

Morning along the Welsh coast was much like dusk—cold, damp and foreboding. The ceiling had risen somewhat during the night, but there was no sign of the skies clearing. The mist in the air was lighter than it had been the previous afternoon and evening, but it still cut through a flight suit like a hot knife through soft butter. It chilled to the bone. The crew awakened, each in their time. Bill Witcomb and Wyatt Gillaspie were the last to rise. Their exhaustion from their ordeal had left them almost comatose. The crew members stumbled down the corridor in the opposite direction from where they had entered the night before and found a dining room. Where once there had been a group of people preparing and serving meals to inmates of the prison, there now stood two matronly women in white cook's uniforms. They ladled out the breakfast of porridge, scones, and coffee to the airmen as they passed by, each with a British military metal meal tray. The boys gobbled down everything given them and returned for a second helping, and then a third. The women were flattered that the Americans seemed to love their cooking, unaware that they'd had only tin rations the night before, and very little of those.

After breakfast, Bill and Hales left the old stone prison for the operations shed before the others. They checked in to see if there had been any change in orders, then they obtained the weather for the remainder of their route. The weather was going to be choppy all day, clouds at varying levels and predicted rain and freezing rain much of the way. It meant an uncomfortably cold ride for all of them all the way through to Thurleigh.

Bill and Hales did their standard walk around the airplane as they prepared for takeoff. They paid particular attention to the landing gear, since the airplane was sitting on a grass field that was soggy and cumbersome. The landing the night before could have splashed up mud or debris that could be easily missed on a quick walk around. They looked for tiny pebbles and blades of grass that might wedge themselves in between the moving parts of the shock absorbers and giant springs. They searched for dust, mud, or twigs that might get lodged in small spaces, only to cause a freeze-up of some crucial equipment later in flight. They moved all the control surfaces by hand and checked all the antennas to make certain they were still fixed in their places. Bill spun the wheels on the superchargers and checked for debris. When the checklist was complete and all were aboard, they got a start-up signal from a ground man standing on the pilot's side of the airplane. The ground crew—such as it was—had done a walk-through with all four engines, circulating the props at least half a dozen times to cycle the engine oil and prime each for starting. There was no external power to boost the electrical system, and no generator standing by for startup. So, after going through the preflight checklist and engaging the battery system, Bill put up one finger outside the cockpit window and Hales threw the switch for the number one engine. The copilot pumped the primer until the motor engaged. It fired up, as did the other three engines in turn. Bill and Hales steered the lumbering giant to the very far end of the field and went through a routine run up. With the engines nearly on full throttle, and the airplane sitting on a wet grass field, the prop wash was a torrent of water and debris that blew into the woods that lined the back side of the field. Unlike other places where they had landed, there were no other aircraft in the area to catch the brunt of the blast from their wake, so it mattered little how much water was blasted behind them.

Finally it came time for takeoff. Bill depressed the brake pedals firmly as he and Hales ran the engines up. It wasn't until the throttles were almost three quarters of the way forward that he finally let go and let her roll. The B-17G rumbled along the soft grass field, gradually gaining momentum. Just prior to reaching the far end of the field that dropped off sharply into the Irish Sea, Norris Hales called out "V-1," and Bill rotated the yoke back ever-so-slightly. As the airplane broke its contact with the ground, Hales reached down and retracted the landing gear, cutting down the drag and increasing the airspeed slightly. As the huge metal craft cleared the coast and began to climb above the water, Bill gave it some rudder pedal and a little wheel, and banked to the port side. All of them except Dorenbush in the tail looked down at where they'd spent the night, amazed at the tiny field they had landed upon, and more amazed that they were able to take off.

– – –

In what seemed like no time at all, the bomber crew was caught in the quagmire of yet another weather front. It was a wonder the German air force had penetrated the island of Britain at all, given the density of the clouds, the bitter cold temperatures even at relatively low altitudes, and the propensity for fog that reached skyward and almost touched the clouds themselves. Unlike the field they had just left, Station 111 at Thurleigh was more-or-less properly equipped for instrument landings. Bill Witcomb and

Norris Hales had been monitoring the radio beam at Thurleigh almost from the moment they took off, as had Wyatt Gillaspie. It was to be the clearest reception of the radio beacon that they would ever receive. Whether it was the terrain or the lack of German jamming in the area to the north and west of Station 111, it was a clear and uninterrupted signal that allowed them to home in on the base. The pilot had an updated navigational chart with all the radio frequencies annotated, and a runway template for the field that was as accurate a map as he'd ever seen. It was only necessary for the pilot to verify this altitude and his position relative to the beam in order to situate his airplane to a runway. The overcast was thick with what the bombing reports would later call 10/10ths (or complete) cover. Pilots without instrument expertise were doomed until they broke through the clouds. Bill Witcomb had those extensive hours in that air-conditioned simulator, thanks to the immoderate heat of the Florida weather, and countless hours as a pilot instructor, teaching younger inexperienced pilots how it was all done. Witcomb hadn't quite reached his twenty-fourth birthday when he aligned his airplane for a final approach on runway 24. The chronological age of a pilot was not determined by his years since birth, but rather by the number of hours he'd had in the air. By those standards, Bill Witcomb was at the far edge of middle age.

Touchdown at Thurleigh was uneventful, like most daytime landings that weren't associated with a combat mission. A quiet pass of Buryfields Farm, then a quick turn over the hamlet of Hatch End before lining up on final approach. Occasionally, a young pilot who'd been pushed through the system too quickly overreacted to conditions and crashed his bomber, but this was rare. At Thurleigh in Bedfordshire, air mishaps were usually the result of the pilot and copilot being killed in action aboard the ill-fated aircraft, or disabled so that they were unable to control the airplane. Many navigators and bombardiers were washed out flying cadets and considered as good backups. But in the end, the flight chief was the guy who understood most about the mechanics of the airplane and knew how to keep it flying. Landing was merely a matter of slowing the airplane down at the right altitude at the right time over the right spot and being headed in the right direction. On the grass-covered runways of some of the RAF bases, using smaller airplanes, this was relatively simple—all you had to do was find the field and set her down. But Thurleigh was a giant triangle of concrete and pavement runways that required a specific approach by heavy aircraft in order to touch down on one of the active runways: two parallel short strips running southwest to northeast (almost true headings) and the wide monster runway running virtually west to east. Landing crosswise, bisecting any runway, could cause multiple collisions with other airplanes, or cause your own airplane to crash when it bogged down at high speed into the muddy grass that was not-so-long-ago a dairy pasture. B-17s were considerably heavier than the fighters and pursuit planes flown by the RAF, and hardened runways were essential for the big birds. For bombers laden with bombs, fuel, munitions, and men, it was the runway or else. Gill's navigation had been perfect again, Bill's flying precise, and the shiny new B-17G screeched out her presence at the northeast end of the field for the first time.

An Army jeep with a black-and-white checkered flag pulled in front of the bomber as it slowed and turned onto an apron near the south end of the field. Bill and Hales cut their inboard engines and used the outboard props to help steer the giant airplane around the tight radius of the acute angle they had to make in order to taxi back toward the control tower and the operations building. The airman in the back of the jeep waved at Bill to follow him, and Witcomb did so. They were led to a large open apron that sprawled out in front of a set of hangers near the heart of the base. The tower was the typical brick-and-concrete box building found all over central England—a ground floor of offices with a lavatory; a second floor that was accessed by an internal staircase and which consisted of a number of small rooms surrounded by windows and a balcony that covered the three sides of the building facing the field and runways; and a third floor consisting of a single cubical radio room, glass from the chair rail to the ceiling, a flat asphalt and gravel roof, a staircase leading from the balcony below, and a railed platform extending out toward the field for observation. With the exceptions of the peak of the hangars and the ball atop the flagpole, it was the highest point on the base.

When Bill Witcomb reached the open area of the tarmac near the tower, the airman left the jeep and walked in front of him, signaling with his arms to turn his airplane. Bill followed the commands of the ground man and when the airman crossed his arms in front of him and above his head, Bill parked his airplane as instructed. He and Hales began shutting down the outboard engines and securing the airplane. Each in their turn, the crewmen began to filter out of the airplane from their respective positions. Dusenberry was the first out, followed by Dorenbush and Dinger. Ringwald was the last out of the aft hatch. Gill and Bob Wilson swung down from the nose, as did Norris Hales and Eli Nelson. Bill was the last to firmly plant his feet on English soil. The whole crew stood a moment and took in the base that was Station 111—their new home. Dinger caught Bill's attention just for a moment and gave yet another thumbs-down for the landing. Bill just smiled and shook his head. As usual, no one else seemed to notice.

"Well," said Bill, clutching his flight kit in his left hand and motioning with his right, "let's report." The group made its way to what was clearly the operations building—a simple brick single-story structure common to most English military posts. Thurleigh had originally been a Royal Air Force base, before America's involvement in the war. But early in 1942 the base was consigned to the United States Army Air Force by the British crown—the first such base in England to actually be handed over to the Americans. Much of what was the original RAF base remained.

The original runway configuration was utilized, and they were surfaced with a thick aggregate in order to accommodate the heavy bombers. The big runway—numbered 27 or 09, depending on whether you were headed west or east respectively—was added to provide the heavy bombers of the USAAF with an expansive strip. And it was needed too, being a third again longer than the other two runways. The addition of the big runway cut off the old road from Bucknoe End, just north and a little east of Thurleigh, from Hatch End, which was the easternmost point of the base. The acreage that made up the base had originally been a huge pasture in Bedfordshire. There once were only herding paths from one end to the other where goats, sheep and cattle roamed at will. Now, the only way to traverse the entire station was to hopscotch along one narrow country road after another until you got around to the other side—to what end, one could only guess. There was nothing around the base except woods and farms. To the north lay Galsey Wood and Red House, to the west Park Farm, to the east Mont Pleasant, Hatch End and Bucknoe End, and to the south the town of Thurleigh itself. Thurleigh was a thriving little farming community with three pubs. There were few eligible females in a town marked by quaint stone cottages, unimproved carriageways, and a bumper crop of farmers who had endured four long years of war by this time and were unsympathetic to the loneliness of American flyers. There were only three problems with the Yanks, as the locals saw it—they were overpaid, oversexed, and over here! The pub owners sang quite a different tune, although the crews of the 306th spent less time in pubs than did most 8th Air Force airmen. This was partially due to the inordinately small number of public houses available around the station; those existing pubs were barely able to handle their regular clientele. But the command staff of the 306th Bomb Group had something to do with this as well, placing a heavy training and combat load on the crews assigned to the four squadrons that made up the group. Combat crews had little time for pub-crawling, and parched officers most often had to settle for a quick diluted beer at the officer's club, while airmen usually had to go thirsty or settle for warm Coca-Cola® when the USO was on station.

Bill and his crew waddled up to the headquarters building in their flight gear and reported in to base operations. The men were directed to take a seat on wooden benches in an austere outer office while a sergeant escorted Bill down a hallway to an office a few steps away. Lieutenant Bill Witcomb found himself in the Group Commander's office, standing at attention before Col. James S. Sutton, his new commanding officer. Sutton had the look of real USAAF. He was a slender man with a finely tailored uniform that fit him perfectly. He sat at his desk wearing his dress blouse, conducting business like a business tycoon dressed in a businessman's suit. His hair was beginning to thin slightly, and there was just the suggestion of gray at the temples.

"Sir, Lieutenant Witcomb reports as ordered, sir," barked the junior officer as he stood erect in front of the commander and held his right hand to the polished brim of his garrison cap in a crisp salute.

"Lieutenant," said the colonel condescendingly, "despite being in a combat zone, we don't wear our covers indoors." Bill quickly removed his hat with his left hand while bringing his hand salute to his right eyebrow. The colonel slowly rose, came to attention and returned the junior officer's salute. "Stand easy," said Sutton, resuming his seat.

"How was your flight down from Scotland?"

"Bumpy, sir. And cloudy," Bill replied. "We were diverted from Scotland by weather and had to put up in Wales for the night."

"That's normal flying weather around here, lieutenant. Get used to it."

"Yes, sir."

"How was the crossing?" asked the colonel.

"Uneventful," replied Witcomb, trying to be a bit more circumspect.

"Welcome to Station 111. You're being assigned to the 368th Bomb Squadron. Your squadron CO is Major Huling. He's just back from his honeymoon, so he's a bit backed up on paperwork. It may take him a little time to get sorted out completely."

"You'll be flying two to three missions a week, rotating with other crews. For the first few missions, you'll fly as second seat with an experienced combat pilot. He'll show you the ropes. Your assigned copilot will fly with another airplane for those missions. I saw your 201 file, Witcomb—you've got quite a bit of four-engine time. How is that?"

"I was a flight instructor, sir," replied the young lieutenant.

"You were a B-17 instructor?

"That's right, sir."

"You'll find flying combat is a world of difference from what you've been doing, Witcomb. Formation flying here isn't a matter of exercise—it's a matter or life or death. Formations over here are not for appearance; they're for defensive firepower. Each airplane's guns are integral to the defense of the group—the tighter your formation, the less likely that some Nazi hotshot bastard will try to penetrate the group. When we fly sloppy formations we lose airplanes, and I don't like losing airplanes. Do you read me, Witcomb?"

"Roger, sir."

"You and your officers will be billeted together in one of the Quonset huts near your airplane's revetment. Your men will be housed together in a nearby barracks. The sergeant outside will show you the way to your squadron." Witcomb snapped back to full attention and saluted the colonel once again. Col. Sutton returned his salute, then extended his hand across his desk for a shake. Bill leaned forward and shook the commander's hand. "Good to have you with us, Witcomb," he said with a smile.

"Thank you, sir," replied Bill, returning the smile. Bill executed a perfect about-face and marched out of the office where he rejoined his crew. As they walked, the sergeant that had led him through the headquarters building started pointing out various locations on the base like the mess hall, the infirmary and the post exchange (PX) —three essential locations for all flying personnel. The briefing room was another huge Quonset structure near the operations building.

"I'll show you your quarters first, sir," instructed the sergeant, "then I'll show you where to park your airplane. Of course, I imagine you'll want to check in with your squadron commander first?"

"That will be fine, sergeant," announced the lieutenant/pilot, as though he were a war-weary veteran with years of combat experience to his credit.

– – –

Within the hour, Bill Witcomb, Norris Hales, Wyatt Gillaspie, and Bob Wilson found themselves standing at attention in the squadron commander's office. Major Huling was a square-shouldered man whom they estimated to be in his late twenties or early thirties. He had a square jaw and an equally square face, and his head rested upon shoulders that were as broad as they were square. He wore his garrison cap toward the back of his head in a roguish fashion, seemingly unaware that regulations prohibited the wearing of hats inside. Like Colonel Sutton, Major Huling was a man who came to the point in a hurry.

"Sir, Lieutenant Witcomb and crew report as ordered, sir," said Bill while he and his three cohorts were at attention and saluting their new commander.

"Stand easy, gentlemen," said Major Huling,

"I saw your record, Witcomb. In fact, I saw the 201 files on all your entire crew. You've got quite a collection of instructors aboard your airplane."

"Yes, sir," was Bill's abrupt reply.

"How do you account for that, Witcomb?"

"It's just the roll of the dice," said Bill.

"Roll of the dice, aye? Well, luck around here isn't determined by the roll of the dice or by the luck of the draw. It's determined by following orders, flying tight formations, by every crew member doing his job, and every airplane commander carrying out his mission. You're flying a G model?"

"Yes, sir."

"Cheek and chin guns?"

"Chin only, sir. They said in Manchester that we'd get a retrofit on the cheek guns when we got over here."

"That still gives you some decent firepower forward and a good chance for survival. When we first started over here, all we had were E and F models without chin or cheek guns – nothing but a little thirty-caliber popgun stuck through the nose of the Plexiglas® with next-to-no field of fire. The krauts really kicked us in the teeth in those days. But these new G's really set them down. They can't risk a head-on attack anymore for fear that all those fifties facing forward will eat 'em up." He moved behind his desk and reclined in his chair a little, rocking a moment before continuing.

"I'm gonna split you two up for the time being. You'll each fly second seat with an experienced pilot."

"The colonel said you'd do that," said Witcomb with a nod.

"It's for the best. I know you've probably flown a lot of hours with your own team already, but combat is not like anything you've ever flown before. You'll have to plan the use of every ounce of gas, the expenditure of every round of ammunition, and the placement of every bomb. You'll have to ration your oxygen at times, and get used to the bitter cold at bombing altitudes. Most of all, you'll have to get used to the fighters and the flak. Unlike any other flying you've ever done, missions are where you get shot at, and it takes some getting used to. I want you to get used to the noise before you're responsible for the whole airplane by yourselves. Witcomb, you'll fly copilot with me for a couple of days. Your copilot will fly second seat in your airplane with one of our experienced men. We'll be doing sucker raids and local hops so I can see what you're made of."

"Before you fly combat," continued the major, "you'll spend some time flying formation and doing practice missions with your crew. We've got several courses laid out and practice bombing ranges for you to hit. You'll be dropping sandbags instead of bombs, but try to keep them on target. The local farmers get pretty upset when we destroy their chicken coops or their barnyards, even if it is only with sandbags." Bill and Fred Hales smiled at the remark. "And no barnstorming! I know the urge is great, given all these thatched-roofed houses—'chocolate box cottages,' the locals call them. But keep your antics to yourselves. We've got a tenuous enough relationship with the Brits without some bomber pilot playing around like he's flying an old Jenny."

"Any questions, gentlemen?" asked Major Huling.

"No, sir," said Bill as he and his officers snapped to attention and presented their salute.

"See you at briefing, gentlemen." The major returned the salute and dismissed them from his office.

– – –

Bill and Hales met Eli Nelson and made their way back to the airplane. The others were shown their quarters by a sergeant from the ground echelon. Bill started up the number one and four engines and taxied the airplane to a revetment on the outskirts of the squadron area. The revetment was a large mound of earth fashioned in a circle around a hardstand: a circular concrete parking apron for the airplane. It was designed in such a way to prevent small-arms fire being used by saboteurs to damage aircraft on the ground. The theory was that before anyone could do sufficient damage from an area just outside the airbase, the MPs would have the culprits in custody or shot dead. The revetments only made the task of sabotage that much harder.

Waiting for Bill Witcomb and his airplane was their newly assigned crew chief, Red. Red was a quiet man, lanky and bland. He spoke softly and slowly whenever he addressed Bill or Eli, and he would nod his head up and down whenever anyone would speak to him, as though he were pumping the words into his head with each motion. Red lived in a tarpaper shack he had constructed himself that sat directly adjacent to the revetment. It was tiny in size, crude in design, and dismal in appearance. But Red spent little time inside the shack, and almost all of his waking hours tending to his assigned airplane. As much as Bill and his crew deemed the U.S. Army Air Force B-17G number 43-38711 as theirs, in reality it belonged to the ground crew chief, Red, and his younger assistant. The care and nurturing of a B-17 was no easy task, given the damage levied upon these planes by Hitler's Luftwaffe and Wehrmacht. Crew chiefs like Red were not ordinary airmen. They didn't fly the airplanes, nor did they participate in any of the actual combat—less the occasional German fighter that strayed over the base and strafed it with random machine gun fire. But these mechanical wizards were vital to the missions. Without them, more than half of the planes that flew missions would not have made it to the target or home again. Men like Red would patch up the battle damage, repair broken parts, replace shot-out windshields, mend bullet holes, change motors and wings like they were putting on a set of snow tires, and refurbish radio and navigational equipment as though they were changing light bulbs. It was second nature for them to scrounge parts and materials. It was commonplace for them to fabricate or even re-manufacture airplane parts. Their industry and inventive nature was what kept the Air Force flying. If they didn't have the needed parts, they improvised. When it came to improvisation, Red was among the best.

And so 43-38711 was tucked neatly into its revetment and into the hands of an expert mechanic. The crew began to nestle into their quarters—enlisted men together in a barracks shared by another crew and the officers in a Quonset hut not far from the airplane. This was business as usual at Station 111. Bill Witcomb and his men would call this place home for the duration of the war in Europe.

Chapter 14

Newla D-Dog – Lassie Come Home

That afternoon, Bill learned from jabbering with the other pilots in the squadron that it was bad luck for any airplane to fly a combat mission without a name. It suddenly became clear that he was going to have to come up with something other than 43-38711. Instead of exerting the privilege of being the airplane commander and naming the plane unilaterally (which many pilots did), Bill decided to put it to a vote. Naturally, after a protracted bond tour in the states, Bill and his crew had heard about Bob Morgan's airplane, the "Memphis Belle." Morgan had named it after his fiancée back home. It would have been a nice gesture for Bill to name the airplane after his wife, but doing so would not have brought the crew any closer together, nor would it have drawn the others any closer to him. Maybe if they had a say in naming the airplane, they'd be more inclined to fight for her.

Bill polled the men and officers for ideas for an airplane name. There was talk about using the last three tail numbers—a common-enough practice among many airplane crews. One of the more famous examples became the airplane 42-31909, named the "Nine-O-Nine" by her first crew at the 91st Bomb Squadron in Bassingbourn. The Nine-O-Nine went on to capture the 8th Air Force record for the number of combat missions flown without a single abort or a single casualty: 140 in all. But the crap-shooting connotation associated with the numbers 7-11 drew mostly sniggers from the crewmen who hadn't suggested it. Bill, by then, had been assigned a radio call sign for his aircraft—"Newla D-Dog." "Newla" was the radio designator for the 368th Bomb Squadron, and "D-Dog" was the specific airplane identifier. On the fuselage of his airplane, the letters BO were painted, indicating the 368th Bomb Squadron, with the letter H in black surrounded by a triangle and a bold yellow horizontal stripe adorning the tail and rudder. The H was the designator for the 306th Bomb Group. Below the airplane number 338711 on the tail, a large letter D was painted. The only other designator markings on the airplane were the giant USAAF star and bar on the wings and fuselage.

Prior to this crew's entry into Europe, Hollywood had produced a feature film starring Roddy McDowell. It was a sophomoric tale of a boy and his dog, but the title of the film had come to have great meaning to both Anglo and American fighting men whose primary goal was to get home safely. *Lassie Come Home* had great appeal to American audiences. It had a special appeal to this crew. It was suggested that it would be an appropriate name for the airplane by the young waist gunner, and it was eventually unanimously agreed that *Lassie Come Home* would be the name of their airplane. Bill pondered the name, thinking to himself that it was more of a prayer than a name, but he was satisfied with the choice. It had been a rare exercise in democracy for his crew, and one that he hoped would reap great rewards.

After the name decision was made, the crew assembled on the tarmac the following day to find that the name was painted in bold lettering on the portside nose of the airplane. Below and beside it was a beautiful painting of a collie dog. Red and his assistant had worked on the airplane all night preparing the artwork. *Lassie Come Home* and her crew were now almost ready to go to war.

– – –

Practice bombing in England was not like the practice missions they had flown in Florida or Alabama. First, there was the weather. England in December and January was not a hospitable place weather-wise. There was a dense cloud cover most of the time, with a ceiling usually well under five thousand feet and a cold drizzle virtually every day. While the drizzle had little effect on the crew or the airplane at bombing altitudes, the cloud cover below them was formidable, making precision bombing through visual sighting impossible. Gill had to rely upon his mathematics and Bill's instruments to properly fix their position. Bob Wilson had to rely upon the bombing radar systems that had been installed, like the PFF and the "Mickey" equipment. PFF stood for Pathfinder Force (a term acquired from the British air war), which came to mean the lead ship with special equipment installed specifically for bombardment with cloud cover. "Mickey" was the code word for an electronic transmitter and receiver that was in addition to the Norden bomb sight. The Mickey equipment stood for devices that allowed the bombardier to "sight" the target electronically rather than optically. Given the winter weather over Europe, this capability was essential, since most of the more recent missions were done in 10/10ths cloud cover. It was difficult getting used to this method of acquiring the target, but Bob Wilson was a training bombardier and instinctively and instantly acclimated to the technology and the techniques.

For the first time, Bill and his crew were flying missions at the same altitudes that they would encounter in combat. Missions over Europe were flown as high as possible in order to confound German artillery and radar and to elude Luftwaffe fighters. Stateside, missions seldom rose above twenty thousand feet. Combat missions to Germany were being flown at twenty-five thousand, twenty-nine thousand and thirty-three thousand feet on a daily basis. Six and one quarter miles in the skies over the Fatherland in January was a bitterly cold environment, and all nine men began to better comprehend the necessity for the insulated flight gear and the electrically heated suits that were issued to them. Class A uniforms were out of the question, even for Gill. Oxygen use was necessary to sustain life over 10,000 feet, and an oxygen mask clogged by frozen saliva or moisture condensation could mean asphyxia for the crewman who failed to clear it regularly. The frigid air alone could bond bare skin to metal. With the exception of the ammo boxes that were made of wood, virtually everything inside the B-17G was made of some kind of metal.

Their first practice mission went successfully; but then the problem presented was a relatively simple one and designed to give them confidence in their abilities. The second mission was much more difficult, flown at a much higher altitude, and had the added burden of a seasoned command pilot kneeling behind Bill Witcomb and Norris Hales during the entire flight. This pilot was young, younger than Bill, with probably half the number of logged flying hours. But the key difference was where they had acquired their hours: Bill Witcomb had logged his over the tepid skies of rural America, and the young command pilot had logged most of his flying cold-weather combat. The young man was critical of Bill's handling of the airplane, and of the casual way Witcomb had of handing over the control of airplane to his bombardier as they approached the bomb run.

"After you hit the IP (initial point), the shit hits the fan," he snarled. "You gotta be on your toes the whole time. From the AP (aiming point) to the target can take as long as twenty minutes, depending on your mission. You gotta fly the plane through fighters and flak. You can't maneuver, you can't evade. When you hand the plane over to the bombardier at the last possible moment, you gotta do it quick, and he's gotta know for certain that he's got the controls. Don't be afraid to talk on your command set." Bill nodded his assent, as did Hales. Both drank in what the young man had to say, but neither completely understood his insistence upon minutiae. All too soon, they would come to understand the importance of the little things.

– – –

In addition to the weather, the local culture (of which Bill and his crew saw little), and the realties of combat that would come in time, Bill had to get used to bunking with his fellow officers. The four were assigned to a cramped Quonset hut near their assigned revetment. It was far from the plush surroundings of some military officer's quarters; a Spartan space with a tiny coke stove in the middle of the open room; four metal bunks with metal springs and paper-thin mattresses; four small wooden shelving units to hold toiletries and personal items; and four short rods fixed in place to hang uniforms. Each man was issued two blankets, two sheets, and a pillowcase, and linen was changed once a week. The latrine was a relatively short walk away and consisted only of a set of commodes and a couple of sinks. There was only one officers' shower that served all the officers on that side of the base. The limited accommodations available in the small shower building was of little importance in the winter. Hot water was a rare commodity, and no one showered when there was no hot water. Bill Witcomb soon learned not to venture over to the shower building unless he saw steam rising into the air from the block building that was several hundred yards beyond his window.

The central mess hall was another Quonset structure, only much larger. Sections of the curved metal composition were cut away near the base of the arc and squared off appendages were added to the base of the building. It allowed the large steel superstructure to be used as an open hall, and permitted the kitchens and service lines to be set up along the linear sides of the building. The mess halls at Thurleigh were open to all personnel, even though enlisted men and officers ate in segregated seating areas. Aircrews tended to stick together, sitting at tables with one another, with ground echelon and support personnel wedging in here and there as they could. Combat crews wore their flying clothes to breakfast, and then made their way to the morning briefings before each mission.

Unlike the chow lines in the States, there was plenty of food. The problem was the kind of food. Since it was winter, produce was in short supply. Good produce was even scarcer. The predominant winter vegetable—available at virtually every meal because they were raised in hothouses locally—was Brussels sprouts. There were Brussels sprouts for breakfast, Brussels sprouts for lunch, and always Brussels sprouts for dinner. The infamous creamed chipped beef on toast and powdered eggs provided most of the protein to the troops, with the limited selection of greens providing vitamins and the necessary carbohydrates. The freshly baked bread and the white fish that the mess sergeants occasionally obtained was a welcome change from the monotony.

Bill and his crew had only been on the station a few days when the group began bombing missions. They noticed after each daylight mission, the returning crews feasted on a meal of roast chicken, mashed potatoes, gravy, and all the fixings. The ground personnel and the crews that didn't fly that day were stuck with the Brussels sprouts. That chicken dinner was one of the two rewards for successful crews—being alive and back safely at their own base was the other.

– – –

On New Year's Day, 1945, the 368th was off on another mission—this time to Limburg and Kassel. Bill and his crew were still assigned to practice missions, still bombing obscure places along both sides of the Bristol Channel or tiny uninhabited islands of rock in the Irish Sea. The next day, the squadron was off to nail a communications center hidden in a tunnel in Kyllburg, and the following day Major Huling led the group to Hermulheim. On both days, all the aircraft returned safely, which was cause for celebration across the station, but especially at the 368th. That same day, January 3rd, the 368th lost a number of experienced officers to other groups and squadrons that were woefully short of combat-hardened pilots who could lead their formations. This left the 368th short of pilots, which dictated that Bill Witcomb was destined to move out of training status and into a combat assignment immediately. He and Fred Hales would be separated at first, which didn't sit well with either of them. But it was for the best. Combat flying—flying in formation—was not the kind of flying that any pilot would willingly do. It was arduous, tedious, and most of all, dangerous. Add to that the flak from the antiaircraft batteries on the ground and the lethal strafing fire of hit-and-run German fighter planes, and formation flying was downright deadly. Bill Witcomb and his crew were about to learn firsthand about combat. As prepared as they were—this crew of instructors—they were ill-prepared at best for what was to come. Regardless, *Lassie Come Home* and her complement of men were about to be thrust into the white-hot plume of the flame.

Chapter 15

The Legend of Old Dobbins

In the predawn hours of January 5th, 1945, Second Lieutenant Charles W. H. Witcomb was awakened from a sound sleep by a corporal holding a dim flashlight to his face. It was a bitter cold morning; damp and typical of the midlands of England in the midst of winter, and chilly even under the scratchy woolen covers. This was the day for which Bill had spent the previous three years of his life training. In a forced husky voice, the young enlisted man announced that it was 02:00 hours and time to get ready for the day's mission. Bill propped himself up on an elbow, and watched as the corporal made his way around the Quonset hut waking the other officers. Gill and Bob Wilson were slow to arouse, but Norris Hales was on his feet and getting dressed in no time at all. The four men shaved very closely that morning, as they had been warned to do. Each then pulled on extra layers of clothing—including their electrically-heated suits—and donned their heavy flight jackets of fleece and leather before lumbering to the mess hall for their first of three of the day's installments of Brussels sprouts. All the crews ate hearty; some of the men grabbed a last leisurely smoke before briefing. Bill and his officers headed off for briefing while the enlisted men went to the armory to draw and clean their machine guns and report to the airplane. The natural anxiety within all of them over it being their first mission was subdued only by their outward desire to absorb every detail at briefing or to take every measure to ensure that the guns wouldn't jam during the mission.

Bill and Fred Hales sat toward the front of the hall for the mission briefing—the area reserved for pilots. Gill and Bob Wilson were in the next section where the navigators and the bombardiers gathered. In the rear of the hall, the radio operators crowded into the few remaining chairs, or stood near the back of the hall to get the frequencies, codes, and call signs they would need to keep communications in order. The hall was dimly lit by hanging metal lamps, except for the stage area. It had flood lamps that would illuminate the large map that reposed on the far wall enshrouded by a large black drape. There was a tripod easel set to one side of the stage that had a detailed timetable, and there was a five-foot long pointer leaning against the drape for the briefing officer's use. The few tiny windows along the sides of the Quonset hut were cloaked in black curtains that maintained the blackout conditions. The room was filled with chatter, and the natural arc of the metal structure made it difficult to hear. A person who was standing anywhere near the sides of the structure heard a cacophony of muted sound from throughout the room, but a whisper from someone standing on the far side of the arch could be heard above all else. The perfect natural arc of the metal caused sound to travel from one side to the other without interruption, allowing eavesdroppers to listen in on conversations on the other side of the hall. It had been a common-enough gambit for some of the founding members of the United States Congress, who used the natural arc of Representative's Hall in the Capitol building the same way. Suddenly, the main door of the hut opened and the captain standing beside the door yelled, "Ten hut!" The order was heard clearly throughout the hall.

The room sprang to attention and quickly went silent. All that could be heard was the sound of the squadron commander, Major Huling, and his new air executive, Major Williams, just transferred in from the 369th, marching into the building and up the center aisle to the stage, their heels clicking in precise military unison. Once they climbed the stage, the two majors faced their squadron and stood a second or so at attention. Major Huling then ordered the room to their seats, and the men quickly seated themselves quietly. The commander offered a few pleasantries, including a welcome and an introduction of Major Williams.

"Major Williams will be replacing Major Miazza as air exec. Major Miazza has been transferred to the 423rd to replace the air exec over there," informed Huling. He then cut right to the briefing and the assignments. Bill Witcomb's plane was assigned as one of the spares of the 40th A Group—an airplane that wasn't to be counted among the necessary mission aircraft and one that carried no bombardier. The navigator—or one of the enlisted men—could drop the bombs when the time came if the automatic electronic release failed. For missions when an actual bombardier wasn't used, the man who actually dropped the bombs was given the affectionate title of *toggelier* because he was the one who threw the toggle switch that released the bombs. The function of a spare airplane in the combat box formation was merely to play "follow-the-leader" with the airplane in front of it, drop the bombs when the lead plane dropped its bombs, and maintain formation no matter what. A seemingly simple task provided the crew wasn't immersed in actual combat conditions.

"I'll be in the lead," instructed the major. "The 368th will have three high squadrons, so you should fare better with the flak than some of the others. Colonel Salada is the 306th group air exec today and he'll be in the air with us, so be on your toes. Tight formations at all times, and no screw-ups! You know how he is about getting the bombs on target. Good luck, men, and God bless." The major passed control of the meeting to the new air exec and took a seat in the front row for the orientation.

The full briefing for the mission that morning had been long and detailed—longer than any training briefing Bill ever remembered. Weather was going to play a major role in the events that were to follow, and Bill Witcomb and Norris Hales both made copious notes of the conditions being outlined during the session; routes and timing, formation instructions, and combat tactics. They knew their lives and the lives of their crew depended on it. Gill did the same from his chair, knowing that pinpoint accuracy in navigation would be crucial, especially during the multiple course corrections that would be required en route. Aerial photos of the target area were shown, although the crews were told that the weather over Germany would make actual sighting of the target very unlikely, requiring the pilots and bombardiers to rely upon the GEE-H (an airborne receiver that worked in conjunction with two ground stations) for the actual sighting.

As the briefing came to an end, all of the men filed out of the hut into the darkness of the English early morning. Those whose airplanes were a considerable distance away climbed aboard trucks and were delivered to their airplanes. Those whose revetments were close by the squadron area rode bicycles or walked to their airplanes.

Norris Hales was pulled away and assigned to another airplane, as was Bob Wilson at the last moment. Hales would fly with an experienced command pilot who could show him the ropes in combat. Bob Wilson would replace a bombardier on another airplane who was rotated out for R&R[1], or who was recovering from wounds sustained on a previous mission. Bill was a highly experienced training pilot. But combat piloting was unique, and 8th Air Force had evolved a method whereby pilots familiar with the demands of combat would shepherd new pilots, inexperienced in air battles, on their initial missions. Bill Witcomb would still fly as the pilot on the airplane assigned to him, but his copilot would be a combat veteran experienced in aerial warfare. The mission that day was the airdrome at Niedermendig. Bill and Wyatt Gillaspie, accompanied by radioman SSgt. Ringwald,

---

1 R&R, depending on the branch of the service, stood for *rest and recreation*, or *rest and reorganization*.

made their way to *Lassie Come Home* where they met the other crewmen, Dusenberry, Dinger, and their replacement tail gunner; all fixing their fifty-caliber machine guns into the gun mounts, while Eli Nelson was busy inserting the mechanized receivers into the chin guns and snaking the belts of ammo through the aluminum feed trays. Louis Dorenbush had been grounded due to a severe inner-ear infection and a substitute gunner from Lt. Claeys' airplane was in the tail.

Gill climbed into the nose of the airplane and settled in. He checked the two fifty calibers set up in the window mounts on either side of the fuselage to make sure the actions were clear and the ammo belts were lined up inside their feed trays. He then sat down at the tiny chart table on the port side and snapped on the flashlight that he used to read his navigational charts and the packet of information that was handed out to each navigator at briefing. Until Bill started the engines and the generators, Gill conserved electrical power aboard. In the packet were air charts, operational signals, radio and radar frequencies, and detailed information for aligning the PFF and the Mickey, which had been installed in their airplane but had yet to be used on a mission. On the charts were marked suspected and known locations for enemy gun emplacements where heavy flak could be anticipated, as well as Nazi-held airfields where fighters would certainly be trouble. Gill noticed that many of the locations in southern and western France had already been marked over, indicating that these locations were now in Allied hands and no longer a threat to American bombers flying overhead. Still, plenty of active sites remained on the unoccupied areas of the charts along the path that the 368th was about to fly. Gill opened one of the candies that had been handed out at briefing and popped the ball of sugar and fruit flavoring in his mouth. He sucked on the sweet, moving it from one side of his mouth to another, clicking it against his teeth as he went over the charts once again.

Bill did his walk around the aircraft, inspecting all the points of importance on the ship. As he got to the tail wheel and checked the exposed shiny metal on the shock absorber, he nodded to the replacement gunner, who was just climbing into the tail via the door under the starboard stabilizer. The young gunner nodded back. No words were exchanged, a silent mutual respect was all there was. Bill then walked forward and completed his preflight check, making sure that everything was in order. When he was finished, his experienced copilot—a captain—was standing at the nose of the airplane waiting for him, right below the fresh portrait of the collie dog that Red and his assistant had painted.

"Let's go," said the young captain. Bill motioned with his hand for the senior officer to climb aboard first. The captain tossed his kit bag up through the hatch opening. He then grabbed the bulkhead with both hands and swung himself up feet first into the hatch. Bill did the same. Once inside, he climbed up to the upper flight deck and turned to find the captain sitting in the pilot's chair on the left side. This had been Bill's exclusive domain from the moment the airplane was delivered to him, and Bill was somewhat shaken by the notion of flying the airplane from the right chair. As he was about to climb into the copilot's seat, the captain suddenly jumped up and remarked:

"I'm so used to flying on this side I just naturally sit over here. Here, take it. I'm flying second seat today," he said as he stepped across the cockpit to the copilot's seat and strapped in. Bill Witcomb climbed into his chair and prepared for takeoff. He went over the checklist with his overseer and awaited the signal from the tower—a green flare from a Very pistol—start engines on the first flare, taxi and takeoff in squadron order on the second flare. Bill nervously awaited the command to begin. Below in the navigator's seat, he could hear Gill shuffling a deck of cards and hoped that the experienced pilot next to him hadn't heard the noisy flutter. Bill looked aft through Eli Nelson's legs and could see Dusenberry, Ringwald, and Dinger all sitting around the radio room talking with each other. Eli remained crouched behind the pilot and copilot with flashlight in hand, watching the various instruments, awaiting the signal from the tower. He kept the vigil throughout takeoffs and landings to make certain that *his* engines were all performing properly. It wasn't as though he was needed as a gunner right then. He kept that flashlight on throughout the ritual as insurance in the event that the panel lights failed.

The green flare in the pitch-blackness of an English January morning was the perfect medium to paint a portrait with colored light. The minutes dragged on endlessly. Finally the signal came—a brilliant green meteor streaking across the sky from the tower. One by one, the engines of all the airplanes began to start in their numeric sequence. Bill's plane was no exception. Each engine started up with a roar, and each engine sent a shiver of vibration throughout the airplane. It was almost as though *Lassie Come Home* was as scared as the men flying in her on their first combat mission. Unlike the stateside ritual of doing the run-up on the taxiway just before takeoff, the captain in the copilot's chair told Bill to do his run-up right there on the hard stand, where the earthen walls of their revetment would direct the blast of wind from the prop wash upward, thus interfering with no other aircraft. Bill did his manifold pressure checks with Eli craning his neck over his shoulder to see all the engine readings on the panel.

The second signal flashed skyward from the tower and Bill Witcomb waited his turn to taxi and form for takeoff. The squadron order had been laid out at briefing so that each pilot knew at which point his airplane was to file onto the taxiway and make its way to the runway for takeoff. *Lassie Come Home* was assigned to the rear of the second section of airplanes; the middle squadron airplanes and the squadron leader came first. Major Huling was in his own airplane, the lead airplane of that section. After the first group of six bombers made their way to the active runway and began taking off, the high squadron airplanes, falling in behind their lead ship, ventured onto the taxiway. Lt. Witcomb pressed the rudder pedals and turned the yoke to move the giant *Lassie Come Home* toward the causeway that led to the strip for takeoff.

Alongside the concrete path that led out to the field was a fenced in corral of sorts. Visible within the dim peripheral light of the headlamps of the airplane, behind the white rail fence stood a horse, staring at the airplanes in a quandary as they passed him. He would raise his snout slightly as though saying hello as the giant airplanes taxied by.

"That's Old Dobbins," informed the captain.

"Old Dobbins?" questioned Bill over the command set.

"Seems as though he's out there at the beginning of every mission. Rumor has it that if he's standing up as we file past it's going to be a good mission – no losses. If he's laying down ..."

"If he's laying down, what?" beseeched Bill.

"Watch out," was all that the captain replied, turning his attention to the end of the taxiway and pointing the way for Bill. The captain was right. It had become almost legend that this tired old white horse, seemingly overweight and scruffy as a rabid badger in appearance, was the true prognosticator of events surrounding the 306th Bomb Group. Old Dobbins had many a time foretold the fate of those who flew on any given day simply by standing or sitting. Although there was absolutely no correlation between the horse standing or lying and the loss of airplanes, pilots and crews were like any group of young men engaged in a struggle of any kind—they became superstitious. If Dobbins was standing and airplanes were shot down, with many men killed or wounded on a mission, the myth was simply rationalized by the men saying that it could have been worse. If the horse was laying down on takeoff, anything that went wrong on the mission—from someone being shot down to a crewman stubbing his toe—was attributed to the foresight of that mangy equine. Bill shook his head in disbelief. Gill shuffled his cards for another round of solitaire.

Lassie Come Home was aligned with the center of the runway and the nose was pointed between the two flaming smudge pots that sat at the far end of the field. Aside from those two burning barrels of oil and the wing lights on the airplane, there was nothing with which to illuminate the runway. The headlamps were fine for taxiing, but as the airplane reached the speeds necessary for takeoff it was actually outrunning the effective range of those headlights on the tarmac. The only way a pilot had to judge distance was the pair of fifty-five gallon drums that were set ablaze in the early morning darkness. The young pilots knew those barrels sat at the far edge of the runway. They knew there was a short apron beyond them that represented a short and steep glide slope, and then a row of trees beyond. They knew also if they weren't airborne by the time they reached the smudge pots they were ultimately doomed. Bill walked the throttles forward as he had done countless times before and, as he did, whispered his now familiar prayer, "Lord, make this a good flight."

– – –

"Navigator to pilot—this is it, Chief," said Gill into the command set, "we're at the rally point." Bill looked out across the brightening morning sky and saw the silhouettes of dozens of groups of airplanes converging upon a single acre of territory in the sky. They were five miles in the air, above the dense cloud cover below, and the vision of American air power before them gave the young pilot a discernible lump in his throat. He'd seen large formations of airplanes before, and had, himself, flown in many. But this was different. These airplanes weren't there for training purposes, nor were they there to bolster civilian resolve with some startling show of force or precision flying. These airplanes were the heavy bombers of the 8th Air Force, laden with ordnance, on a combat mission to blast an enemy target with fire and explosions that would crumble the very foundations of their buildings.

There was another reason for Bill to be choked up with emotion over that morning's mission. The rally point that Gill announced was directly over the city of Nancy, France, where Ken Witcomb had met his fate a few short months before. Now held by the Allies, Nancy was an easily discernible location from their altitude and a natural point at which to form the bomber stream for runs that penetrated deep into German territory. It completely avoided the coastal emplacements that battered airplanes all over the western approaches, and allowed for the bomber stream to approach targets with the sun at their backs, making it difficult for the few remaining enemy interceptors. Bill wrestled with his emotions as Gill identified their location. Suddenly, all that he had dammed up inside him during the memorial service for his younger brother came spilling out, and Bill Witcomb turned his airplane in the sky on cue with a stream of tears flowing down over his oxygen mask. The captain seated next to him noticed but said nothing, attributing the tears to some physical reaction to the altitude or a combination of fear and intolerance to the oxygen.

Regardless of his emotional state, Bill tucked his airplane tight into the formation assigned him, right wing of the high squadron from the 368th. Major Huling's airplane was below and ahead by half a mile with the lead and middle squadron. The air exec had the low squadron, far off to Bill's right; a quarter mile below and a half mile behind. Witcomb was in an enviable position for his first run. Fighters would have to cut their way through a lot of fire from the ships below him in order to get a straight run at him, and the flak batteries would likely draw a range on the low and middle squadron before getting a fix on his altitude. Had he been allowed to ask for a formation position, he couldn't have chosen a better one.

Bill gave the order to test guns, and all the gunners and Gill chambered ammunition into the throaty fifties and let go a couple of bursts to make sure everything was working. After the gun check, Gill made his way to the bomb bay to arm the bombs. He carefully pulled the safety pins at the tail of each bomb. This released the safety mechanism within and allowed the bombs to explode upon any contact with the firing pin in the nose of the bomb. If one of them jarred loose in flight and hit the bomb bay door, it could explode if the firing pin was depressed in any fashion. Now *Lassie Come Home* was herself a flying bomb.

Hours of boredom passed before Gill informed him that they were coming up on the IP. Bill noticed the lead plane in his squadron making ever-so-slight course corrections now—just a touch of rudder trim to adjust was needed. There was absolutely no way to discern where they were, since the target had been described by "Buckeye Blue" as 10/10ths cloud cover. Buckeye Blue was the code name for a forward vanguard that collected weather data in advance of a bombing run, and that spread "chaff" in the air ahead of the bomber stream. Chaff consisted of tons of shredded strips of aluminum and metal foil thrown out the waist gun ports of a B-17 from 35,000 feet. It sometimes took hours for these extremely lightweight strips of metal to gently fall all the way to earth. Their presence posed a serious problem for German radar operators who could not interpret the return signals properly. The metal reflected the radar beam, just as an airplane would, and caused a clutter on their screens that often masked an entire division of B-17s. Even when airplanes were clearly discernible, the chaff created enough ghost echoes to make determining course, speed, and number of the actual aircraft virtually impossible. Antiaircraft artillery batteries also relied upon radar for targeting aircraft under overcast conditions, and chaff made nonsense of their calculations as well. AA bursts were seen as far as a mile away from any airplane in the stream. The strange thing to Bill was that they saw no fighters going into the target. He'd heard so much about the devastation that fighters caused, and this he and the others had feared the most.

Lt. Arthur Maenner, a senior pilot of the "Eager Beaver" Squadron (the 368th), and the eight airplanes assigned to his formation, bombed with the 381st Group. As often happened, one of the lead aircraft of the low group had a rack malfunction and failed to dump its load. Because the bombs from the lead plane did not drop, the other airplanes in that group did not drop their bombs, either. Lt. Col. Salada, the air exec flying with that group, decided to bring the bombs home rather than risk a second run on the target. Salada reckoned that saving the precious bombs was preferable to unloading on something that wasn't a viable target, and second runs were considered an invitation to suicide. If enemy aircraft had not caught up to the lethargic bombers at that point, the ground artillery would have surely pinpointed their positions and altitudes by then and made short work of the fragile aircraft before they ever reached the target for a second run. As a result, six of the aircraft in the 306th Bomb Group failed to drop their bombs over the target and brought them home instead.

Bill watched the lead aircraft in his section intently. The bomb bay doors parted and arced back to the sides, exposing the bombs that lay in the center of the fuselage. He commented to Gill, who immediately opened the bomb bay of *Lassie Come Home* and got ready to let go the load of bombs aboard. The seconds ticked by like hours as Gill stared at the lead plane, waiting for the sign of the first bomb or the signal light on the panel indicating it was time to release. By now the AA fire from below had found the general area of the bomber stream and the enemy had taken a good guess as to the altitude of the invading bombers. Bursts of black smoke and shrapnel exploded in their path—in front of them, to the sides, and behind. It wasn't thick by normal standards, but this was Bill's first mission. Any flak at all was more than he'd ever encountered working in the training commands. The noise of the explosions could be heard faintly over the roar of the motors—more an interruption in the routine sounds rather than a distinct sound of its own. The shrapnel that did make its way to his airplane sounded like pebbles being tossed onto a metal roof. It wasn't starkly alarming, but the disconcerting nature of its presence helped to build stress within every member of the crew. The horror of its potential was a passive weapon that flak brought with it.

"Bombs away, Gill!" shouted Bill, as he witnessed the bombs falling to ground from the lead bomber. Gill toggled the switch on the panel to the left of the bombardier's chair and held it in place while repeating Bill's order. "Bombs away!" The bomb load dropped from the airplane as though a giant bird were laying her eggs. Instantly the airplane began to rise in the air from the loss of the enormous weight. Gill waited for the last bomb to clear the rack before releasing the toggle switch.

"Closing bomb bay, chief," he announced as he pulled the lever that retracted the giant bomb bay doors in the belly of the airplane. Gill began searching the skies again for enemy aircraft, but there were still bursts of AA coming sporadically so the likelihood of fighters was slim. Realizing this, the young lieutenant slipped back aft through the passageway and opened the hatch door to the bomb bay to make certain that all the bombs had dropped and that the doors had closed securely.

Gill returned to his station and hopped onto the chin turret guns and again panned the sky for fighters. The AA had stopped as suddenly as it started and every man aboard strained their eyes for the first glimmer of incoming airplanes. Bill held tight to his formation, tucking the wingtip of the B-17 as close as he dared to the neighboring airplane. Gill moved the yoke of the turret now and then to show any unseen fighter pilot that he was awake at his station. In fact, all the gunners did that. Raymond Dinger pivoted the ball from side to side, probing the sky below the airplane for any sign of the German Air Force. Eli Nelson swiveled the top turret around so that it was facing mostly forward, in the hopes that he would find the first bogey (enemy aircraft). It meant facing the two hundred and twenty-five mile an hour wind smack in the face through the machine gun openings in the canopy, but not doing so meant the possibility of death for all aboard.

Ringwald and Dusenberry moved their guns from side to side in the waist of the fuselage. Ringwald had rigged an extra-long cord for his headphones that allowed him to step out of the radio room and man the open waist gun while still focusing his attention on the radio. The tail gunner scanned where they had been, looking down on Niedermendig and the smoky trail left behind in the wake of the bombers. In the few breaks between clouds he could see most of the town still standing, even the marshaling yards that were the intended target. Most of the bombs dropped that day had been wasted. Most of the German manufacturing and transportation capability in Niedermendig remained intact. But then, there was little enough of either there to begin with—the lack of a major air assault from the Luftwaffe and the thin saturation of antiaircraft artillery were testimony to that.

"BANDITS, twelve o'clock high!" shouted Eli Nelson over the headset. Every gunner instinctively pulled back on the charging handle of the fifties to make certain they were ready to fire. Just as instinctively, the captain in the copilot's seat cautioned them all to hold their fire until the fighters were in range. They all fought hard against the temptation to start blasting the instant that they could see the tiny blips that were enemy airplanes, except Dinger and the tail gunner, who couldn't see them because the Germans were above or forward of their vantage points. Dinger just kept the ball turret moving and his guns waggling to let anyone else out there know that he was still looking for a target and not asleep at his station. The experienced tail gunner moved his guns now and then, but his view included only the B-17s in formation directly behind him. Within seconds the enemy airplanes were on top of them, streaking past at an alarming rate.

"What the hell are those?" yelled Gill into the command set.

"Jets," announced the copilot, as a pair of Lance Wolf Ones blitzed overhead. Eli Nelson fired a couple of bursts as they zoomed by, but there was little likelihood that he would have hit anything with a closing speed that fast. They had to be traveling at better than four hundred miles per hour. Coupled with the two hundred and twenty-five mile-per-hour airspeed of *Lassie Come Home*, it meant that Eli had less than a second to acquire the target, aim the fifties with a proper lead, and fire. A hit would have been more likely if he'd simply aimed the guns in their path and fired continuously until the jets flew through the stream of bullets.

"Tighten up your formation," barked the Captain to Bill, "get right in next to your wing man. That's the safest place there is with these bastards. The tighter you are, the less likely they'll even come in at you."

Bill maneuvered his shiny silver airplane in close to the O.D. green B-17 model F that was in the lead of his flight. Being in tight meant that incoming fighters suddenly faced that wall of fire that was offered by multiplying the number of machine guns concentrating their fire on a single position. Too many Luftwaffe pilots had learned this bitter lesson over the previous two years in the air campaign, and even the great speed of the German jets could not overcome the raw and awesome firepower of a flock of B-17s flown in close formation. The jets made that one pass, as though to say the German Air Force exists and it won't let the Allies have a free ride over Niedermendig. But there were only a few short bursts of inaccurate machine gun fire from the fighters, and then they were gone as quickly as they appeared.

The five hours of flying back to the base were reasonably uneventful. There were flak fields along the way that the group leader seemed oblivious to, and an occasional ME-109 would wander toward the group, only to turn tail and run when it saw the cohesiveness of the bomber stream on the return leg. Bill made mental notes of some of the landmarks below—a river here, a town there—in addition to taking mental note of where the most flak came up. Gill did the same thing, only he documented his observations on the charts before him. He was certain it would prove to be valuable information at the debriefing, and even more important on future missions. He was right.

– – –

Debriefings were done differently at the various bases of the 8th Air Force, but their objective was always the same—to ascertain what had happened on the mission. At Thurleigh (like at all bases), the wounded were always tended to first, receiving first aid in the field or transported to the infirmary by ambulance. Four men were often loaded into the back of the cramped field ambulances and hauled away like so much freight. Their care at the hospital was good, but those delivering them to a doctor's care were a far cry from the combat medics that accompanied troops in the field. The wounded were evaluated by simple criteria: if he was still bleeding, the patient was unconscious, or there was a limb missing, they were immediately hauled to the hospital. If the patient was disoriented, dazed, or dopey, but still able to function, they were herded to the debriefing room. Those doing the evaluations in the field took their cues from the air crews themselves. If a flare from the built-in on-board Very pistol was seen as the airplane made its final approach, someone aboard needed to be transported to the hospital. The triage that was performed in the field by medical personnel in other places was done at the hospital at Thurleigh. Scoop-and-run was the standing order for the Station 111 medics.

The survivors of the mission—those not killed, captured or physically maimed—reported to the ready room where they had received their mission briefing that morning. Here the crews were ushered past a table that was covered with small glasses of whiskey. Each crewman would take a drink to jolt him somewhat and brace him for the verbal recounting of the mission. The alcohol was designed not only as a reward, but as a facilitator to loosen the tongue.

Bill and his crew, with the young captain in the lead, marched past the table and each took a glass from it. Only Gill refrained from imbibing. The young replacement tail gunner took two drinks. The crew was directed to a table where a young officer sat with a note pad. They each took a chair around the table and the young officer began to question them about the mission as the crew members began shucking their safety equipment and loosening their clothing slightly. The young captain that had flown as copilot carried on most of the conversation. Eli Nelson reported the jets that they had encountered, and the other crewmen that had seen the Lance Wolves chimed in with their recollections. There were no reports of enemy fighters being shot down, no loss of airplanes during the mission, and very little flak damage to any of the airplanes that any of them could see. The young officer questioned the tail gunner for his estimate of the bomb damage that he had observed from his position in the tail. There hadn't been much to see due to the weather, so there was little to tell. But his evaluation of things made it difficult to tell whether or not the 368th had done their job that day. The young officer brushed it all away by saying the aerial photographs taken by the PRU (photo reconnaissance unit) should give them the answers to those questions once they were developed and analyzed.

At the beginning of the debriefing, the entire crew (less the copilot) was as reticent as could be. The newness of the exercise made them so. The tail gunner was used to debriefings, but not with this crew. But as their time in the hot seat wore on, and the alcohol began to take effect, each one contributed to the story of the mission in some way. They had no way of knowing what value was to be found in telling and retelling a story that was so bland. But the 8th Air Force evaluated all the debriefing information and analyzed it thoroughly. The lack of precision in the bombing that day could be attributed to a combination of factors. Weather was certainly the biggest factor. A 10/10ths cloud cover is never easy to bomb in. Alignment of the PFF and the Mickey required considerable precision, and a miscalibration of the instruments at any one of the critical points along the way—the rally point, the IP, the AP, or even at the point of bombs away—could account for a complete miss of the target. At an altitude of five miles (26,400 feet) above a target, being just half a degree off in a calibration from the IP to the AP would miss the target by several thousand yards. At that same altitude, inputting the information into either the Norden bombsight or the H2X radar just a few seconds late could result in missing an entire targeted town.

One factor that Bill Witcomb attributed in his own mind the poor bombing results to that day was that Bob Wilson was not in the nose of *Lassie Come Home*. Bill was confident that if Wilson had been the lead bombardier on that mission, the bombs would have been in the proverbial pickle barrel and the need for another mission to Niedermendig would be superfluous. Whatever friction may have existed at one time between pilot and bombardier did nothing to deter Bill's respect for Bob's ability in his job. Wilson's precision in his job was equal to Bill's in his, or Gill's, or Norris's for that matter.

The crew completed the debriefing and filed out of the building past Red Cross ladies who handed them a cup of hot coffee and some kind of scone. Stateside they would have been served coffee and a doughnut. In England, they were served scones. They returned to their quarters—the enlisted men to their barracks and the officers to their Quonset hut. They removed their bulky flight suits and washed their hands and faces. Dinger sat on the edge of his bunk with his shoes and socks removed while the others milled around the open bay.

"What the hell are you doing?" asked Ringwald of the ball turret gunner.

"Counting my toes," snapped Dinger.

"Your species still have six on each foot, right?" questioned the radioman.

"Hey listen, wise ass, you any idea how cold it is in that God damn ball when you're five miles up? It's friggin' freezin', dat's what. You know what I mean?"

"So how bad was it?" questioned Louis Dorenbush as he was penning another letter to his wife, Joyce.

"Lou, you don't want to know," said Ringwald as he tossed a towel over his shoulder and headed for the latrine.

"We saw jets," said Dusenberry in an excited voice.

"You saw what?" questioned Dorenbush.

"Jets, you yokel," cracked Dinger as he continued to massage his cold feet with his hands. "You know—really fast airplanes."

"And you wonder why you wind up in the stockade all the time, Dinger," said Eli Nelson as he fastened his collar button and finished fixing his tie.

"I never wonder that," said Dinger with a confused expression.

"I know what jets are," defended Louis. "How close did they come?"

"We were nose-to-nose with 'em," said the Kid. "Lieutenant Gill took a shot at them, but they were gone before you knew it. Eli had a shot, too."

"Really, Eli?"

"I saw 'em, and I fired, but I wouldn't call that gettin' a shot at 'em. They were too damn fast."

"I was talking to this guy from the 423rd over at the hospital today," explained Dorenbush, "and he said the whole mission of the 8th Air Force right now is to knock out the plants that are building those planes."

"And who'd he get his info from, Ira Eaker direct?" snapped Dinger.

"He also told me, Mr. Dinger, that they got an airplane over in the 367th called *Lassie Come Home*."

"NO WAY," cried Raymond Dinger.

"He said it's been there since June," informed Louis.

"Is that bad luck?" questioned Dusenberry of Eli Nelson.

"Only if we run into each other on takeoff," explained the southerner calmly.

– – –

Dinner for the air crews that had flown the mission was a treat—roast chicken with mashed potatoes, homemade gravy, dinner rolls with real butter, and milk for a beverage. There remained the ever-present Brussels sprouts for a green vegetable, but the meal was a feast compared to the usual fare. They all "chowed down" and enjoyed the abundance while it lasted. After dinner, there was a casual stroll back to their quarters, and many of them enjoyed a smoke as they walked. The day had been what was known universally as a milk run—a combat mission against a strategic target with little enemy interaction and no losses. Had the bombs been on target, it would have been a successful milk run … but they weren't.

Bill Witcomb nestled into his bunk for the night, exhausted from the work of the day. Earlier, upon landing and before reporting to the debriefing, Bill had wandered away from the others to a quiet place at the edge of the field. There, beneath the barren trees and the bleak January overcast sky, he kneeled and prayed to his God for forgiveness. His subconscious mind had labored during the entire return leg of the mission about the lives that he might be responsible for taking that day. He was prepared to some degree to accept the deaths that he caused at the target, because these people were actively engaged in a war. But the bombs of the 368th had not found the target that day and had come to earth thousands of feet from where they were intended. This meant collateral damage—a modern term for civilian casualties. Bill buried himself in his blankets and tried to banish the thoughts of these casualties from his mind. Neither would the feelings that swept over him at the RP (rally point) dissolve in any way. His brother Ken was still foremost in his mind. Those combined emotions would not go away, and sleep that night for the fatigued pilot was to be short and far from restful—far from the desired rest that he would need for another mission the next day.

CHAPTER 16

Medals

Again, a corporal with a flashlight stumbled his way into their Quonset hut and awakened the young officers at some ungodly hour. Once again they came groggily to their feet. It was different this morning—it was as though they had just gone to bed. A single lamp was turned on in the metal hut to provide light for the quartet of lieutenants as they shaved and dressed. They were cranky and slow this morning, unlike the previous day. They weren't as eager to face combat now that they were actually combat veterans. But they prepared themselves both physically and mentally this time, with the experience of the previous day to guide them in their preparations.

Again breakfast was a clamorous event, the droning sounds of young men all vying for the attention of their crewmates, the clanking of metal utensils against the Spartan metal mess trays. Any day after a mission where no aircraft were lost was cause for more boisterous interaction. It was the noises of Jefferson Barracks all over again, and the bitter damp chill of the English morning had Bill flashing back to those days when he learned all the fundamentals he needed to know: discipline and training. After breakfast there was the detailed briefing by the command staff, then the preflight prep and the walk around the airplane in the pitch blackness of the January chill. The target that day was Cologne (or Koln, depending upon the inclination of the clerk who typed the morning report). Their primary target was obscured by cloud cover, and the ground clutter on the in-flight radar equipment made sighting the secondary target difficult as well. They struck at the marshaling yards with marginal success. Although manufacturing facilities were considered prime objectives at all times, elimination of distribution capabilities was considered a close second in the event that the primary was obscured or unattainable. Marshaling yards were railroad centers where war materiel was disembarked for destinations at the front. At any given time, a marshaling yard could contain hundreds of railroad cars filled with equipment, weapons, ammunition, food, supplies, or even support troops that could be thrown into the fight against the Allies. Destruction of trains and the rails upon which they ran was prized very highly.

From the middle years of America's involvement in the European theater, the 8th Air Force was a military force consisting of two major elements. There were the bombers: the heavies, B-17s and B-24s, and the mediums, B-25s and B-26s. There were also the pursuit airplanes, later called fighters—the P-38s, P-47s, and eventually, the P-51s. Although these smaller airplanes were tasked primarily with the in-flight defense of the bombers to and from the target, there were periods of time (especially later in the air war) when the Allied high command unleashed the smaller aircraft to seek out targets of opportunity. Railroad trains were among the most favored of these targets. Called "choo-choo runs" by the pilots who flew them, American fighters would swoop down and strafe the enemy supply trains with a firestorm of mixed fifty-caliber rounds. Their primary objective was always the engine, and they would giggle like school girls when their machine gun fire triggered an explosion in the boiler of the steam locomotives. Having stopped a train dead on the tracks, the pilots would then rake the cars behind it with a torrent of bullets—some, regular rounds; others, incendiaries that would quickly ignite or explode volatile chemicals or explosive ordnance that was stored within. These raids from above would rip into passenger cars that carried troops, and even civilians, to untold destinations. The random nature of the killing was the most unsettling aspect of the raids, and cause for consternation among the troops who endured them.

Putting a halt to German industry was no easy task. Hitler's war machine was a highly developed and formidable system of both military might and civilian ingenuity and industry. It was a two-stage process: making the weapons for war, then delivering those weapons to the front. Both the means of production and distribution were essential to the German war effort and, therefore, cherished equally as targets of opportunity by the allies.

It was on this second mission that Bill and his crew first encountered the tracking fire of AA. Although it only lasted two minutes or so around Cologne, he observed a pattern to the fire. Four bursts of reasonably accurate fire would come up. Then there would be a pause. Then four more bursts would come in close succession, with another pause. Each time, it was as though the guns were following them. With the lack of enemy fighters around, Gill swung away the joystick that controlled the chin guns and glanced through the barren optics of the Norden bombsight to see what he could. Without the highly-guarded "football" portion of the sight—the portion maintained under the strictest security conditions—the system was almost useless. But Gill had brought a small conventional telescope aboard with him and was able to manipulate it sufficiently amid the jolts and vibrations of the airplane, to discern the image of a rail line running ahead and beneath their formation and in direct line with their heading. He saw flashes from below—four of them—and tried to focus on their exact location. He could barely make it out, but there were German 88-millimeter guns mounted on the flat cars of a train that was speeding along below them. The German gunners would get a fix on altitude by primitive sighting techniques then, using simple mathematics to calculate speed and distance, let loose with a barrage from all four cannons. It was amazingly accurate, given the simplicity of their technique coupled with the additional variable of both target and attacker movements in the equation. But then, German gunners were amazingly accurate with their highly developed 88-millimeter cannon under a wide range of adverse conditions.

There was another prayer at the beginning of the mission and another chicken dinner that followed, and yet another trip to the far edge of the field for Bill, where he attempted to atone for his actions that day. The other crewmen found their absolution by visiting the nearby church. It being Saturday evening, it seemed almost inappropriate, but the vicar was more than accommodating when it came to the salvation of a soldiers' soul, even though it interrupted his Saturday evening supper and his preparations for Sunday's sermon. Bill's absence did not go unnoticed by the crew. They had all somehow found their way to that church on their own, but their leader was not with them. He was removed from them physically, which widened the gulf that existed already. That Saturday evening, they began to question in their minds Bill's motives for flying and his ability to lead, primarily because the emotional grief he was suffering was not shared. To them, it was as though Bill believed his problems were somehow more important than their own.

In the week that followed, the squadron was called upon to fly missions three out of seven days. But *Lassie Come Home* was not among the airplanes that would go to Euskirchen, Speyer, or Gymnich. Some of Bill's crew members were pulled into other airplanes due to shortages of gunners and the like, but the officers all stood down for the week, giving them a much-needed break after their initial missions. Bill still demanded that they drill, practicing various emergency procedures. Whenever Red wasn't busy tuning engines or repairing holes and flak damage, Bill and his crew were in the airplane drilling, both on the ground and in the air. Any opportunity available to fly was spent conducting practice bombing missions.

Dinger had agreed to ride the ball turret in another airplane at one point. The 35-mission requirement applied to gunners as well as pilots, and Dinger was interested in ending his obligation as soon as possible. He often hectored the first sergeant for assignments in order to complete his requirement early and get home. He flew once on a raid along the German eastern front when 8th Air Force bombed the enemy from behind. The temperatures were so cold, and the conditions aloft so bad, that Dinger was hospitalized afterwards for several days with frostbite on his face and his fingers. While in the hospital bed he pleaded with the doctor to credit him with injuries sustained in combat. When the doctor refused, Raymond Dinger argued that it might be the surgeon's only chance to award a Purple Heart to a ball turret gunner without it being given posthumously. The doctor did not budge—frostbite was far too common among 8th Air Force flyers to be considered a wound. Besides, even if it were considered a wound, it wasn't inflicted by the enemy. So, Dinger would remain one of the very few ball turret gunners who would escape the war alive and who also went without being awarded the "Purple George," as it came to be known.[1]

On one of his "alternate missions," as he put it, Dinger was supposed to handle the ball. But when he first got aboard the airplane and drilled the green waist gunner on the technique for cranking the ball around in an emergency, the young recruit had no idea how to do it. Dinger told the pilot when he finished his preflight walk around that he'd fly in the waist, but he refused to fly in the ball when that pilot's crew had no idea of emergency procedures. In most cases, refusals of this nature could result in a court martial. But Dinger told the young lieutenant before they took off that he was willing to go before the commanding officer and put it to him directly—Dinger was willing to risk the wrath of the brass, but not certain death if he were trapped in the ball. The feisty gunner knew that it was the pilot's job to make sure that every crewman

---

1 The Purple Heart is a medal awarded to members of the United States Military who sustain wounds of any kind at the hands of the enemy. A gold profile of George Washington rests inside a heart-shaped medal, suspended from its clasp by a purple ribbon.

knew his job, and a waist gunner that didn't know how to crank the ball around was really the fault of the pilot. The young lieutenant pilot sheepishly agreed that Dinger could handle the second waist gun and made no attempt to force the question. The ball in that airplane remained locked into position for that mission, and it was at that moment that Dinger began to comprehend the value of flying with Iron Ass Witcomb. He may have been a martinet, but his crew knew their jobs right down to the last detail, and Dinger never feared being in the ball when he knew any of his crewmates could crank the ball and extricate him in an emergency. Although he never came out and said so, his silence was tacit approval of Bill Witcomb's methods—that, coupled with Bill bailing him out of trouble and the stockade now and then.

On Sunday the 14th of January, Bill and most of his crew flew to Cologne again, this time aiming at the Hohenzollern railway bridge within the city. The raid that day brought at least one of Bill's crew members back to him—Louis Dorenbush was in the tail again after a short recovery period from his illness. He sat stoically in the back of the airplane, nearly silent as always. Hales was still farmed out to sit as copilot with another airplane, and Bob Wilson had been assigned as bombardier with one of the lead ships. Again, the 368th was assigned to 40th A Group and Bill's plane was considered only a spare. Bombing was done electronically, and their bombs were released electronically and automatically when the lead ship dropped hers. The navigator was merely a back-up toggelier to the electronics.

Colonel Sutton, the first air division leader assigned to lead the mission, in an airplane specially equipped for the job, was unable to assume the lead due to engine failure at takeoff. This put the air exec in charge, and elevated the level of responsibility for the remaining airplanes that were properly equipped. *Lassie Come Home* was such a ship. Gill worked the Mickey equipment and stood by to toggle the bombs on cue if needed.

The 368th raised hell with the approaches of the bridge, and the low squadron hit the marshaling yard to the west. The high squadron concentrated on the bridge itself, dropping bombs all around it, but only a single five-hundred-pounder landed on the bridge directly. Upon their return, Louis Dorenbush scribbled a note onto a piece of paper that began a comprehensive diary of the remainder of his missions.

> *January 14, 1945. 1st mission to Cologne. Target was bridge on Rhine. Flak was heavy. Our R wing hit bad and so was pilot. Lt. Claeys. 711*

Lt. Richard Claeys may have been "hit bad" that day over Cologne, but he was able to rally for yet another mission the following morning when the 368th flew to Freiburg, Germany. Their target was another railroad bridge that was the artery of supply for the Colmar pocket. The thick cloud cover over the target meant bombing would be done by PFF, and Bill's airplane was equipped appropriately. The 306th put up 36 aircraft that day, three of which were outfitted with the Mickey equipment. The 368th was assigned as high squadron and, for the first time, Bill Witcomb had Norris Hales and Bob Wilson back aboard for a combat flight. Bill was no longer under the watchful eye of a seasoned veteran pilot. He was a seasoned veteran with three missions under his belt. So too were the rest of his crew, with varying numbers of missions on their records. The group had full fighter support all the way in and all the way out, even though no enemy aircraft were sent up to oppose them. The flak was ridiculously light, with less than a dozen bursts seen prior to bombs away, and absolutely no battle damage reported by any of the crews. Debriefing was fast and furious—another milk run, if a mission over Germany could ever be considered that. Again, Louis Dorenbush jotted down his brief synopsis of the flight:

> *Jan. 15, 1945 2nd mission to Freiburg. Target was marshaling yards. Flak was light. No damage done. Flew full crew. First mail from home. 474*

The three-digit number at the end of each of his entries would perplex his family years after his death, but it was his simple code that showed the versatility of the tail gunner and the resolve he had to fulfilling his mission requirement. Those three digits identified the airplane in which he rode (the last three digits of the tail number). The crews knew their airplanes by name. So too did the press correspondents that often wrote human-interest pieces about the boys flying them, offering a glorified promotional slant to increase the war effort at home and boost enlistments. But to command—and to Louis Dorenbush—the tail number was the means of identification for airplanes. It was the way the military maintained an ordered accounting of their equipment and crews, and it was the way Louis documented his thirty-five missions.

Two days later, *Lassie Come Home* would rise into the frigid European air again and make its way to Bielefeld. On January 20th, Bill had his entire original crew back aboard. The nine that had assembled on that tarmac a few short months before in the warmth of the States climbed aboard their lifeboat and headed off to Rhines, Germany for a leaflet drop from five-and-a-half miles up. While the heart of the group was occupied with dropping explosives on strategic targets around a synthetic fuel plant, *Lassie Come Home* was tasked with dropping propaganda pamphlets all over the city. Instead of raining bombs on the position, 43-38711 carried only paper—paper that presented the realities of terror bombing to the very people who had codified the practice over London in 1940. The explosive horror of the actual bombing was a demonstrative reinforcement of the sentiments that were contained in the psy-war (psychological warfare) material that fluttered to earth as the smoke began to clear. The mission was a snap, and again Dorenbush relegated the entire effort to his own simple shorthand.

> *Jan. 20, 1945 4th mission to Rhines. Target was marshaling yards. Flak was very, very light. A milk run. We carried propaganda leaflets. A milk run. 711*

The missions continued—Aschaffenburg, Cologne, Koblenz, and Mannheim. Each one drew on the energy of the men flying it, and with each new mission came a new understanding of the demands of combat. The crew of *Lassie Come Home* was teetering on the brink of some manner of madness. Regardless of the crew station that they manned, the fear that comes with the risks they were taking began to take its toll. Combat mathematics—a formula that says your odds begin to run out when you keep exposing yourself to danger—played a big role in escalating the trepidation. Bill Witcomb continued to remain aloof from the others, finding what little grace he could scrounge in his solitary trips to the edge of the field at the end of each mission. The others immersed themselves in the rituals of religion and clung to the superstitions that were common among air crews—the legend of Old Dobbins being high on the list. Had they not been able to see that mangy old nag as they passed by, it was questionable if the 306th could have launched a mission, the superstition being so thoroughly pervasive by 1945.

By their third trip to Cologne in three weeks, Bill and the crew—indeed, the entire group—had a pretty good sense of the target. There were no fighters to be seen this time, but the flak on that third run was the heaviest they'd seen yet. The group managed to drop their bombs while once again avoided touching the twin church steeples in the center of the city that had become their bombing benchmark. During the terror bombing of the Blitz over London, German pilots had unsuccessfully attempted to take out Big Ben, despite numerous attempts at leveling the giant tower. It was obvious by their bombing patterns that the huge square spire on the water's edge was their intended goal. But, like the Londoners themselves, Big Ben stood tall and erect throughout the bombing and remained a stalwart emblem of the British resolve. Eighth Air Force had no intention of striking at such a target within the Third Reich, unless of course it was a structure that was at the heart of the Nazi regime. Church steeples were objects to be avoided, because bombing them meant inflicting collateral damage. The crews had no problem with killing the enemy, but they found the deliberate murder of civilians difficult to resolve. More to the point, tall steeples were visible identifying landmarks that assisted in Allied aiming. The Allies knew precisely where the steeples in Cologne were, and they assisted the bombardiers in calculating their ultimate target no matter what part of the city it was in. Steeples were also extremely difficult to camouflage, unlike other elements of the landscape.

The mission report of January 28th for the 368th was almost as succinct as the one offered by Louis Dorenbush. The official version read:

> No E/A were seen. We encountered accurate, predicted flak at bombs away, damaging four a/c severely and seven slightly. Incendiary AA shells were also fired at us.

The tail gunner encapsulated the entire day this way:

> *Jan. 28, 1945 6th mission to Cologne. Target was marshaling yards. We took off late and flew with different group. Flak was pretty rough. We didn't get hit. Several did tho. Altitude 25,000 temp -42° 711*

In all, it had been a rough day—one of the roughest thus far. The 306th reported their losses, but Bill and *Lassie Come Home* had tacked themselves onto another group because of their delay in take off. They weren't even part of the official summary equation for the 306th. Even though Bill did exactly the same things he would have done had he been able to catch up to his own squadron, his crew grew restless and fearful of the outcome because of the belated takeoff. As the enemy flak began finding targets all around them at four-and-three-quarters miles up, Bill's crew became more and more terrified by the possibilities. They could fight back when attacked by fighters, but flak … there was nothing to do but wait. Either your number was up or it wasn't. And until the noise and the fiery, billowing black clouds and the ominous flames inside those clouds stopped erupting all around the airplane, the crew had no idea if this was their time or not. It was predictably unsettling and unnerving. Bowels no longer functioned normally, and bladders were quick to empty without warning as jagged metal shrapnel ripped through a fuselage. The success of the mission may have rested in the hands of their bombardier, Bob Wilson, but their lives lay in the hands of Bill Witcomb and God.

When they cleared the coast and were over English soil headed back to Thurleigh, the bulk of the crew assembled in the radio room. Dorenbush was still "Tail-End-Charlie" and remained in the tail looking for stray fighters, and the Kid remained on alert at his station in the waist. But the rest of them crowded into the tiny radio cabin and sat kibitzing before landing. They were disgruntled and angry, upset that Bill had decided to fly the mission after being late on take off. They were peeved at the severity of the attack from the AA; peeved because of the unsettling effect of flak. Their grumbling took on an air of authority because two of those grumbling the loudest had bars on their collars.

Upon landing, the bulk of the crew assembled outside the airplane, behind the right wing. Some of them lit up smokes, despite the precautions concerning the proximity to the fuel tanks. They began to form a plan of attack. Louis Dorenbush was still tucked away in the tail, and Eli Nelson was busy on the flight deck inspecting and documenting the sparse flak damage that they had sustained. Some of the instruments had been severely jarred during the assault in the air and needed to be checked, but all seemed to be working during landing. The reverberation of a plot began to foment among the men, something along the lines of refusing to fly with Bill Witcomb. But as they griped and complained to each other about the risks associated with being on Bill's crew, they polled each other for reassurance that they all felt the same way. When they got to the Kid, his blonde round face beamed out through the fleece collar of his jacket and he shook his head from side to side.

"The lieutenant's gotten us back every time," he said. "I'll stick with the lieutenant. He's going to get us home again."

The others were suddenly left standing with their mouths open and nothing to say. The solidarity that they'd hoped for didn't exist. Without a unanimous front, it would not be a combat crew offering higher command a uniform evaluation of a pilot gone sour. It would be—put in classical military terms—a mutiny. Those who had complained the loudest knew this well. What they didn't know was that Bill Witcomb did not exit the aircraft that day through the nose hatch, but instead through the side hatch that was aft of the waist guns. He had decided to walk through the airplane to check for flak damage himself, and he and Norris Hales had overheard the entire conspiracy from a few feet away. They silently looked at each other in disbelief as the incipient mutiny evolved. When the Kid chirped up and put down the rebellion with his honest faith in their pilot, a lump formed in Bill's chest. He swelled with pride. In the years after his service, Bill would say that one of the medals he was awarded during the war were the words spoken that day by the youngest member of his crew. Those words meant more to him than the Distinguished Flying Cross. A few short days later he would receive what he called his second medal.

Chapter 17

Crosses in the Sky

"Berlin." That was the only word that Major Huling needed to speak at the morning briefing. Palpable fear and a discernable groan were the initial responses as the curtain was pulled away from the operational map on the briefing stage showing the route to be followed by the 306th. Every man in the United States armed forces knew that Berlin was the most prized target in the European theater. Every man knew equally the inherent dangers in going there. Even though the Luftwaffe had been dramatically diluted by February 1945, Berlin was still the most heavily defended city in the world. Hitler's army had recalled thousands of cannon from the various fronts in order to defend the Nazi capital against air attacks. The US 8th Air Force might have been able to drop bombs on Berlin regularly, but only at substantial risk, and routinely at a terrible price. The German Army had no intention of going quietly into the night.

Bill Witcomb and Fred Hales sat quietly in their seats, making notes about engine start-up, taxi, and takeoff times. Hales chewed a stick of gum feverishly as he scribbled numbers on his pad that were later barely legible, even to him. He had been rocked by the news that the target was Berlin. Bill remained erect and seemingly unshaken by the announcement of the mission. He had long figured it was just a matter of time before Berlin would again become a primary target for the 306th. The group had been there many times before, prior to the addition of

43-38711 to their ranks. This was to be another 1,000+ bomber sortie, with airplanes from virtually every 8th Air Force station in England participating. B-17s and B-24s were the weapons of choice this time, due to the extremely long range of the target. Fighter support would be substantial, with P-51 Mustangs accompanying the Fortresses and Liberators all the long way to and from Berlin. But those cannon …

To his surprise, Bill Witcomb's name was called out to lead a flight of six airplanes on the screening aspect of the mission. *Lassie Come Home* would literally lead the mission that day, dropping chaff ahead of the bomber stream in order to confuse and confound enemy radar. Flying vanguard for such a mission was an awesome responsibility. It required being first over enemy territory, first to encounter fighters, and first to draw the dreaded flak. Everyday formation flying required a blind faith in the guy flying ahead of you. When his plane veered one way or another, you played follow-the-leader in order to maintain group integrity in the combat box. But Bill Witcomb was about to be in the lead ship, and he had five other planes chasing his slipstream all the way to the target and back. It wasn't as though he could just follow along now—the entire mission of 8th Air Force was truly resting upon his shoulders. Fortunately, Bill Witcomb had broad shoulders.

Lassie Come Home was assigned to the high squadron, which was where Bill always preferred to be, and assigned as an element to 40th D Group. Being out front and armed with nothing more devastating than shredded metal foil gave him and the entire crew an indescribable feeling of vulnerability. It shouldn't have—in the event of a direct hit, chaff was unlikely to explode like 500-pound bombs might. But the thought that they weren't actually dropping bombs made it seem as though they were superfluous.

The plan was to pull ahead of the main body of aircraft and spread chaff along the route, like a flower girl dropping rose petals ahead of the bride at a wedding. The main bombers would thunder along a few minutes behind the screening flight and be almost completely obscured on German radar screens by the blizzard of metal foil floating at altitudes just below them. For the airplanes with the bombs, it meant that the radar-controlled guns would be ineffective against them, and gunners on the ground would have to estimate their altitude and speed. For Bill and his six airplane crews, it meant complete exposure to the wrath of the Third Reich's artillery below.

The briefing officer emphasized the strategic importance of the targeted sites that day, but truth be known, hitting anything in Berlin was considered good. Even if the only thing that came of it was that streets were closed around a bomb crater, it slowed down the Reich and drove home to Berliners the reality that they were now vulnerable to attack from the Allies. Hermann Goering had once guaranteed Adolph Hitler and the German people that not a single bomb would fall upon German soil. But Hitler, safely ensconced in his subterranean bunker, would feel the impact of every bomb that fell upon the city that he had chosen as his capital. The reverberations of 500- and 1,000-pound bombs shook the foundations of every Nazi edifice and shockwaves found their way to every crevice of the warren where the Fuehrer hid. Bombing may have been a morally challenging ordeal for those who were dropping the bombs, but it was among the most terrifying aspects of warfare for those being bombed. It wasn't dissimilar to the feeling of helplessness that the air crews felt when subjected to flak from below. There was no telling where the next bomb would hit, and the only defense was to be entombed deep within the ground, far from the blast and cushioned by tons of earth. Even the relative safety of bomb shelters did nothing to mitigate fear. With each impact, streams of loosened sand and dust would cascade down from shelter ceilings, pointing to the skies from which the horror came. While the bombs dropped from above, those finding refuge below the surface couldn't help but speculate whether the hole in the ground they turned to for shelter would soon become their tomb.

Pilot's briefing was long that morning, and the navigator's briefing even longer. Gill had the flak chart open and was reading it by flashlight as he walked toward the airplane. Dozens of little red blossoms appeared all over the chart denoting where the airmen could expect the heaviest flak. After climbing aboard *Lassie Come Home*, Gill spread the chart out on the tiny table in the nose and scrutinized the assigned route. Along several points on their path, the group was to traverse known heavy flak zones. Even though they had been assigned to the high squadron—which, in theory, put their airplane further away from danger than those below them—German flak had a nasty way of climbing to all altitudes, and Bill's flight of six airplanes was destined to be first into the fray sent up by radar-controlled antiaircraft artillery. Since a chaff drop would not precede *Lassie Come Home*, German radar could accurately plot altitude as well as speed, heading, and exact location in the sky. Gill knew that Bill Witcomb would demand a close, tight formation from the airplanes assigned to him, and although flying tight formations was clearly the best defense against enemy fighters, it actually increased the chances of being hit by flak from the ground. Flak was an imprecise weapon, much like a grenade or a sawed-off shotgun. Enemy gunners only had to time their bursts to be at the right altitude in generally the right place in order to wreak havoc with the somewhat fragile Allied airplanes. All that shielded the aircrews was a thin layer of aircraft aluminum—hardly a defense from molten steel shrapnel traveling at the speed of a bullet; enough could rip an airplane to shreds.

Red stood by in the darkness of the revetment waiting for Witcomb and Hales to arrive. He and his young assistant had spent the two days and nights since the last mission installing additional armor plating around some of the inhabited areas of the airplane. The added armor plating was scrounged from hangers at Station 111 at the request of Bill Witcomb and his crew. The cockpit was now a cocoon of three-eighths-inch steel and an added layer of Plexiglas® to the windscreens. The same was true for portions of the nose where Gill and Bob Wilson lived. Red had ignored the aft fuselage, due to intelligence reports that noted German pilots had recently been ordered to concentrate their fire on flight decks of B-17s rather than going toe-to-toe with the gunner's stations. The stoical flight mechanic pointed out that these additions would make significant changes in the trim characteristics of the airplane, making it nose-heavy as compared to before. This was nullified to some degree by the fact that their cargo for that morning's mission was relatively lightweight chaff as opposed to several tons of bombs. The additional armor was a safeguard from the flak they were sure to encounter, but it offered little security from aerial attack by strafing aircraft. Armor-piercing rounds could easily penetrate the relatively thin plating. Even worse, once such a round entered the cockpit and the energy of the bullet had been reduced considerably, it could ricochet around against the armor plates until it hit something that would absorb it, like an instrument panel or seat cushions, or, worse, a human body. And that is one of the many truths about combat—every measure that can be taken to ensure safety and security is invariably a double-edged sword. In minimizing exposure to enemy fire, one must sacrifice something—position, field of view, timing—something. Red's only hope was that his efforts would work to defend his aircrew and not jeopardize it.

Bill and Norris did the preflight walk around and climbed aboard. The others were already at their stations. Red's assistant stood behind the number one and two engines with the fire extinguisher trolley, while Red positioned himself where the pilot could see him. Once Bill was strapped in, he and Hales completed the checklist and he filled out Form A as always. Red held up his index finger and pointed a flashlight into the engine cowling of number one as Hales pumped the fuel primer on the right side of the panel and Bill threw the switch for startup. The engine came to life quickly and they moved on to number two. When all the engines were roaring, Red's assistant dragged the trolley out from under the nose and broke to the right side of the airplane, where Fred Hales could see that he was clear. Red held his ground a moment or two, crossed his fingers on both hands in front of him, and held them up for Bill to see. He gave a double thumbs-up to the lieutenant, then snapped to a sort of attention and saluted the airplane. At 05:41hours, exactly as briefed, Bill Witcomb began to push the throttles forward and *Lassie Come Home* started her journey to Berlin.

– – –

Being assigned the screening portion of the mission meant that Bill was among the first to take off that morning. He and the five other planes assigned to his flight would assume the point position of the formation and head straight for the Dutch coast once they were formed. The squadron, group, and wing commanders were all flying behind them, but well within viewing distance. Lt. Witcomb talked to the nearby aircraft in his charge on the liaison radio which they identified as "channel B." It was a short-range radio used for plane-to-plane chat. As expected, Lt. Witcomb demanded a tight grouping from his five flyers and he got it. The command staff in the airplanes to the rear was being treated to a clinic in formation flying from a young lieutenant. Along the route, each element of the bomber stream would slip into their assigned places. Dorenbush announced over the intercom the addition of each new group as they tacked on. There was a teeming river of bombers that stretched for miles and miles, and their thunderous sound could be heard roaring like a lion, even five miles below on the ground. Had Adolph Hitler been able to see the air armada being wielded at him that morning, he would likely have capitulated on the spot, or at least reconsidered his options. But then, Adolph Hitler could retreat to safety in his bunker, oblivious to signs that the end of his Reich was only a few short months away.

Lassie Come Home nosed her way over the English Channel and approached the coast of Holland. The gunners tested their guns, Gill labored over the charts in the nose, and Bob Wilson pushed his way through the bomb bay and nestled into a seat in the radio room until they got within range for dropping the chaff. Since spreading chaff through the air was done from the side openings in the fuselage rather than by being dropped like bombs, there was no need for a toggelier or bombardier to remain in the nose. Gill was perfectly capable of handling the chin fifties, and Wilson could quickly grab the second waist gun if fighters suddenly appeared.

"Bill, we got a problem here," said Gill through the intercom.

"What's the problem, Gill?" asked the pilot.

"They've got us routed directly over a primary flak field in Holland, according to this revised flak chart they gave me at briefing."

"Any way we can avoid it?" asked Bill.

"Sure we can, but not without leaving the briefed route."

"Give me a heading, Gill," was the order from the flight deck. Gill didn't quibble. He plotted a course that veered five degrees to starboard, then back on a parallel course to the assigned route. Bill signaled the other pilots in his flight, then shifted the rudder slightly to make the giant bird slide subtly to the right. The other five planes followed right along. The rest of the air group and the wing behind were aghast at the sudden change in direction of the screening force, until they found themselves in the midst of an enemy barrage from the ground. The flak there was thick, and three of the thirty-six airplanes of the 306th were hit and knocked out of the sky before ever reaching German soil. Having successfully bypassed the flak field, Bill and his flight were given a new heading by Gill and the six aircraft returned to a position in front of the bomber stream. The 8th Air Force was on course and on target, and Bill's six airplanes were unscathed by the murderous attack from the charted flak field below.

When the mission concluded and the group assembled in the briefing room for a formal debriefing, the colonel stood at the podium and called Witcomb to accounts for his unauthorized change in course.

"Witcomb, you broke formation this morning over Holland. What's your excuse?"

Standing at attention, Bill Witcomb stared directly into the face of the Group commander and boldly announced his actions in his Yankee accent.

"Sir, I was assigned six aircraft at morning briefing. I lead those six aircraft to Berlin, Germany this morning. I also lead those six aircraft home this afternoon. All six crews are in this room." He said nothing more. The colonel paused before speaking and realized that his own record that day wasn't as good. He had 36 airplanes assigned to him and three of them went down—each one a victim of the very flak that Bill and his flight had avoided. Realizing that everyone in the briefing room understood that, he was left with only one thing to say.

"Be seated, Witcomb."

– – –

Putting Holland behind them, Bill Witcomb and his flight finally broke from the bomber stream just north of Hanover and pushed the throttles forward all the way. They zoomed ahead of the other airplanes that continued to lumber along. At 26,000 feet, the temperature that morning was still forty-five degrees below zero. The machine gun stations along the side of the fuselage were wide open to facilitate the spreading of chaff, and the crew had all it could do to survive the elements. Bob Wilson and the Kid both had to rely upon the warmth generated by their own bodies and the limited protection that they would get from their protective clothing. Due to the bending and stooping they had to do, the plugs for their electrically-heated suits kept coming out of the electrical outlets mounted on the bulkheads near the oxygen outputs.

Upon command, Bill's six airplanes altered their formation so that they resembled a V formation, like a flock of geese. This allowed the chaff they were dropping to cover a wider area, and ensured that none of the metal foil would be sucked into the props of the trailing aircraft.

At exactly 10:49 hours, as planned, Bob Wilson and Francis Dusenberry began filling the sky with metal foil. A metallic cloud that took only twelve minutes to create formed in the wake of the six escort bombers and gradually descended toward earth. As it fell, it completely obscured from Nazi radar screens the bomber force of the mighty 8th Air Force that followed just minutes behind Witcomb's flight. Bill and his airplanes turned after the chaff run and realigned themselves into a small combat box, creating a diversion for any fighters that might come up to intercept. But none did. The deadliest aspect of the mission was the flak that came up from below. It seemed as though every Berliner had his or her own antiaircraft artillery and was shooting at the American bombers. There was a light cloud cover at lower altitudes, but the skies were as clear as they ever got over the target. The only things above 10,000 feet that morning were a hail storm of metal chaff, one thousand or more bombers, and a carpet of blackened cotton balls that burst all around the American airplanes. One pilot claimed the flak was so thick you could walk from airplane to airplane on it. Bill didn't know if that was true, but it was certainly heavy—so heavy, in fact, that for the first time in his combat career Bill could smell the burnt gun powder from the flak bursts even through his oxygen mask.

Normally, Bill and Norris Hales were nervously idle during a bomb run while Bob Wilson controlled the airplane from the bombardier's seat. But there were no bombs to toggle today, so Witcomb and Hales struggled to thread their way between the bursts of flak. There was no avoiding the flak fields around Berlin. In order to place bombs anywhere in the city, the airplane commanders were required to expose their aircraft to extreme concentrations of coordinated cannon fire. The radar may have been confounded by the chaff, but advanced optical aiming devices and old-fashioned triangulation, combined with dead-reckoning by German gunners, were all brought to bear against the invading airplanes. Berlin was not a flak field that could be sidestepped, as Bill had done over Holland. It was a densely populated, sprawling metropolis that was thoroughly and heavily defended.

Regardless of Bill Witcomb's earlier maneuver to avoid flak, he was now faced with having to maintain course and speed over the path of the bomb run in order to draw Nazi fire away from the following bomber stream. He flew at an altitude well above the main body of airplanes in order to give the Germans a fix on his group of airplanes. The remaining bombers were better than a thousand feet below his little group of six airplanes. Since he was first over the target, it was presumed that the ground gunners would fix on his altitude and not adjust when the main body started their run from the AP. In order for the ruse to work, Bill and his five companion pilots had to pretend they were doing a standard bomb run, which meant holding a close formation and going through all the motions of a standard run. The ground forces never seemed to notice that those lead six planes never dropped any bombs. But being more than five miles away, it would be difficult for people on the ground to actually see the bombs exiting the airplane.

A standard bomb run, from IP to "bombs away" varied from twenty to thirty minutes. Navigators would get a fix from a known position on the ground and from there plot a course to the target. Once the final heading was established, the airplane was committed to that course until it reached the target. The longer the bomb run, the longer the exposure to enemy fire and the more time the Germans had to calibrate their gunfire for altitude, speed, and distance. It was bad enough for those crews that had bombs to drop on the target—it was an exasperating absurdity for those who didn't.

With each explosion near the airplane, shrapnel could be heard clanking inharmoniously against the outer skin of *Lassie Come Home*. It was as though some kid were throwing pebbles as hard as he could against the aluminum skin. With each blast came a disconcerting wave of terror for the crew, who sat at their stations praying for enemy fighters to shoot at. If there were fighters there would be no flak—the Germans wouldn't risk shooting down their own extremely limited number of airplanes. Eli crouched slightly in the top turret so that he could still see the horizon outside the airplane, but he withdrew his head and upper body below the bubble that made up the top of the turret. As good a windshield as Plexiglas® was, it was no protection from the shrapnel of flak. Dinger spun in the ball, this way and that, trying to lessen his exposure as the ominous black clouds erupted along both sides of the airplane. Bob Wilson had returned to the nose after the chaff drop, where he and Gill huddled behind the newly-installed armor plates. The rest of the crew did what they could to shield themselves from the horror of the flak, but there was really no protection, other than luck. If your number was up, it was up, and all the armor in the world wouldn't have shielded a man from his fate. At times like those, Bob Wilson could be heard on the command set saying, "Have a little faith boys, have a little faith." Wilson was the unofficial cheerleader of the crew when it came to viewing the glass as half full. Bill didn't mind the cheerleading; he only minded that Bob's little pep talks often tied up the intercom.

Toward what could be considered the end of the bomb run, Bill Witcomb sat in the pilot's chair grasping the black yoke and wincing with each explosion that surrounded his airplane. He'd never before experienced such a barrage. His Christian faith had always been strong, even though he'd never exposed his beliefs to the others in his crew. Even Fred Hales had never really seen a religious side to Bill. But true to the notion that there are no atheists in foxholes, men surrounded by flak become men of faith in a hurry, and Bill Witcomb was no exception. He clutched the controls harder than ever before, and he whispered a prayer out loud for the first time during his combat flying.

"Jesus, please save me," he beseeched his Maker as the sun became completely eclipsed by the black Nazi clouds. He sat shivering in fear, his eyes mere slits. Bill Witcomb saw death and destruction all around him, but for the first time he felt certain that his time had come. He decided to face it head-on and gradually began to open his eyes. There, outside of the cockpit, in front of the windshield, enshrouded by thunderous bursts of orange flames and huge balls of ominous black smoke, was a pure white light that shone from a face that he knew to be that of Jesus Christ. It was a vision of peace and tranquility amidst the conflagration of war. The figure spoke to him and said only two words, "Fear not." Instantly, the fear that had nearly consumed Bill a moment before was completely gone. The frigid below-zero temperatures five miles into the air were replaced by a rejuvenating inner warmth that reassured the pilot like nothing else. That one moment of glory completely restored his strength, his courage, and his resolve. As quickly as the image appeared before the airplane, it vanished, leaving Bill's memory the only record of the episode.

After completing the bomb run, *Lassie Come Home* banked off away from the city of Berlin, and Bill Witcomb and his crew headed back to Station 111 for their debriefing and another chicken dinner. Whether the image that Bill saw that day over Berlin was real or merely some hallucination brought on by hysteria amid the ordeals of combat is of little significance. It was real to him, and the results spoke for themselves. Thirty-six airplanes flew that mission to Berlin—only thirty-three came home. Bill, his eight crewmen, and the other five crews that flew in Witcomb's formation that day had been sitting ducks against the Nazi defenses. Their altitude, and their course and speed were all calibrated by the Allied command to use them as bait for the Germans. Yet they were spared, either by arbitrary fortunes of war or by the intervention of a Divine Providence. Bill Witcomb would ever after claim the latter to be the case. Twenty-eight of their fellow flyers from the 306th Bomb Group would be missing, killed, wounded, captured or dumped in the English Channel, to be saved only by the grace of God and the swift rescue actions of the Royal Navy. Louis Dorenbush summed up the mission this way:

> *Feb. 3, 9th mission to Berlin. We flew screening force. No bombs. The boys got hit pretty hard. 3 ships went down. Very long mission. Altitude 26,000 Temp. -45^{0}*
> *711*

Chapter 18

"10th Mission Went Haywire"

From the Berlin mission forward, Bill Witcomb was a regular attendee at the local church. The vicar of the Bedfordshire parish welcomed the young lieutenant with open arms, as he did all of the airmen from the American base at Thurleigh. The congregation was a mixture of the local inhabitants and military personnel from the entire area. The war had done much to fill the seats of the tiny Gothic chapel, even if the collection box didn't reflect the rise in attendance. At the outset of American involvement in the war, the local people were barely tolerant of American troops in their midst. But by the time Bill Witcomb and his crew had arrived on the great island, at least the country people of England had become quite hospitable to the boys. The hackneyed saying, "overpaid, oversexed, and over here," was seldom heard anymore. American valor on the shores of Normandy, at the crossroads called Bastogne, and in the air over Germany time after time had convinced the English people that the Yanks were considerably more to them than a mere nuisance. They were welcomed in the churches, in the pubs, and even in their homes—especially the young clean-cut officers from the airfield at Thurleigh.

Bill's sudden appearance in church each week had its greatest impact on the rest of his crew. They had long feared that Bill was either an atheist, or some Godless heathen who approached his flying duties with a reckless abandon that was the exclusive dominion of non-believers. His sudden religious regimen seemed somewhat incongruous with the crisp military bearing and the business-only attitude that had been Bill's hallmark since the crew was first assembled. But in time, the crew came to recognize that their captain's deep abiding faith and devotion to Christianity was completely consistent with his performance as a warrior. Witcomb abhorred killing, yet he flew missions with precision and discipline that were responsible for countless deaths. He hated being the tough-assed bastard that his crew believed him to be, but it was the only way he knew to get done the terrible job he had been assigned. After their first mission to Berlin, the crew began to understand just how much of their luck had been the result of the rigid discipline that Iron-Ass Witcomb had demanded of them. And they also began to understand that it was his own sense of survival and his deep Christian ethic that motivated him to protect those who were assigned to him. Coming home with those six airplanes and crews was no small feat, and the crew of *Lassie Come Home* was now a cohesive fighting unit that was bound together by Bill Witcomb's discipline and training, by their mutually hard-earned combat experience, by the realization that Witcomb had always been doing what was in their best interests, and by their mutual faith in God. They had, in themselves, become a force to be reckoned with.

After that trip to Berlin, the crew was seen together almost all of the time. Bill would join them at the local pub once a week for a pint or two of black beer, and all nine of them would walk together to church on Sunday mornings when they didn't have a mission that preoccupied them. They socialized amongst themselves and mingled very little with other crews, especially at the pub. When Dorenbush, Dinger, or the other gunners would fly a mission with another crew, they were all business. There was no socialization after the mission, even though they had experienced the rigors of combat with another crew. They were quick to get back to the barracks and tell their fellow crewmen of

Lassie Come Home how the mission had gone. Often, the tenor of the discussion had to do with the lack of preparedness of the crew they'd just flown with. Other times there were complaints about the capability of the officers, the lack of repair of the airplane flown, and even the level of training that existed among a crew. They didn't realize, as they voiced their complaints, that their griping was actually a vindication of Bill Witcomb's training methods. The demand he had placed upon every crewmember for efficiency in emergency procedures stood in stark contrast to other crews that seldom drilled and that seemingly knew nothing about what to do when disaster struck. Dinger's brush with such a crew, when he refused to fly in the ball because the waist gunner had no idea how to crank the ball around in an emergency, was commonplace. The demands of combat command leadership in flight had been ingrained in Bill Witcomb and Fred Hales from the beginning of their brief military careers. Somehow, those same values had been neglected with the young pilots and copilots that had been whisked through training and pressed into combat service all too soon. And even if they never uttered it out loud, the crew was thankful for Bill Witcomb being in the pilot's seat of *Lassie Come Home*.

– – –

Fulda, Germany was their next mission. Once again, in the pre-dawn hours Bill and his crew climbed aboard their aircraft and made their way to the runway. There were no lines painted on the tarmac, in order to help camouflage the airbase from enemy fighters. The only way to visualize the runway was to see the patchwork of pavement and concrete in the airplane's headlight beams, and to see the tiny flaming smudge pots on either side of the far end of the runway a mile-and-a-half away. The Eager Beavers of the 368th were assigned to Lieutenant Risk that day—little did they know at takeoff how risky the mission would be.

The weather over Europe in February can be reliable—reliably bad. During February of 1945, it was exceptionally bad. As the 306th Bomb Group lifted off from Station 111 that early February morning, they were attempting to climb to an altitude where they would assemble. A weather ship had been airborne for some time, reported that altitude was completely socked in, and advised them to try 12,000 feet. When the group arrived at 12,000, the pilots couldn't see the nose of their airplanes due to the thickness of the clouds. Risk ordered his squadron of twelve birds to meet at 6,000 and the 368th finally assembled over Mt. Farm Buncher.

Lt. Risk did his best to keep the squadron on course to the target, but formation flying within the bomber stream is all about following another's lead. As such, one has little choice in where one goes. Such was the case that day. The group leader's navigator either missed a checkpoint, or failed to follow the briefed course to the target. The result was a colossal waste of time while the lead ship searched all over Germany for the little town of Fulda. In the aftermath of the raid many of the crews mistakenly reported that they'd actually hit Giessen, but radar plots from Bill Witcomb's airplane and several other pilots put their hits that day directly on the assigned target. The notion that the town actually hit was Giessen had some merit, though. In past missions to Giessen, dozens of airplanes were lost due to collisions over the target when various groups would approach the town from different directions. The planned air routes took many things into consideration, but often failed to consider the intensity of the weather over that hamlet. Crosswinds, visibility limited to the length of a wingspan, and precipitation that would instantly adhere to the surface of the airplane, adding enormous drag, were normal. The cumulus clouds over Giessen seemed impenetrable—their very density seemed to render 1,200-horsepower motors ineffective. "It was like flying into a brick wall," one pilot commented. But the midair collisions were what took the real toll, and those were attributable to the weather and a mission plan that failed to account for it.

Gill spent the mission scratching his head through his wavy hair and wondering where in the world they were going. He would comment now and then to Bill on the intercom, but Bill—ever faithful to orders—followed Lt. Risk wherever he went. Gill's primary concern that day was not the flak from below, which seemed inordinately light. Fulda was a trek under favorable conditions. With the delay in assembly, the climb to 12,000 followed by a drop to 6,000, then another climb to 26,500 for their briefed bombing altitude, and the wandering that they did all over Germany in search of the target, fuel was what preoccupied Gill. As the bomb bay doors opened and Bob Wilson crouched over the Norden bombsight, Gill postulated that they'd already used more than fifty percent of their fuel. Navigators and pilots both relied upon a three-wheel calculation table that helped them judge fuel usage while in flight. It was a form of a slide rule for determining how much flying time was available to them. Gill pored over his wheel, scribbling notes and figuring.

Dinger spun the ball around now and then, searching for enemy aircraft in the skies below, but none were there. Eli Nelson searched above the airplane, while the Kid moved from starboard to port amidships. Louis Dorenbush sat quietly in the tail, chewing some gum and happy to see the five other ships attached to *Lassie Come Home* trailing behind them in a tight formation. Bob Wilson was doing the bomb sighting, even though he had set the system to automatic. When Lt. Risk's ship dropped its bombs, the bombs in the remaining airplanes of the 368th would drop as well. But Bob Wilson—like Bill—was not someone to leave things to chance. If he sighted the run properly and the electronic systems failed, he could still make a successful bomb run by toggling the bombs himself.

Suddenly, the airplane began to rise as the whistling of the falling bombs could be heard trailing away from the bomb bay. The entire crew breathed a slight sigh of relief, but remained ever-vigilant for fighters. Bob quickly closed the bomb bay doors to reduce the profile of the airplane in an effort to conserve fuel. Bill Witcomb would have turned off the run sooner than they did, as Lt. Leon Risk would have done, but they were consigned to follow the group leader who brought them there, and instead made the wide slow turn that put them on the path to England. Fuel was critical.

Gill shuffled through charts of the Channel ports and along the English coast looking for bases that could accommodate a bomber. He first checked to see if they were concrete or aggregate runways instead of grass, fearing that even the dry weight of a B17 would bog down in the wet conditions. He eliminated any field that didn't have at least a mile-and-a-half of paved or concrete runway. Although France was certainly an option in an emergency, it wasn't the option of choice. The Luftwaffe may have been reduced in size and potency by then, but it was far from dead, and tempting French targets were still well within effective striking distance for German raider pilots.

Bill Witcomb and Fred Hales listened intently to channel B as the group made its way toward Belgium and eventually to France. *Lassie Come Home* wasn't the only ship running desperately low on fuel. Most of the group, including their own squadron leader, was reporting similar problems. There was another problem as well. The clouds that had hampered assembly that morning had expanded well beyond the shores of Britain, and now engulfed the entire coast of Western Europe. It was impossible to keep visual track of any flight, squadron, or group, and word came from the group leader to strike formation and get to the nearest base before fuel was completely expended.

"Gill, give me a heading," announced Witcomb in relief.

"Two-seven-six," was the instant reply. The pilot pushed the rudder pedal and turned the yoke, banking the airplane sharply away from the rest of the squadron. He headed straight for the nearest landing strip that Gill could find. The other airplanes in the flight gradually broke from each other as their navigators caught on to what Wyatt Gillaspie had been doing for hours.

Emergency procedures—planning for disaster before disaster befell you—that's what Gill had been doing. Within minutes they were on the ground and safe, while other pilots dodged about all over the sky searching desperately for a place to land.

All thirty-six airplanes from the 306th eventually returned to England, but twenty-two of them had to divert to other bases due to their fuel shortage. When the clouds cleared and the damage could be assessed, the group had hit Fulda as planned, even though many still felt they had been someplace else. The wandering bomber stream that day found its way home, despite a number of close calls in midair and the threat of losses due to fuel exhaustion.

For *Lassie Come Home*, it was yet another day that served as an example of how leadership can trickle down. Wyatt Gillaspie was a really good navigator under any circumstances, and his initiative that day got his crew and his airplane to a safe haven before disaster could strike. Every man on the crew had maintained his faith in God, and they had evolved to a point where they had a similar faith in each other. Every man did his job—that was how it was.

Louis Dorenbush would encapsulate the entire mission with his short and simple scribbling on note paper:

> *Feb. 6. 10th mission went haywire. Our group got lost & flub-dubbed all over Germany. We dropped our bombs on mission. Longest mission I've had. We ran out of gas so landed at Becclis, an English field. Spent night there. Come back next morning. Flak was light. Altitude 26,500 temp. -45⁰ 711*

CHAPTER 19

ME262s

"How close were you to the crew?" asked the doctor.

"Not that close," said Bill, with a note of remorse in his voice. "Hales and I remained good friends after the war, but I wasn't that close with the others. I mean, we respected the jobs that we all did and we had faith in each other being able to handle a job, but we weren't good buddies like some crews."

"Why was that?"

"I suppose most of it was because of me," said Witcomb solemnly.

"How so?"

"Because of what I demanded of them."

"But isn't that part of what brought all of you home?" questioned the doctor.

"It probably was. But ..."

"But what?"

"Being a good Christian is more than that," he said instructively. "I should have been more than just a good leader to them. I suppose I should have been more of a friend to them."

"Why weren't you?"

"Because the military during a war is a different place—a different thing—with different rules of conduct and different demands placed on everyone. I was an airplane commander in the middle of an air war. I had to maintain discipline."

"And you couldn't do that any other way?" questioned the psychiatrist.

Bill didn't answer. He stared right through the doctor into the past and found himself reliving the war once again. The group had been assigned to attack Wittstock, Germany. Instead, the 368th attacked Ludwigslust due to a misunderstanding by the squadron leader, Lt. Claeys.

It was a long mission that day, but in theory an easy one. Their plotted course bypassed almost all of the known flak fields, and their altitude was to be very low, prompting Gill to report to the airplane in his Class A uniform again instead of his flying gear. The enlisted men all grinned and giggled as the lieutenant stepped out of the jeep looking like a poster boy for the Army Air Force. They remembered the time when Gill flew in Class As and got drenched in urine. The only concession Gill made that day was wearing regulation low quarters instead of his now-infamous pointed-toe cowboy boots.

Once again, *Lassie Come Home* was toward the head of the bomber stream in the high squadron, flying one of the four PFF airborne radar systems used by the 306th. The 368th Bomb Squadron was flying its 300th sortie of the war, even though it was only Bill's 17th mission. Twelve of the thirty-six airplanes of the 306th that made up 40th A Group were Eager Beavers. Lt. Richard Claeys was a distinguished senior pilot with the squadron. He had flown dozens of missions and was routinely chosen by command as a leader of the group. He was fearless and bold, but never careless. His flying skills were superior and he maintained an excellent crew, among them his bombardier, Sam Hatton. Regardless of the misunderstanding at the IP that had the lead third of the group turning away from the bomb run, the 306th continued to the target.

Instead of trying to regroup and come around for another run on the primary, a maneuver that would have exposed the 368th to both enemy flak and fighters, Claeys judiciously decided to go for one of the secondary targets, Ludwigslust. Lt. Hatton had only moments to grab a fix from one of the known points on the ground and set up the bomb run. Crouched in the nose bubble of the lead ship, he scrambled to align the Norden bomb sight and plot the run. Bob Wilson and the other bombardiers scrambled as well, preparing for the possibility that the electronic triggering might fail on the run. Bill Witcomb pulled the vertical control bar of the autopilot toward him, releasing the controls of the airplane to Wilson. The bombardier was now flying the airplane by the bomb sight as he focused the optics on the marshaling yard at Ludwigslust.

"Fighters, twelve o'clock high!" yelled Eli Nelson as he caught a glimpse of two fast-moving airplanes dead ahead of them and slightly above them. Bob Wilson looked up for just a second, then fixed his eye back on the bomb sight. Gill leaped from his seat and crowded in behind the bombardier to man the fifty caliber on the port side. Dinger spun his turret forward, feeling the rush of frigid German air pumping into the ball.

"How many fighters? Be specific," demanded Witcomb.

"Two fighters and they're screaming at us nose to nose," shouted Eli.

"Port or starboard?" questioned the Kid in the waist, moving from one side to the other. Before an answer could be given, the two enemy aircraft closed on the bombers at an alarming rate of speed. These weren't conventional fighters—these were the jets again, and no one on Bill's crew could get a clear shot at them due to their tremendous speed. Every hand tensed on the grips and triggers of the deadly fifty-caliber guns. Every eye strained down the sights, searching for the targets. But the speed of this relatively new form of airplane was twice that of a normal fighter, and the brace of ME262's blew right over *Lassie Come Home* from nose to tail with a thunderous roar. As good as those gunners were the men on Bill's crew couldn't acquire the targets quickly enough to even fire a shot in desperation. The tail gunner was the only one who had any chance at all. With the airspeed of the bombers at 225 miles per hour, and the jets racing along in the opposite direction at 450 miles per hour, closure speed grew close to the speed of sound. This gave the men less than half a second when the jets were in range. Normal human reaction time is half a second, and even though aerial gunners faced with combat conditions react quicker than that, it was still not enough time to engage this particular enemy. Louis Dorenbush saw the hazy, dark exhaust trails from both the German airplanes as they passed by, but at their speed, he still could barely see them through their contrails, much less get a bead on them and fire successfully.

The presence of superior fighters might have been cause for panic among some airmen, but the Eager Beavers were focused on the marshalling yards below, and continued the bomb run with deadly precision. Sam Hatton took his final fix at the AP and toggled the bombs. All twelve aircraft began dropping their eggs as the electronics worked perfectly. Bob Wilson waited for the bombs to clear the rack, then closed the bomb bay doors and swung the chin gun controls into place in preparation for another pass by the ME262s. None came. The deadly fighters had made that one pass and moved on. No one was certain if it was the tight formation maintained by the 368th that held the Nazi jets at bay, or whether it was something else, but they didn't come back for another strafing run just like before. The slow-moving bombers would have made easy pickings for the jets, even with the tight formation and the sophisticated combat box they were flying. Air speeds over 400 miles per hour rendered the traditional defenses of the B-17s somewhat ineffective.

But this day would again not see any destruction from the jets, because ironically, neither airplane fired a shot. Either their airplanes weren't armed, or their pilots were too inexperienced in combat maneuvers at those speeds to engage. Whatever the reason, the easy prey of twelve fat bombers lumbering along at half their speed wasn't enough to make their machine guns open up.

Below, the bombs of the 368th hit the target with unerring accuracy. The marshalling yards at Ludwigslust were eradicated in a hail of explosions that blew trains and track in every direction.

It was a long and tedious flight home that day. Despite the scare from the two German jets, there was no flak going into the target or on the way out. Aside from the routine of remaining on alert and searching the skies for enemy airplanes, it was a somewhat restful flight home for most of the crew. Bill Witcomb and Norris Hales were hard at work flying the airplane. Eli Nelson would search the heavens for fighters and intermittently check the fuel systems, the cabling to the control surfaces, and the dozens of things that a good flight chief watches over. The others relaxed somewhat. It wasn't until they were safely on the ground that Bill Witcomb discovered just how relaxed one of them was.

Both Bill and Norris Hales had felt through the yoke a gradual deterioration of the responsiveness of the tail control surfaces. Whether it was just a loosening of the cabling or one of the cables had jumped a pulley was unknown, but Bill mentioned it to Eli before they landed. Once the airplane was shut down for the day, Bill and Eli did a walk through to check cables that ran along the dorsal spine of the ship. They traversed the bomb bay, where just a few short hours before, death and destruction had rested, awaiting the marshalling yards at Ludwigslust. Bill tugged at the cables as they crossed the narrow catwalk into the radio room. Ringwald sat at his desk, completing his log and shutting down the radios for the day. Bill said nothing to him as he passed through. Eli just nodded and smiled.

As they stepped down from the radio room, Raymond Dinger was just extricating himself from the ball. He had locked it down for the night after extracting the fifties and was preparing to exit through the side hatch. It was then that Lt. Witcomb discovered something unusual. There were blankets strewn about the waist area of the airplane; the waist more resembling an unmade bed than a combat station. It had been some time since the airplane commander had explored that part of the ship. Francis Dusenberry had just removed his two guns from their mounts and was headed out the side hatch with the others.

"What the hell is this?" barked the pilot in an angry voice.

"What?" asked Dusenberry, with a dumbfounded expression upon his face.

"What is with all the blankets?"

"Ahhhhh ..." was the only reply from the Kid.

"Straight answer," said Bill firmly.

"Well, on the long trips," said Dusenberry sheepishly, knowing full well that his answer would enrage the lieutenant.

"Go ahead, on long trips," prompted Bill.

"When we clear the coast on the way back, I throw a blanket over me," said the kid before being cut off by the angry pilot.

"And you SLEEP?" demanded Bill. The kid merely nodded shamefully. "You sleep? Did you ever stop to think what would have happened if all that fabric got hit with an incendiary round or a piece of molten shrapnel? The whole ship would go up in flames! That doesn't even address the matter of you sleeping during a mission!"

"I think he needs to clear this stuff out of here, sir," said Eli Nelson in a preemptive attempt to calm Bill down.

"You bet your ass he needs to get this out!" said the pilot with a searing tone of voice.

Other pilots had to contend with crewmen hanging pinup girls from the exposed control cables that ran along the inside of the fuselage. Bill Witcomb felt he had a bigger problem. A crewman nodding off during missions was not at all unusual. Flights to Germany were always long and arduous, and the tedium of war took its toll on every man, draining him of energy and making what little sleep he got restless and unfulfilling. The occasional catnap during a lengthy mission was essential for staying alert during the tense times when enemy fighters attacked or flak threatened.

Dusenberry, the Kid, flew in the toughest position for long flights. Unlike most of the crew, who sat at their various combat stations, his fighting position was standing in the waist. Eli Nelson was the only other crewman who stood during flight in the top turret. But even there, Eli had a flat surface on which to stand, and he could brace himself against the sides of the tiny cylinder and rest somewhat. The kid had to balance himself in the middle of the arched fuselage. Trying to stand that way for eight to ten hours in a moving aircraft was exhausting. To combat the problem, Francis would grab a few winks once they'd crossed the Dutch or French coasts and were back in relatively safe skies. It wasn't as though he was sleeping all the way to the target and back with a brief pause in his napping for combat in between.

Despite the blanket episode, the mission that day had been a good one. Everyone came back that day, which was always an excuse for celebration. They all enjoyed a chicken dinner, and most of them got a day off before the next mission. The official report showed how, in combat, one can make lemonade when handed a bunch of lemons:

> To Lt. Richard Claeys and Lt. Sam Hatton, lead bombardier, go the honors of the day for a job well done.

Louis Dorenbush had his own way of putting it:

> *Feb. 22, 14th mission to Wittstock. Target was a marshalling yards. No flak today. We were attacked by 2 fighters. No damage done. Fighters were so fast none of us got a shot. Long mission. Altitude 17,500 Temp. -15°*
> *711*

Chapter 20

Combat Rations

Witcomb's crew continued flying without interruption after the Bremen trip until March 11th. That particular mission wasn't the toughest the crew had faced together, but any trip to Bremen was a challenge, both technically and for endurance. Flak over Bremen was always formidable, and airplanes were often lost to the ominous black clouds of death from below. *Lassie Come Home* was part of the lead element, again running slightly ahead of the flak instead of in the thick of it. It wouldn't have mattered though, because that day was a very lucky day for the 306th—there was no battle damage to any of the aircraft and no casualties. Everyone came home safely for a quick debriefing and the usual and most-welcome chicken dinner.

Mission debriefing was a ritual that was used for assembling more than just the facts of a mission. Crews would sit at tables and talk about the mission to a debriefing officer who would scribble down the information on paper. Hits on target, damage from flak, hits from fighters and the gunners that downed enemy fighters were all topics of discussion—it was the same after every mission. There was ample coffee and doughnuts or scones available to munch on while crews waited, occasionally apples or pears, and for those who needed their nerves steadied there were what the crews called combat rations—a shot of straight whiskey. The liquor was poured out in shot glasses and available to anyone passing by the table that sat near the entrance to the debriefing room. What crews often discounted was that the bartenders were no ordinary stewards, but medics chosen for their observation skills. Each corpsman was trained to watch for specific signs of battle or combat fatigue in the flyers, especially in the officers. A man who took a single combat ration was considered normal. A man who took two after a mission was worth watching. But a man who stood for a third shot of whiskey or more at debriefing was cause for serious concern. Even though the run on Bremen that day had been a reasonably safe and uneventful one, it was long and stressful, and the culmination of two full months' worth of stop-and-go combat for Bill and his men. Virtually everyone on the crew had amassed more than 100 combat hours in the air, and the stress was beginning to show.

Bill Witcomb and several of his men walked straight past the coffee and doughnuts and quickly made their way to the combat rations. Bill slugged down one shot, then another right behind it. The eyebrows on the corpsmen began to rise. When he clutched the third glass and started to drink it slowly, he and his crew were called to the debriefing table for their interview. One of the corpsmen tagged along to listen and watch.

The average infantryman had the stress of combat as a constant companion whenever he was assigned to the front. In some cases, one could be exposed to the enemy for months at a time. The same was true for many seamen who would advance the fleet by probing ahead, searching for a fight with the enemy in order to report their positions. But one of the most difficult kinds of combat stress to deal with was the on-again-off-again kind that Eight Air Force combat crews faced routinely. Waking up to a shower and clean clothes, and eating a meal at a table that was covered with a clean cloth and set with solid and spotless cutlery, was hardly what one would perceive as the antecedent to the barbaric warfare that would follow. But within a few short hours of that somewhat civilized meal, those same young men would be engaged in Neolithic struggles five miles up in the sky, where the brutal realities of the air war were all-too-vivid and commonplace. And just as quickly as the hostile environment came upon them, it was gone again as they landed back in England and re-immersed themselves in the gentile civilization that they'd enjoyed a few short hours before. Having to throw that switch inside them on, then off, then on again exacted a special kind of stress upon air crews that other soldiers and sailors never experienced. Although many may have had to deal with a similar dynamic of now-and-then combat, seldom was the turnaround achieved so quickly.

England in March 1945 was a quiet and somewhat serene place, with the exception of the vibrating drone of airplane motors when hundreds of bombers would make their way to their altitudes and to the continent, then back again. The Luftwaffe seldom ventured across the channel by then. Only once did Bill and his crew even hear a German airplane over English soil. One night in February, a stray Messerschmitt swooped down over the base and made a single strafing run on some of the hangers and a couple of aircraft. There was virtually no damage, there were no injuries, and there had been very little alarm before and during the raid. Some nervous stomachs existed afterward, but most of those belonged to crews that were close to fulfilling their thirty-five mission requirement. Aside from that one isolated incident, the English countryside had been a peaceful retreat for those who returned from the arduous rigors of aerial combat. It was this contrast in environments that weighed so heavily upon air crews. The effect it had upon psyches was similar to the physical effect that would occur if one were held in a refrigerated locker all day, then suddenly thrown into a vat of hot water. And once the body had assimilated the temperature of the hot water, it was tossed back into the refrigerated locker. The rules of civilization were many and rigid; the rules of combat were simple and few: survival at all cost.

One had to keep in mind at all times that the American airmen, soldiers and sailors fighting the war were, for the most part, very young men—kids by almost anyone's standards. As such, they had to blow off steam regularly in order to keep their sanity. After one particularly grueling mission, Bill Witcomb had seen that his crew was overstressed. Each member wandered back to his Quonset hut in a near-catatonic state. Seeing this, Bill retrieved one of the colored flares from behind the pilot's seat of *Lassie Come Home* and climbed atop the hut that he shared with Gill, Bob Wilson, and Fred Hales. He dropped the incendiary shell down the chimney spout and slid down the curve of the structure to the snow below. The pilot then took up a position near the door and waited for his roommates to come bursting out. As anticipated, the flare ignited in the tiny coke stove and exploded into the room. The three young officers inside responded by racing for what they thought was their lives out of the hut, unaware that the sparks and smoke that filled their quarters was not some strafing run by the Luftwaffe but merely a harmless signaling flare. After evacuating the hut, the trio learned that it was all just a pilot's prank, and all four officers enjoyed a good laugh together. The reaction of the three to the exploding flare became the focus of their conversation and energy, and helped to dim the horrors of their recent mission. The episode went a long way toward dissipating the abundance of adrenalin in each of them that had remained stored up after the mission. The most latent and debilitating aspect of combat was the stress caused by unspent adrenalin.

As the interrogation continued, the medic leaned in close to listen to the men speak to the debriefing officer. Dinger punctuated each of his statements to the young captain with the words, "Ya know what I mean?"—Dinger's trademark comment. For the others at the table, it had become their way of recognizing that the ball turret gunner was nervous or upset. He would point his finger like a pistol at the person to whom he spoke in order to drive home his point. Louis Dorenbush said little, as usual, reticence being his strong suit. The Kid and Ringwald had little to offer, since it had been a truly uneventful mission in the waist. Eli Nelson mentioned the lack of fighters and the officers all spoke of the inaccurate flak that was encountered. It was a very businesslike debriefing—no sentiment, no emotion. Only Dinger's pointed comments alluded to the escalating rage that was harbored within each member of the crew, Bill Witcomb included. The medic found the flight surgeon and conveyed his suspicions, and the doctor, in turn, eavesdropped on the end of the interrogation. As the captain finished up his notes and began to excuse the crew, the flight surgeon interrupted.

"How many missions does this make for you, lieutenant?" asked the doctor.

"Twenty-one," said Louis Dorenbush after a long silence from all the officers.

"Actually," said Eli Nelson, "this was our twenty-third mission."

Bill Witcomb was speechless, as were the other three officers standing with him. They had lost track of their missions—another telltale sign the medics used to judge a crew unworthy to continue flying. The flight surgeon asked to see the records, and the squadron adjutant made a note about the crew in his notebook. The crew was excused and allowed to return to their barracks before their evening meal.

The flight surgeon followed up and reviewed the combat record of *Lassie Come Home's* crew. All of them had fulfilled twenty-one missions—most of them had twenty-two or twenty-three. After a short argument with the squadron CO, the flight surgeon sent a runner to the Quonset hut where Bill Witcomb and his officers were either lounging around the tiny coke stove, or shaving again in cold water.

"Lieutenant Witcomb?" questioned the corporal.

"What is it?" asked Bill of the runner.

"The CO says your crew is to stand down on tomorrow's mission."

"Stand down?" questioned the pilot. "What the hell for?"

"You've been grounded by the flight surgeon, sir," replied the corporal.

"Grounded?" asked Fred Hales. "How come?"

"You've been grounded too, sir," said the young man. "In fact, all of you have. You're ordered to report to the major's office as soon as you've finished chow, along with the rest of your crew."

Bill stroked his chin a moment or two, then asked the corporal to make his way to the enlisted men's hut and instruct them to dress in Class A uniforms for dinner.

"Class A's?" barked Dinger. "What the hell for?"

"Yeah, what the hell's going on here?" asked Ringwald and Dusenberry.

"Lieutenant Witcomb has been grounded."

"GROUNDED?" came a chorus from the enlisted members of the crew.

"How come?" asked Eli Nelson as all the men encircled the corporal.

"I don't know why, Sarge, I only know that your entire crew is ordered to report to the CO's office after dinner."

"That explains the Class A's," said Raymond Dinger with a snarl.

"What the hell did we do now?" questioned Louis Dorenbush, for the first time becoming somewhat vocal about their situation.

– – –

The chicken dinner for the combat crews was a feast, as always, but it wasn't sitting well with the crew of *Lassie Come Home*. They fussed and fidgeted throughout dinner, seemingly uncomfortable in their chairs and unsatisfied with the meal. Each man questioned in his own mind what any of them might have done to cause the entire crew to be in trouble with command. They'd flown good missions and been a substantial part of the most accurate bombing the squadron had ever recorded. None of them could understand what they'd done wrong.

All nine men assembled in the orderly room and awaited the nod to see the commander. Bill inspected each man to make certain that they were all clad in strict military fashion, crisp and clean, insignia and medals all in proper order. After checking the enlisted men, he surveyed his officers. Captain Gillaspie was spit and polish all the way, except for wearing his cowboy boots instead of regulation low quarters. Bill was about to say something when the commander's orderly appeared at the door.

"The major will see you all now." Bill's crew snapped to attention and marched into the commander's office as though they were on the parade field. The crew stopped in front of the CO's desk—eight of them, two abreast. Bill ordered them to halt, and two steps later they came to a sharp and unison attention. Bill ordered left face, and all eight men turned crisply on the order to face their commander. The major, in awe by the display, came to his feet. As he did, Bill Witcomb drew his right hand up to his eyebrow in a rigid salute, and spoke:

"Present arms!" The entire crew brought their right hands to their right eyebrows and held a salute to the CO. "Lieutenant Witcomb and crew report as ordered, sir."

The major returned the salute and grinned ever so slightly at the military show before him.

"Ready, two," ordered Witcomb and the crew dropped their hands and resumed their position of attention. Bill and his men reported exactly the way military men are supposed to report to their commander, but seldom do.

"Stand easy," said the major as he resumed his chair. "Witcomb, you've been racking up some flying time lately, haven't you?"

"Yes, sir," replied the pilot.

"So has the rest of your crew, hasn't it?"

"Yes, sir."

"I've been reviewing your records and find that you've logged twenty-three missions in just sixty-five days. That's pretty impressive."

"Thank you, sir," said Bill, wondering where this conversation was going. He knew he wasn't going to be singled out for punishment, because command would never punish an officer directly in front of enlisted men.

"No thanks necessary, Witcomb. You've all been doing a fine job. I see you turned back only once," said the major.

"Yes, sir, but that was due to mechanical failure just after we got to the rally point. We lost our number three engine and had to come back."

"It says here you brought your bombs back with you."

"Yes, sir," said Bill matter-of-factly.

"Wasn't that kind of risky? Landing with a full bomb and fuel load?" Dinger was standing in the back row unconsciously nodding his head up and down as the major asked the question, agreeing that landing with that much explosive and volatile material aboard was a huge risk.

"The squadron was short of bombs and gas, sir. I figured we'd need both of them."

"Well, Witcomb, it's clear you and your crew have been doing an excellent job. From what my flight surgeon tells me, maybe too good a job." Bill was more confused than ever, as were the rest of the crew.

"The medics keep a pretty close eye on your guys, you know? They watch for signs that crews might be reaching the breaking point. They tell me you nine guys are almost there."

"Not at all, sir!" defended Bill.

"It's not unusual, Witcomb. It's nothing to be ashamed of. Combat is tough on all of us, and it has a way of deteriorating things within us unless we take a break from it. That's why I called you in here this evening. At the suggestion … no … at the insistence of the flight surgeon's office, I'm grounding your crew for a ten-day furlough. There's an R&R center in Edinburgh, Scotland and you, and your crew, are assigned to travel there tomorrow for a well-deserved rest."

Despite being astonished by the orders, a tiny smile came to Bill's face for the first time in months. The week before, the crew had stood for a photograph before their airplane, similar to the crew photo taken the previous August back in the states. This time the officers stood in back and the enlisted men kneeled in the front row. This time the enlisted men all wore staff sergeant stripes on their sleeves—all but Raymond Dinger, who had temporarily lost his stripes again for yet another brawl. But that wasn't the only difference. In the first group photo, the fun-loving, jovial nature of the young men was evident in the carefree expressions on their faces. In a few short weeks of combat, those expressions had been replaced by determined scowls and the grim expressions of those who had witnessed the horrors of combat. In less than half a year they had been altered from nine carefree young men and boys to nine combat-hardened veterans and a comparison of their crew photos reflected this stark and sudden transfiguration.

– – –

A sequence of train rides through the English and Scottish countryside whisked them to the ancient city on the east coast of Scotland. It had been the capital since the year Columbus discovered America. The Scots were delightful hosts, recognizing the sacrifices being made by young American flyers in an effort to save the Scottish civilization as well as their own. The crew was booked into a primitive form of bed-and-breakfast where the officers slept together in one big room and the enlisted men in another. They had all imbibed on the train ride and had all indulged at the local pub before bedding down for the night. Hangovers were something that Bill Witcomb was unaccustomed to, and he clutched at the sides of his head as he awoke late the next morning. As he opened his eyes, he was staring into the face of a beautiful young woman who possessed dark gray eyes and long chestnut hair that was streaked here and there with a brilliant splash of henna.

"Good morning, Lieutenant," said the lass in a soft brogue, seemingly in deference to Bill's condition. "Care for some tea?"

"What time is it?" was all Bill could muster.

"It is half past nine," was the reply in a deep Scottish brogue.

"Where's my crew?"

"Right here, chief," said Bob Wilson standing in the doorway across the room with his arm around the shoulder of another equally-attractive girl. She was buxom and blonde and offered a broad smile to Bill in his grog. "Hales and Gill already went down for breakfast. Care to join us?"

"I'll be along shortly," said Witcomb as he started to remove the bed covers then stopped when he remembered there were women present. He clutched at the blanket as the young brunette moved toward him.

"Don't worry, Bill, she's here to help you dress," said Wilson.

"I'm quite capable of dressing myself," said the blushing pilot.

"Americans," said the girl with a sigh. She shrugged her shoulders and moved to the door from where Bob Wilson and the blonde had just departed. "I'll leave you to it, then." With that she left the room and latched the door shut behind her.

Bill Witcomb shook his head in amazement—wherever they went, gorgeous women seemed to find their way to Bob Wilson. He was like a magnet that attracted them like no one else could. His charm and good looks had much to do with it, but there was a charisma that the bombardier possessed that transcended mere looks and calculated charm. Gill and Norris Hales were just as good looking as Bob, as was Bill Witcomb himself. But the women all seemed to spark when Bob Wilson was present. Bill couldn't explain it, nor did he try any longer to do so.

– – –

The nine men of *Lassie Come Home* wandered around the streets of Edinburgh, poking their heads into shops and standing for photos here and there in front of famous buildings and monuments. They had nothing to do, no training to do, no assignments to fulfill, no missions to fly. They gradually moved back toward being the carefree kids they once were, wrestling with each other now and then, joking and laughing. They ate and drank together, blowing off steam and acting foolishly. That was precisely what R&R was supposed to be—a release from all the things that had brought them to this place.

Just as soon as their furlough had started, it seemed to be over, and the nine of them climbed back aboard the Scottish Flyer and headed south to the Bedfordshire rail station and their base at Thurleigh. It had been a wonderful break from the strain of combat—a much-needed break indeed.

During their furlough, *Lassie Come Home* was refitted with a new PFF radar unit, and Red and his crew had repaired or replaced all the questionable systems that Bill and Eli had included on their repair punch list. 43-38711 was in terrific shape and ready to return to war. It was as though the furlough had recharged her systems, just as the trip to Edinburgh had revitalized the crew.

The 368th continued their relentless attacks on Hitler's Third Reich during the absence of Bill and his crew. The day they got on the northbound train, the squadron flew lead again to Swinemunde, where they bombed the dock facilities. Swinemunde was home to the German nuclear research effort. Two days later, they put up nine airplanes out of the 36 flown by the 306th. Only one airplane was damaged on that mission. On the Ides of March, nine more Eager Beavers flew to Zossen, headquarters for the entire Wehrmacht. Again, Lieutenant Claeys led the way. On Saint Patrick's Day, the squadron went to Molbis, led by Captain Matzke.

On March 18th, the 368th mustered nine airplanes that were attached to the 40th C group. Their mission: Berlin. Captain Robert Dodge was in the lead. He took a noteworthy list of pilots along with him: Captain James S. Law and Lts. Dick Claeys, Ben Olsen, Harold Altshuler, Gordon Dobbs, Dick Jones, Jim Burgess, and

George Purnell. Despite low cloud cover and persistent contrails, the squadron zeroed in on the marshalling yards below. Just 30 seconds before they were to drop their bombs, John Weber, the lead bombardier for the squadron, picked up an error in the instrument calculations and made a visual run on the target. The results were bomb hits north of the aiming point, but complete destruction of the "choke point" in the marshalling yards—the point where vast numbers of side tracks taper down to just a few main arteries. It was a formidable battle to be sure, with thirty-three out of thirty-six airplanes sustaining damage from either fighters or antiaircraft artillery. The Luftwaffe was very evident that day, with roughly two dozen ME-262s attacking the group. A single ME-109 made runs at the bombers as well. All the crews were delighted to have their "little friends" with them that day, the P51s that followed them to and from the target.

On the 19th, the Eager Beavers went to hit the oil fields at Molbis again, but it was obscured by a dense haze and contrails, so they moved on to Plauen. The crews actually counted only six bursts of flak on the entire mission; hardly the formidable defenses that they'd faced at other targets.

After their week of relaxation in Scotland, Bill Witcomb and crew returned to Station 111 and resumed their position in the flying rotation that had done without them. *Lassie Come Home* was fit and ready for combat, and so was her crew.

Chapter 21

Flak Jackets and Bales of Hay

Bill and his crew were back in the Quonset huts in the late afternoon of the 20th of March. The squadron was already alerted for a mission the following day, and Bill and his men readied themselves mentally in order to get back to the business of war. The mission on the 21st was Rheine, with Lieutenant Claeys was designated to lead again. By all accounts, it was a milk run where they attacked an airfield that housed jets. Despite the relative ease of the mission, it was a harrowing experience for Bill and Fred Hales, who had all they could do to control *Lassie Come Home*. They were carrying a load of antipersonnel bombs, which were lighter and less cumbersome than the heavy stuff they usually trucked to Germany. The bombs were fused differently and timed to go off before hitting the ground in order to spray the area with deadly shrapnel. There was a lot of fuel on board, but not so much to account for a nose-heavy airplane that was sluggish on takeoff and hard to hold up during flight.

"Eli, I thought Red said he took the extra armor plates out?" questioned the pilot to his flight engineer standing behind him.

"He did, skipper," said Nelson as he stooped down behind the pilot's seat and talked directly to Bill without the intercom.

"This thing wants to drop the nose constantly. It's as if the bombs are loaded in the nose bubble rather than the bomb bay," said Bill.

Eli glanced at Hales, who turned to look at the sergeant and nod affirmatively to him in agreement with Bill.

"I can't imagine what's causing it, sir. Maybe the horizontal stabilizer is jammed?"

"It was fine at preflight," said Hales. "I moved it through its entire travel, up and down. Smooth as silk."

"Ailerons?" asked Eli.

"Nope, they're working fine," replied Bill. "It's like trying to fly an elephant with a two-hundred-foot trunk."

All the way to Germany that day, *Lassie Come Home* kept bowing toward the ground, as though a canard had been added to the front of the airplane and cocked at an angle that forced the nose perpetually downward. Witcomb and Hales wrestled the monster all the way to the target before discovering the source of the problem.

As they reached the IP and began the bomb run, light-to-moderate flak began breaking through the slight overcast. There was a natural buffeting that came with the winter crosswinds over Germany, and there were the added bumps and jolts that came from the flak. The closer the flak bursts were to the aircraft, the bumpier the ride. It was especially noisy if flak was directly alongside the fuselage because of the peppering that the hot shrapnel caused along the skin of the airplane. If the bursts were just above or below the wing, where they could disrupt the flow of air over the airfoil, the plane would bounce violently upward or downward in midair.

Bob Wilson was on the bomb sight as the flak began to come up. He sighted clearly and stood ready at the toggle switch in case the electronics were off. As the lead ship let loose with her bombs, the bombs in *Lassie Come Home* began to rain down upon Germany. Wilson closed the bomb bay doors and everything seemed in order for the trip home. It was then that the front half of the airplane was rocked by a tremendous jolt and metal could be heard hitting metal in the compartment below the flight deck. They'd been hit by flak, and hit hard.

Bill Witcomb screamed on the command set for the navigator and the bombardier to check in, but only Gill responded.

"You guys okay?" screeched the pilot.

"All set, chief," replied Gill with a discernable laugh in his voice. Bill turned and looked at Hales who merely shrugged his shoulders in bewilderment. Eli Nelson ducked down out of the turret and swung his head between the two to make eye contact with Bill. Witcomb nodded his head in a gesture for the crew chief to go below and check on the two officers. Eli dutifully stepped off the turret swivel and climbed down to the lower deck to check on the brace of lieutenants. As he pushed past the oxygen bottles and the pulleys that directed the cables for the control surfaces of the airplane, he saw the problem.

The tiny compartment, that was barely big enough for the two men who manned that space and the equipment they needed to fight the war, was filled with spare flak jackets. Gill and Bob Wilson had literally lined the nose with as many flak jackets as they could find to provide added protection from flak. Since the additional armor plating had been removed, the pair decided that they wanted some added protection. They scrounged all the heavy flak jackets they could find in order to carpet the nose of the airplane with a protective layer. Flak jackets were heavy shields that aircrews would don as they entered flak fields. They were cumbersome shrouds in which to work due to their extreme weight, their awkward design, and their rigidity and inflexiblity. But they were the airborne equivalent of a bullet-proof vest, and no crewman wanted to be without one in the middle of a flak field.

The thump that had jostled the plane so badly a moment or two before had been a large chunk of molten metal that had ripped through the bottom of the aluminum fuselage near where the ammo box was mounted and directly below where Bob Wilson had been sitting. Wilson had been tossed to the other side of the compartment by the blast, causing a bruise on his butt and Wyatt Gillaspie to burst into laughter. The bombardier was draped over the carpet of flak jackets and rubbing his backside when Eli poked his head into the compartment. Gill, dressed in his Class

A uniform, was seated at the navigation table, chuckling, and Bob Wilson said nothing to the crew chief. Nelson shook his head when he realized what had happened and climbed back up to the flight deck.

"I can tell ya why the nose is so heavy, skipper," he said as he crouched behind Bill's seat and spoke directly into his ear over the din of the four motors and the artillery assault from the ground.

"What's up?" asked Bill.

"They've got the whole nose loaded down with flak jackets."

"Flak jackets?" questioned Hales as he listened in.

"Flak jackets!" insisted the crew chief.

"How many?" asked Bill.

"Dozens!" replied Eli.

"Pilot to navigator," said Bill into the intercom.

"Yo," replied Gill.

"You and Bob move some of that ballast aft to the bomb bay so we can finally trim this bird."

"Yes, sir," was the reply.

By the time the pair had finished moving the bulky flak jackets out of the nose, the flak had disappeared. They were heading home, and the pilot and copilot were finally able to steady the airplane for the trip. Nothing more was said about the incident by Bill to either the navigator or the bombardier. Gill and Bob Wilson realized how their zeal to protect themselves had actually jeopardized the airplane, and they never again carried more than two flak jackets in the nose. It was suggested that the bruise on Bob Wilson's backside was actually a wound sustained in combat which entitled him to the Purple Heart. But Dinger was quick to point out that the circumstances under which he had obtained his "wound" would have to be spelled out on the citation when he was awarded the medal.

"*While protecting himself with a layer of flak jackets, nearly causing the aircraft he was in to crash due to altered trim characteristics, Captain Wilson bravely pointed his posterior toward the enemy barrage of flak, exposing himself to grave danger and thereby sustaining a large bruise on his ass when the German flak tore a hole in his airplane and slammed against the very flak jacket that he sat upon,"* mimicked Dinger, as though he were reading the citation. "Yep, that'll sound real good at the presentation ceremony."

Bob Wilson never put in for the medal. But then none of them ever put in for any medals. The squadron policy was simple: if you wanted a medal, you had to do the write-up for it yourself. The squadron adjutant was far too busy with death notifications and crafting telegrams to the loved ones of wounded men to be drafting commendations so airmen could sport fruit salad on their chest. Since no one in the military ever wanted to do paperwork—particularly the self-aggrandizing variety—medals awarded to members of the 368th were very few.

That is not to say that squadron members were not worthy of recognition for countless acts of courage and initiative under extremely adverse conditions. But squadron tradition called for a kind of toe-in-the-sand approach to recognition, and Bill and his crew were perfectly suited to that tradition.

– – –

Gill and Bob Wilson, as it turned out, were not the only ones aboard *Lassie Come Home* to jeopardize the airplane for their own purpose. At the end of the mission, Bill Witcomb decided to do another complete walk through of the airplane to check things out. His ship had been hit hard in the nose by flak and that was sufficient reason for the commander to inspect the rest of her. He and Hales left the nose and climbed up to the cabin door that led to the bomb bay. They looked for signs of daylight in the aluminum skin as they crossed the structural girder that led to the radio room. They checked the mechanical and electrical fixtures as they moved aft. The radio room was probably the best-lit compartment of the airplane, due to the opening overhead where a machine gun was usually mounted. There was a window that could be inserted there if the gun was removed, and *Lassie Come Home* was outfitted that way. The pilot and his assistant found everything in order.

As Bill opened the radio room door that led to the waist portion of the airplane, he saw that the floor below was covered in straw. Both Dinger and the Kid had exited the aircraft right after the mission. All the gunners had removed their weapons to clean them, even though the only shots fired that day were done when the guns were tested over the channel. As Bill and Fred stepped past the ball turret they found themselves ankle deep in hay.

"What the hell?" said Bill as he tried to figure out how and why hay was in the back of his airplane. He looked at Hales, who merely shrugged his shoulders in a quandary. "Dusenberry!" he said in earnest.

The Kid hadn't wandered far away—he was nearby and heard the lieutenant calling for him. Ringwald raised his eyebrows at the young gunner alerting him that he was probably headed for trouble.

"Yes, Lieutenant?" said the Kid as he poked his head inside the fuselage door.

"What the hell is all this?" asked Bill Witcomb as he lifted hay up from the floor and let it sift through his fingers.

"Ahhhhhh, that's hay, sir."

"I know what it is. What the hell is it doing here? Have you been stabling horses in here?"

"Hey, that's a good one, lieutenant," said the Kid with a chuckle, hoping it would lighten the mood. One look in Bill Witcomb's eyes told the young sergeant there was no humor in the pilot's question.

"I'm waiting," said Bill sternly.

"Well, ya see lieutenant, that floor is pretty hard, especially when you lay down on it."

"Lay down on it?" asked Hales.

"Yea …"

"So the blanket episode wasn't enough? You weren't satisfied with blankets? You needed a mattress as well?" asked the angry pilot.

The young crewman said nothing. He merely lowered his head in remorse.

"Sergeant, have you any idea how fast this airplane would burn if this kind of fuel ever got ignited?" questioned Witcomb.

Dusenberry paused a moment before answering, then said, "Pretty fast, I suspect."

"Do you see that extinguisher on the aft bulkhead? That wouldn't begin to put out the fire that hot shrapnel could start back here with all this hay. And on your best day you don't store enough piss to ever put down the blaze that this fuel would cause."

"I never thought about that," said the Kid.

"Well, you won't need the hay any more because you won't be lying down back here ever again," instructed Witcomb. "You've got half an hour to clean this mess up before I inspect it and if I find so much as one piece of straw back here …"

"You won't, sir," promised the Kid as he began scooping the hay in his hands and dumping it on the ground outside the hatch.

Bill and Fred Hales stepped outside the airplane as the young sergeant set about his task. The pilot swung himself under the right stabilizer and opened the small access door to the tail gunner's position.

"What are we going to find in here, a four-poster bed?" asked Bill as he stuck his head inside and surveyed the solitary and Spartan domain of Louis Dorenbush. Both the tail and the ball were in proper order. But then both the tail and ball were incredibly cramped spaces—barely enough room for the inhabitants and very little space for any sundries.

After that mission to Rheine that day, no one on the crew ever compromised a mission again. The bonding they had enjoyed on furlough and the fact that Bill Witcomb took no punitive action against the offenders that day seemed to refocus everyone on their jobs. Witcomb was no longer some affectionless martinet that lorded over them—there was an apparent reason for all his actions, and his crewmen no longer questioned what he did or why. Gill and Bob Wilson realized that luck played an amazing role in war and so far theirs had held. They elected not to hedge their bets again with flak jackets. The Kid never slept on the job again, but instead remained standing vigil at his post from the beginning of the flights to their end. They were truly a unified crew now instead of just nine individuals that shared the occasional airplane ride.

Chapter 22

Fran

"So, tell me about Fran," said the therapist as he tapped his pencil on the pad in his lap.

"Fran?"

"Yes, Fran. You know, your wife? When did you meet her? Where did you meet her? How did you two get together?"

"It was after the war. I was working for American Airlines in Boston when I first saw her. She worked there, too. She was the prettiest thing I'd ever laid eyes on."

"So you asked her out?" questioned the doctor.

"I approached her, but she wanted nothing to do with me. She was much younger than me, and it was common knowledge around the office that I was divorced."

"That was a problem?"

"In the early fifties, that was a big problem. A divorced man with two young children was no one's idea of an ideal date—too much baggage."

"So, what did you do?"

"I honestly don't recall why she finally agreed to go out with me, but she did. And it didn't seem like a very long time before we were making wedding plans."

"You were happy then?"

"Most of the time," said Bill despondently. "There were times when I found everything too much for me and I'd just go off somewhere until it all passed."

"So, tell me about Fran," said the doctor.

"Like I said, she was a lot younger than me. When I was dropping bombs on Germany, she was in high school. She lived in Newburyport and she and her brother would drive to Ipswich after school each day to work in the defense plant in the center of town. She was assigned to wiring the fusing mechanisms that were used on the bombs I was dropping."

"That's an interesting coincidence, isn't it?"

"Ironic, I'd say."

"Did you ever establish if she helped manufacture any of the bombs you actually dropped?"

Bill simply shook his head in disbelief and a certain amount of disgust that the doctor would even consider such minutia germane to his therapy.

"How long did she work there?"

Bill told of how young Frances Ackerman had dutifully worked at the Sylvania plant along the Ipswich River right up until April of 1945. She was quick with the soldering iron and efficient on the line, which was what every defense contractor was looking for in a workforce. The fact that she was a schoolgirl seemed to matter little, nor did the question of the morality of school kids participating in the manufacturing process of weapons that would be thrust primarily upon a civilian population. The bombing of Pearl Harbor by the Japanese and the terror bombing of London by the Germans had made payback in kind morally acceptable to Americans. The ruthless firebombing of cities in Germany and Japan, where tens of thousands of people suffered horrible and unspoken-of deaths, was the work of the military. American civilians throughout the war justified their participation as supportive of their soldier's efforts. Anything that could be wielded against the enemy to end the war sooner was acceptable, especially if it had the added benefit of saving American lives.

Each afternoon in the winter and spring of that year, sixteen-year-old Fran and her brother would drive at the snail's pace of thirty-five miles per hour (the national speed limit during the war) along Route 1, the coast road, through Newbury and Rowley and report to work in the mill in downtown Ipswich. After hours of tedious work at a bench, they'd climb back into their aged Buick and head north along the same road. The rationing of gasoline had been expanded by then, so the ability to purchase fuel was no longer a deterrent to working fifteen to twenty miles from home. Her work had allowed the family a "B" sticker for the car, which permitted them to buy well above the four-gallons-per-week ration of the average driver. During her breaks from work Fran would walk down the hill from the Boston and Maine railway station into town and look into the shop windows of the stores that lined the river. She'd often stop at the entrance to the Strand Theater and peruse the display posters of coming films. Homework and chores were finished in the wee hours of the morning before school or on weekends when she had a day off. Sorting the laundry, cleaning the bathroom, filling the fire box with wood, and helping with dinner were but some of the tasks assigned to Fran, in addition to her defense work.

And then one day in April, as she and her brother reported for work, the foreman called all the workers on her shift together and told them that they were no longer needed. He thanked them for their work toward the war effort and sent them on their way. There were no pink slips, and no advance notice that work would end on a certain date. It ended abruptly before it began that day, and everyone was sent home. Unlike labor forces that are suddenly and inexplicably shut out of work in peacetime, Fran and most of her coworkers were not displeased with the foreman's announcement because they knew it meant the end of the war was at hand. Fran was pleased that she had contributed, but just as pleased that she no longer had to work in that factory after school each day.

Fran finished high school about the time that Bill's divorce was being finalized. She went on to college and eventually accepted an administrative job with American Airlines where she began to encounter Bill Witcomb on a somewhat regular basis. She was a dazzlingly handsome woman, with high cheekbones, wavy auburn hair, and a smile that lit up a room. It was no wonder that Bill—and every other red-blooded male that saw her—was instantly attracted to her. She was a pious woman from good Christian stock, and great company for like-minded people. In time, Bill and Fran courted and were married, and they were blessed with a pair of daughters, Sandra and Constance. Bill's other two daughters would join them when they could, and the combined family would venture places together where Bill taught the girls how to fish. It was a peaceful existence during a time when America had all but fallen asleep to world affairs that would percolate into civil unrest, a cold war, and a hot war that would eventually split the nation in half.

And as each year passed, Bill Witcomb grew more and more restless with the times and with his life. Sound sleep had been replaced by bed-drenching nightmares, where he tossed and turned so violently that he awakened the children who'd been asleep in a distant room. Even when he was in a relatively good mood, anger would suddenly overtake him and those around him would wince in fright or disbelief at the rapid metamorphosis. Anger and rage were never far from the surface.

Fran gently confronted Bill about his mood swings and his apparent lack of satisfaction with his life, but she was simply ignored. She naturally questioned if she was his problem. He had left the airlines in favor of taking up his father's trade as a silversmith. He had been approached at one time by a medical manufacturing company that needed certain shunts crafted of silver. Bill perfected a method of making the items efficiently and less-expensively than had ever been done before. The manufacturer was so delighted with the new process that they adopted Bill's methods themselves and canceled all of the orders they had given him. He was never compensated for his ingenuity or his efforts, which further enraged the inner man. He was forced to turn his hand to crafting the fineries of silver that silversmiths of centuries past had done. This appealed to the artist inside him, but did little to quell the embers that burned within him. It was also not as lucrative as he'd hoped.

By the fall of 1965, the man who had once commanded an airplane in dozens of combat missions had been reduced to a mass of self-doubt and confusion. He became lost in his own home, unable to remember what he was supposed to do next and unable to communicate with those around him. It was then that Fran suggested that he consider formal treatment. By then Bill Witcomb was past the point of rejecting such an idea—he was in pain and he no longer knew which way to turn for relief. He had to trust in someone, so he trusted Fran. At her suggestion, he signed himself in to the New Hampshire State Hospital for psychiatric evaluation.

Fran graciously offered the doctors enormous help in unraveling the mysteries of Bill's problems but, like most laymen, she was mostly ignored. She knew the seeds of his problem were planted long before she had ever met him, high in the skies over Europe, where he witnessed the fiery deaths of young men on so many missions. The doctors listened to her, but they had so many cases aimlessly wandering the vast wards of the hospital that focusing their efforts on solving this one man's problems was just impossible. The psychiatrists and administrators of the state hospital were confronted with multiple admissions each and every day of the week. Moving one man along would not help them win the numbers game that perplexed them. They were interested in moving groups of patients permanently out the door. So, Bill sat in the ward, staring out the dirty window into a barren yard.

Fran visited him almost every day. She had work and the children to attend to, and the drive to Concord from Hampton along Route 4 is an arduous journey, even today. There was no interstate highway system, not even a divided highway available to her with the exception of a small stretch of Route 1 between Hampton and Portsmouth. The rest of the trip was via a two-lane state road with few passing zones but an abundance of traffic lights, stop signs, and congested villages and towns from one end to the other. Still, she managed.

In the years that followed, Bill was diagnosed as being bipolar. The full definition of the term eludes many therapists even today, but the gist of the problem was that his moods would shift quickly—often without warning—from congenial to near-violent within seconds. Some clinicians felt it was a chemical imbalance that was primarily triggered by certain thoughts or external emotional stimuli. Others felt it had a predictable pattern or rhythm that could be tracked and plotted on a chart, so that episodes of violence would be foreseen and countermeasures taken beforehand. Whether either scenario was correct, or whether the actual affliction was some combination of the two, proved elusive in Bill's case. The only one who seemed to be able to track his mood pattern was Fran. She had an innate sense of her husband and would foretell his coming episodes with an accuracy that baffled the doctors. It was after her predictions that the application of medications was refined to soften his temper and make him socially acceptable in a pluralistic world that had changed in so many ways since his days in combat. The root cause of Bill's bipolar condition was never established. He himself was unsure if it was a condition that was with him from childhood, or whether the first telltale attributes of it began to surface during the war. The many horrors that he had witnessed in combat and the guilt that he bore for the countless deaths he had caused undoubtedly contributed to his particular malady bringing on the age-old argument over which came first—the chicken or the egg. Was being bipolar what pushed him through the war and what later escalated into the abhorrent behavior that he displayed? Or did the stress of combat and command cause some kind of genetic or molecular split that altered his internal chemistry and precipitated the episodes? Was the condition common to everyone, laying dormant in most people but erupting in others? As is common in the practice of medicine and psychiatry, nothing definitive was ever established in Bill's case.

In the end, Bill's love for Fran would be the ultimate means by which he would overcome the many obstacles that life presented. He loved her, he loved his children, and most of all, he loved his faith in God. He and Fran were devout Advent Christians who cherished their marriage and tried their very best to be the Christians that they thought they ought to be. Their distain for abortion was so great that in their retirement—with precious few dollars available to them from Social Security and the little money they had managed to save—they donated a twenty-thousand dollar ultrasound machine to a Dover, New Hampshire prenatal clinic so pregnant women could see demonstrable proof that actual life was going on inside them and choose not to abort. They didn't ask for accolades for their actions, they merely felt so moved by their faith. Where few would risk poverty for the sake of an ideal, Bill and Fran Witcomb were first in line to take up the challenge when matters of principle were involved.

Bill Witcomb often remarked throughout his later life that he was in recovery, as though life was some kind of perpetual twelve-step program. That was what he truly believed; that everyone is in recovery all the time. In the years just prior to his passing, Bill and his wife became acutely aware of certain movements within their community that seemed to favor lifestyles which were in conflict with their religious beliefs. Then in his early eighties, Bill and Fran could have easily retreated from the problems they saw and let them pass by unchallenged. But they chose instead to take on the forces that they felt were attempting to push a radically liberal agenda upon the young people in town. They attended a public meeting in the city hall where Fran recorded the session with a tape recorder. When the meeting concluded and city officials found that their words had been recorded on tape, they threatened Fran with arrest and prosecution under New Hampshire's wire tapping statute if she recorded another meeting. The Witcombs' answer to this was to sue the City of Dover, New Hampshire in Superior Court.

In the suit they brought, Bill and Fran Witcomb asked the court to rule that law enforcement officials don't have the right to intimidate or threaten the arrest of citizens who are exercising their rights under the Public Right-to-Know law. Judge Mohl of the Strafford Superior Court summarily denied the suit and dismissed it without so much as a hearing. One lawyer the Witcombs consulted exclaimed that "the judge took a dive."

Apparently, the local government officials reckoned that the Witcombs were merely a little old couple that could not muster the resources to pursue the issue at a higher level. Filing for reconsideration with the New Hampshire Supreme Court was an expensive, exhausting, and extremely time-consuming proposition, an ordeal that an elderly couple on a tightly-fixed income was unlikely to endure. But the city and court officials that calculated all this failed to consider with whom they were dealing. Bill Witcomb often remarked that as long as you had fuel in your tanks you kept bombing the enemy at every opportunity.

Bill and Fran searched the countryside for a lawyer that would take the case. Politically, the Witcombs were as conservative as two people could be, invariably supporting Republican candidates and those with a non-liberal agenda for office. But the lawyer that grasped their cause and believed that it was a noble and worthwhile question to pose to the higher court was Paul McEachern—a life-long Democrat from Portsmouth who had once run unsuccessfully for governor. Neither the Witcombs nor McEachern saw partisan politics in the case. The issue was open government. The lawyer quickly researched the matter and drafted an appeal to the state Supreme Court and presented it for certification and hearing.

Supreme Court matters are not trials. The proceedings are actually trials of trials. Decisions by that court are made from transcripts, briefs and oral arguments. A witness is never seen or heard, nor is any new testimony taken—there are only arguments pertaining to what has already happened. Therefore, it would seem unlikely that witnesses would be needed for the State Supreme Court to make an informed decision on the question presented. Yet that was the very excuse that was used to summarily throw the appeal out. Fran and Bill Witcomb had both passed away in the late summer of 2002, just a few months before the New Hampshire Supreme Court was to hear their appeal. Despite assurances to them by the legal community that the case would go forward even after they were gone, the court tossed the matter out. Its spokeswoman, Laura Kiernen, stated that the reason was that the defendant (the City of Dover) was unable to cross-examine the plaintiffs. Even though the original issue was the threatening remarks of the police chief and captain, the issue before the Supreme Court was the error of the trial court judge who threw out the case without a hearing. The Supreme Court apparently decided in a cabal-like forum that since the plaintiffs were no longer alive, it was senseless to overturn the lower court because a *trial de novo* (new trial) would be impossible. Although the logic might seem just, the question of whether a Superior Court judge can unilaterally dismiss a case in New Hampshire without the plaintiff having been heard remains unanswered. Also left up in the air is whether a police official can threaten arrest of someone who is exercising their rights in a public meeting.

Bill often lamented before his passing that the situation in the City of Dover was reminiscent of the political climate that existed in Nazi Germany prior to America's involvement in the war—it was the very evil he fought to eliminate from the world. Bill feared that if it was allowed to go unchecked, it would eventually consume our free society.

CHAPTER 23

Hanging on the Props

The laws of probability are far from an exact science, but the average losses of the 8th Air Force during the years 1942 through 1944 were the primary impetus that escalated the combat mission requirement from 25 to 35 missions. The statistics that were used to formulate that requirement were based on the declining losses from enemy fighters due to a rapid disintegration of the Luftwaffe. The German Air Force had certainly taken a beating at the hands of the British during the Battle of Britain, and its effectiveness had been beaten back even more as the result of American involvement in the air war. Not only were fighters compelled to go head-to-head with American fighters, the bombing missions of the 8th Air Force had raised hell with their bases in Europe. Planes, crews, and bases had been primary targets for both British carpet bombing at night and Allied strategic bombing during daylight hours.

But the increase in mission requirements didn't take into consideration a corresponding escalation in losses from flak. When all the numbers were crunched after the war it became clear that men were actually more likely to survive the 25-mission requirement during the early air war, when it was perceived to be more dangerous due to fighters, than they were during the time believed to be more survivable, when 35 missions was the standard. The laws of probability—and flak—were the reasons. Seven-come-eleven was a nice thought, but—as any polished gambler can tell you—the likelihood of rolling that combination time after time is very slim. At some point, the odds dictate that you'll roll craps and lose.

No one understood the reality of the odds and probability more than the bomber crews flying their 35-mission requirement during the early months of 1945. They had the benefit of three years of performance figures from those who had gone before them to support their logical conclusions. It precipitated an underlying element of fear that was never outwardly identified, but clearly present—an element that would exact a toll on all crewmembers.

One thing that is common among military organizations regardless of country is the concept of chain-of-command. Power emanates from the top down, providing a clearly identifiable table of organization for all involved. This holds true right up to the point where combat eliminates significant elements from that organizational flow chart, leaving gaps between the lower and upper portions of the organization. The problem that most military organizations faced was that those on top seldom indoctrinated those directly below them as to the functions of their position, fearing that the underling would literally stab his way to the top. The result was that those on the bottom had no idea what to do when those above them were summarily removed from the picture. The American military—which has always operated under the strict rule of law—is somewhat different. Privates and corporals were all versed in the responsibilities of a sergeant so that they could take over if the sergeant were killed or wounded. Sergeants, in turn, knew the role of a lieutenant and could step in to fill an officer's shoes when the need arose. The World War II legend of Audie Murphy is a tribute to how well the American military system functions. Murphy assimilated the functions of sergeants and lieutenants when they were removed from his chain of command by combat. The young Texas farm boy's ability to assume command amid the din of battle was part of the reason he became the most decorated soldier of the war.

The German army didn't operate this way. Officers weren't interested in sharing the details of command with their subordinates, fearing that those with the knowledge would wield it against them, just as many of them had done to get to the level where they were. German officers were content with giving orders. This meant that removing a significant number of officers from their commands could disrupt the entire Nazi military machine and make it vulnerable to attack. Chopping off the head of the snake, so to speak, ensured that the entire snake would eventually die. On March 22, 1945, the Eager Beavers of the 368th were given an opportunity to create a significant void in the Nazi command structure with their target being the German officer's quarters at Dorsten. It might seem as though housing for officers would be a low priority for defense when compared to a marshaling yard or a gun emplacement. But Dorsten was a heavily-defended target with 88- and 105-mm guns covering the sky. German tank divisions were often left to defend themselves against aerial attacks with their 88-mm guns, but an officer's billet was protected at all costs for fear that a significant disruption in command would occur. This ensured that a raid on Dorsten would be no milk run.

Lassie Come Home was one of ten airplanes from the 368th that made up 40th B group that day. Captain Dorich was in the lead—a seasoned command pilot with plenty of savvy and more than his share of courage. He was a good flyer, but more importantly, he was a good leader. His deputy squadron commander in the air was Captain James Law, another good man that Bill had flown with often. Except for a haze near the ground that obscured the actual target, conditions were CAVU all the way to Germany and back. It made for truly lovely flying, except of course for the flak. The official report listed the flak as, "meager but accurate tracking for four minutes in the target area." Those four minutes would bring Bill and his crew closer to death then they'd ever been before.

From five miles in the air, releasing a bomb rack on a target and expecting the bombs to hit the target is dependent upon many factors. Most of those variables the Norden bomb sight took into consideration. Bob Wilson was among the best bombardiers in the 306th Bomb Group and he was never shaken by the presence of flak over the target. Wilson would soberly acquire the target in the viewfinder, like an optometrist measuring a patient for eyeglasses. He'd focus, set for altitude, adjust for wind drift, and make all the calculations for a perfect drop of bombs on target. He worked hard to achieve the elusive "right in the pickle barrel" standard that 8th Air Force and the Norden Company constantly boasted about. But neither Bob Wilson nor the Norden bombsight could compensate for the sudden yaw (sideways movement) of the airplane as flak struck close aboard at the bomb release. Bursts of flak not only spew out molten shrapnel in all directions, but also create a shockwave from the blast that disrupts the airflow around the wing—the sort of impact to the aircraft that actually moved a B-17 sideways, often as much as several feet. Being a foot or two off on the bomb run, protracted out at five miles' altitude and almost the same distance in linear measurement from the target, meant the bombs would hit hundreds—if not thousands—of yards from their intended spot.

As Bob Wilson took his final sight, his left hand moved to the bomb release button. His fingers slid the red release guard forward, exposing the silver switch. The bumps and jolts from nearby flak often tossed navigators and bombardiers all over the nose compartment of the airplane, and the release guard was essential in protecting the release switch from flying debris or being hit by an arm or a leg as the crew bounced about. Wilson sighted the complex of buildings that had been described at briefing as best he could, given the haze that obscured the target. The GEE-H equipment aboard indicated they were on the target, even though he couldn't see it clearly. As he toggled the release switch, he clutched his throat microphone with his right hand and said, "Bombs away." Before he could finish his words, flak exploded under the starboard wing, lifting *Lassie Come Home* awkwardly into a left bank of about twelve degrees—

well beyond the recommended tilt of the airframe for dropping bombs. Despite the incorrect angle, the bomb load managed to clear the bomb bay with little room to spare as it passed by the open doors. Bob Wilson attempted to retract the doors, but they didn't respond. That blast on the starboard side had also ripped through the cowling and knocked out the number three engine—the one with the electrical generator—and all the AC power aboard suddenly went dead. The Norden bombsight and the GEE-H were out of commission, and tracking the bombs to target was impossible for the navigator. It wasn't until the strike photos were examined that it was found that they'd actually hit Gelsenkirchen, a considerable distance away from their intended target.

Before any of the crew knew what had happened, another burst of flak hit the port wing. There wasn't any visible damage from the cockpit, but the aileron was sluggish in its movement, and no one could be sure whether the flap or the trim tab would work at all.

Bill Witcomb and Fred Hales scrambled to get control of the airplane. Normally, when bombs were released the airplane would rise in the air as lift increased in direct proportion to the weight being shed. But 43-38711 was losing altitude due to the reduced power from a dead motor, a mutilated wing on the starboard side, and open bomb bay doors. Wilson and Gill were jostled in the nose, both winding up slammed against the bombardier's controls on the port side. Eli Nelson popped down from the top turret and quickly surveyed the damage to the right wing from the cockpit window.

"We're losing fuel, Bill," he exclaimed as he opened the cabin door and moved to the fuel transfer pump in an effort to save some of the precious liquid from the bleeding tank. Hales manipulated the flow switches as Eli pumped away with the hand pump like a madman in the open bomb bay, moving the gas not only from the injured wing tanks, but from the large feeder tank that exclusively served engine three. The two-hundred-mile-an-hour winds gusting up through the open bay were enough to keep any man off balance, but the added jolts from flak kept Eli fighting to keep his footing on the central beam that ran along the bay. Hales could see the gas dripping off the trailing edge of the wing at an alarming rate. He knew they had used more than half of the 3,600 gallons getting to Dorsten because of the bomb load. But they'd still need every drop available in order to get back. As Eli's strong arm moved the two hundred gallons of gas in the feeder tank, Bob Wilson finally managed to close the bomb bay doors with the emergency power. Hales watched the leak trickle away to almost nothing. They'd managed to save much of the fuel and stop the leak at the same time. But there was another problem.

"Bill, we got trouble," said Hales as he stared out the starboard window at the number three engine. There was no smoke or fire, but the prop was "windmilling," like a pinwheel, as the giant airplane moved through the air. "Number three is still spinning."

"Feather it," ordered Bill, and the copilot reached down to his left for the pitch control for that propeller. He pushed the number three lever all the way down, but nothing happened. The propeller continued to spin wildly in the wind. He pulled it up in the hope that it would free itself and regain function, but there was still no reaction.

"The mechanics inside must have been gutted from the flak," said Eli as he instantly recognized the problem upon reentering the cabin.

"We've got to feather it, Eli. Any ideas?" asked the pilot.

"If the pitch control is gone, there's no way," informed the flight mechanic. "She'll spin until she burns up. When the shaft gets hot enough, it'll break off and that prop will buzz-saw its way right through the fuselage—or worse, it'll smash into the other prop on number four and rip the wing right off that side of the airplane."

Fred Hales looked at Bill and Bill looked back at him. They both knew that the longer that prop spun, the more heat it would create, and the likelihood of fire was almost one hundred percent. The wing had already been damaged, and an engine fire could quickly spread to a damaged fuel system and engulf the entire wing in a flash. The structural integrity of the wing was questionable because there was no way to assess that kind of damage in the air. They knew they had to stop that prop, or at least slow it down so that the friction inside the propeller shaft didn't reach the flash point.

Every scenario that Bill ran through his mind added up to a bad option. If they couldn't control the windmilling, the engine would ignite and set the wing on fire. If the wing caught fire, the two extinguisher bottles in the engine housings would not be able to control the blaze. The fuel system would most likely explode in a chain reaction as each of the thirteen fuel tanks on that side ignited, ripping the entire wing off and causing the airplane to spin into the ground. In a spin, the crew would be pinned to the inside of the fuselage from the overwhelming centrifugal force and they'd crash and burn along with the airplane.

There was also the possibility that Eli had mentioned—that the propeller shaft would melt from the friction and the prop would fly off in an unknown direction, causing untold damage.

No matter what happened, the problem was time. In any case, everything would happen in less time than it would take to reasonably evacuate the airplane, so ringing the alarm bell would be of little use if the propeller shaft ignited the engine or suddenly flew off. By the time the crew reacted to the alarm bell and started to bail out, the wing would probably be gone, the spin would have begun and all aboard would most likely be doomed.

If he had the crew bail out now, they'd parachute directly into Nazi Germany, where it was unlikely that they'd ever find their way back to England without being captured or killed. Even though each man had his escape kit and a pair of regular combat boots to help negotiate the rigorous winter terrain of the German countryside, connecting with the underground before being captured was risky at best. In addition, the Germans had taken to shooting soldiers in parachutes since the Normandy invasion, and there was the possibility that none of his crew would even reach the ground alive.

As he postulated the options, another burst of 105-mm fire struck near the bomb bay, corrupting and bending the doors and reducing their airspeed due to the drag from the protruding metal. Dinger reported the damage over the intercom, telling Bill it was a good thing the hit came after bombs away or they'd all have had it. Bill remembered that a few missions before this one, he'd lost his wing man to just such a situation. It was at bombs-away as the bombardier took his final sighting that a 105-mm burst exploded inside the bomb bay and triggered all the bombs. The airplane was a ball of fire with wingtips and a tail, dropping from formation like a wounded goose that had been taken by hunters in a duck blind.

"We've got to hang on the props," informed Bill as he pulled back on the yoke and brought the nose of the airplane up at a stark angle as though he were trying to climb to a higher altitude.

"Hang on the props?" asked Hales.

"Never heard of it," remarked Eli as he moved forward between the two lieutenants to watch what Bill was doing.

"We used to do it in flight school, just playing around. We'd shut the engine off and bring the nose up and nearly stall the airplane. It helped us glide for incredible distances."

"How's that going to help?" asked the copilot, unsure what good the maneuver would do.

"Look at the prop," said Bill as *Lassie Come Home* was pitched nose-up. Hales looked out the window and saw that the number three propeller was almost at a standstill. As the airplane began to stall in the air, the nose dropped and Bill would allow it to speed forward until enough momentum was gained to once again hang the airplane on the other three props. The dead prop would speed up in the process, but the intermittent slowing of revolutions allowed much of the heat to dissipate into the frigid German air and keep the engine from bursting into flames.

Lassie Come Home was no longer in formation. Her reduced speed didn't allow her to keep up with the returning bomber stream, nor did it allow her to maintain altitude. Flying without a cloud cover to hide in made her highly vulnerable to fighters, due to her slower speed, and easy prey for flak, due to her reduced altitude and lethargic pace. The crew had seen an FW-190 over the target, but the German pilot made a single pass at the group without engaging, then flew off to parts unknown in order to fight another day. German defenses in the air were thin and the few fighters that were aloft that day either missed seeing the wounded B-17G or weren't interested in knocking down an airplane that seemed destined to crash.

Before Eli Nelson returned to his turret, he reached in and extracted a hunk of shrapnel that had ripped through the fuselage on the starboard side, tore through a support strut extending behind the copilot's seat, and lodged itself in the back of Bill's seat cushion. Witcomb had been so preoccupied with controlling his damaged airplane that he hadn't even noticed that the molten Nazi flak had stopped less than an inch from his spine. The jagged chunk of metal was still warm as Eli held it up for Bill and Fred to see. They glanced at it briefly before returning their concentration to driving their twenty-eight-ton roller coaster in the sky.

In the back of the airplane, Louis Dorenbush sat alone and cut off from the rest of the crew. With the blast of flak that ripped into the bomb bay, the wiring to his part of the command set was severed, leaving him out of touch with his comrades. He tried in vain several times to get their attention, but the headset was dead. The loss of AC power also eliminated power to his electrically-heated suit, and there was a definite chill in the air. Louis saw the squadron and group fade from view as the altitude of *Lassie Come Home* dropped and the airspeed slowed considerably. He had no way of understanding why the airplane was going up, then down, then up again constantly, or who up forward was still alive. He knew the plane had been hit, and he had seen and could smell the fuel leaking, but there was no way he could see the prop on the number three engine windmilling. He had to endure a frozen silence for the next six-plus hours, never knowing what would happen next.

Standard speed for B-17s was well in excess of two hundred miles per hour. Even though *Lassie Come Home* was a G model, with more nose drag than the F model due to the chin gun protrusion, she was equipped with the bigger motors that allowed her to keep up with the faster B-24s. She also had a plain metal finish, which eliminated the weight and drag of the camouflage paint job of previous versions of the bomber. The result was that she could pull at least five miles per hour more speed than her painted counterparts with similar motors. But now, with holes in both wings, a crumpled set of bomb bay doors, and a windmilling number three engine slowing her down, 43-38711 was limping through the sky at less than 180 miles per hour, raising her nose up at an acute angle, then dropping down in a stall that was like belly-flopping in midair. It was nauseating for those inside—a truly gut-wrenching ordeal that seemed as though it would never end.

The prop would speed up, then slow down with each drop and rise of the bird, the heat being minimized in the process. Hardest hit by the requirements of the maneuver were Bill Witcomb and Fred Hales. For over six hours they pulled and pushed at the yoke in a constant ballet to keep the airplane from falling off too far in the stalls. It required both of them to use every ounce of muscle they had to wrestle with the controls and make the airplane obey. It was like riding a wounded horse, trying to get it to respond as it had been trained even though it was in terrific pain and no longer physically capable of executing certain movements.

In the nose of the airplane, Gill checked and rechecked their course and speed to make certain they were following the quickest route home. He had plotted a fairly straight path that avoided the usual flak fields that the Nazis still held in central Europe. Once the crew was back over Holland, some of the tension eased up. There was no more fear of flak and very little fear of fighters at that point. But the question still remained whether Bill could hold the plane in the air long enough to reach England. Each man had his escape kit attached to his chute harness, and everyone had their chutes on in anticipation of the alarm bell sounding without warning. Everyone, that is, except Louis Dorenbush. Bill and Hales didn't say much on the intercom, but Witcomb's grunts and groans as he bullied the controls of the airplane were clearly audible to the few who still had working headsets.

Bob Wilson collected all the candy treats that each man had with him and made his way to the flight deck to pass them along to the pilot and copilot. Bill popped one of the sourballs into his mouth and sucked on the citrus flavor like a starving man savoring his first square meal. The instant burst of energy that the balls of sugar gave him was helpful in fighting the sluggish controls of his airplane. Once they were no longer fearful of fighters, Eli checked out the bomb bay to see what repairs he could make while still airborne. He also worked with Hales in moving fuel throughout the wing tanks to make certain that every available drop was used and the supply was equally spread to the three remaining engines.

As *Lassie Come Home* drew closer and closer to their home base in Bedfordshire, it became apparent to most on board that Bill Witcomb's procedure of hanging on the props was going to bring them home again. But huge questions remained in Bill's mind. The left flap was still questionable, and the aileron on the port side was difficult to control at altitude. When they were close to the ground, it might not respond quickly enough to be of use in a landing maneuver that was buffeted by crosswinds. If the wing dipped suddenly when they were close to the ground, the airplane could cartwheel down the runway and crash. The only trim tab was on the left wing. It hadn't been needed during the roller-coaster maneuver that he'd been executing for six hours, but he might just need that small control surface during landing. The loss of the number three engine meant that the other engines had to be tuned and tapered to compensate for the loss of power from its position. In order for this to work, the airplane was yawed in flight to minimize the attack angle on the number three engine and maximize it for the others. Upon final approach, the yaw angle of the airplane in relation to the runway would be critical and he would have to straighten out the fuselage at the exact moment of touchdown. Every control surface would be needed to do this. Then there was the landing gear—no one yet knew if the electrical loss from the number three engine had made it impossible to lower the wheels for landing. If the power feed to the gear had been severed at the same time as the command set wires, the only method open to them was the hand crank, and that took time. If time was too short, it was possible that they'd have to belly land, and the outcome of that maneuver was anyone's guess.

The bulk of the crew had made their way to the radio room just aft of the bomb bay. This was their assigned emergency landing station. In the event of a water landing, they would evacuate through the overhead window and deploy the life rafts that were stowed in compartments on either side of the overhead. The compartment doors were on the outside of the fuselage and were well above where the water line would be right after landing. A B-17 would take some time to sink if it weren't full of holes, so the crew would have a reasonable amount of time to get out. In the event of an emergency landing on the ground, the radio room was amid ship and high in the fuselage—an unlikely spot for major ground impact damage. It was believed that this was among the most survivable places to be. The other safe haven was the tail compartment occupied exclusively by Louis Dorenbush. Of course, there was barely room for one in that tiny space, and it was as claustrophobic as it could be. The tail gunner was supposed to move forward through the tail assembly, over the rear wheel well, traverse the superstructure that supported the tail wheel mechanism, pass the two gunner stations in the waist, climb over and around the ball turret, then ascend to the radio room that was just forward of the ball. It was an arduous trip in a bulky flight suit, fleece-lined boots, and heavy gloves, but no more treacherous than the trip from the nose, which required balancing on a single beam in the bomb bay with the doors half-open and wind gusts whipping upward with the force and spin of a tornado.

Ringwald radioed ahead their condition to the base and the runways were cleared for the emergency landing. Normally, Bill would approach the field from the southwest after circling around from the northeast. But this was an emergency, and heading straight in was essential. The field was cleared for him so any runway that presented itself was his for the taking. Fire trucks and ambulances sat on the tarmac near the three-story tower, awaiting word from the controller. The ground crew didn't need to know all the particulars—any declared in-flight emergency meant that an airplane and its crew were in jeopardy. And any crash on the base also put the ground crew at risk. Just being near an exploding or burning airplane had the ability to take lives or cause serious injuries.

Officers in their Class A uniforms paced the railings of the tower and along the second floor balcony while the ground echelon sat patiently waiting for their damaged airplane to return home. No one on the ground could do anything but wait.

Aboard *Lassie Come Home*, it was a different story. Bill and Fred Hales were near complete exhaustion from their physical ordeal. Bill's biceps were bulging with pain from pushing and pulling the yoke against the strong will of the airplane. Hanging on the props had kept the wounded propeller in place and stayed the damage to the airplane, and it had gotten them almost home. But the trickiest part of the return trip was the landing, and it was questionable as to which systems were working and which ones weren't. As the terrain started getting familiar to the pilot and copilot, it was time to prepare for the end of the flight. Bill and

Hales went over the checklist for landing and the landing gear was deployed successfully, much to everyone's amazement. Eli Nelson had swung into the bomb bay and rigged some loose wire around the doors to hold them tight for landing. The last thing Bill Witcomb needed during a crucial landing was a bomb bay door flying open.

Hales completed the checklist and stowed it to his right. He then tightened his seat belt and got ready for the final approach. The airplane had descended below four thousand feet and was aligned with the main runway at the base. The gear was down, the headlights were on—even though it was broad daylight—and 43-38711 was as ready as she was ever going to be for landing. Eli braced himself behind the pilot's seat and prepared for impact. Even though he was in the worst possible position in the event of a crash landing, he wanted to be close at hand in case either Bill or Fred needed his able pair of hands. The roller-coaster ride was finally at an end. It was time for straight flying, regardless of the heat that would build up in the number three engine shaft. Bill told Hales to lower the flaps and they seemed to function properly. But it was early—the flaps weren't fully extended yet.

Lassie Come Home crested the trees at the far end of the field, then swooped low over the glide space near the end of the apron. Bill pushed the rudder pedals slightly at first, then harder when the metal behemoth didn't respond quickly enough. The ship began to straighten from its yaw, aligning the wheels with the runway below. It was only then that Bill noticed that his feet were sitting in boots that were soaking wet. He presumed that the moisture was some kind of fuel or lubricant that had oozed out of a ruptured line that ran somewhere in the cockpit and behind the panel before him. He would later learn that it was actually his own perspiration that had puddled in his boots during his extended physical exertion. Power to all three engines had been reduced, and Fred Hales had his hands in position to cut the switches whenever Bill gave the order.

The rough pavement at the end of the apron was where the main gear wheels first touched. From the moment the shrapnel burst under the right wing, the ship had shuddered and shaken and made tremendous noise. As the gear hit the tarmac, the sound of metal bending or rubbing against other metal reverberated throughout the airplane. Those braced in the radio room for impact suddenly had eyes wide open in fear as the sounds sliced through them like a sword. In the cockpit, Eli squinted and pressed his eyes tightly together for fear of something giving way and breaking. *Lassie Come Home* bounced once off her main gear, and then she touched down a second time on the main runway. Just before the tires touched the second time, Bill pulled back on the throttles and slowed the motors considerably. He pushed the yoke forward, holding the nose down slightly and eliminating more bouncing. Fire trucks and ambulances intercepted the big plane halfway down the field and followed along behind it as it raced along the runway. The pilot touched the brakes now and then to see if they would grab but let the craft calm itself down over time instead of demanding obedience.

Gradually, the monster slowed to the speed of an automobile and Bill shut down engine number two. By using just the outboards to assist the rudder, he could more easily steer the giant airplane. Instead of stopping at the earliest opportunity, Bill drove the airplane to its own revetment, where Red and his assistant stood waiting to repair their damaged ship. The fire trucks and ambulances nearly followed the big plane into the enclosure, but stopped short of it to allow the airplane to swing around completely on the hard stand. Hales instantly cut the switches to the outboards the moment that Bill applied the brakes, and they both began the task of shutting down all the systems. The crew filed through the back of the fuselage and out the starboard side door. Ringwald was last out after radioing their location to the tower. Dinger cupped his hand around his Zippo® lighter and lit a cigarette as Dusenberry knelt down and kissed the tarmac. The two officers wandered forward toward the nose hatch and climbed back in to get their gear.

Eli suddenly swung down from the nose hatch and called to the medics to get over there right away. The medics leapt from their ambulance and raced toward the airplane. They climbed aboard and made their way to the cockpit. Bill Witcomb and Norris Hales were still in their seats. They hadn't moved since landing. They couldn't move. Their exhaustion was so complete that neither of them could move. They had expended so much energy during the flight that all of their arm and leg muscles ceased to respond when they wanted to stand up. The corpsmen had to extricate the pair of flyers from their seats—a method of peeling them from the chair as though they were removing wallpaper. Bill and Fred were slung by the armpits and dragged aft to the bomb bay. Eli and Red had pried open the bomb bay doors and where there were litters waiting for both the lieutenants. Hales was first out and Bill soon followed.

As the corpsmen were strapping Hales onto the litter and packaging him for transport to the base hospital, Bill lay on the litter in the bomb bay prostrate from his ordeal. Eli moved over to his litter and knelt beside him. The flight chief clutched the pilot's wrist and spoke softly and privately to him.

"Bill, you ever get orders to fly to hell and back, I'll fly as your crew chief," said the sergeant in his soft southern drawl. Bill smiled outwardly. In the years after that day, the pilot of that airplane would always say that one of the two medals he received during the war was when Eli Nelson made that statement to him. But the accolades didn't stop there. The rest of the crew stood just outside the bomb bay doors looking on and showing their concern for their pilot and copilot. Each man knew what a job Bill Witcomb had done that day, and each was grateful for another lease on life that he had been granted by the ingenuity, resourcefulness and dedication of the flight crew.

Before Bill's litter was loaded into the little olive-drab cracker box ambulance, it was placed on the ground so the medic could open the truck doors and tie them back out of the way. Bill turned his head to the side and looked back on *Lassie Come Home*. He could see the entire right wing. It had been crumpled some by the blast of flak and there were holes everywhere. He saw Red and his crew moving the scaffolding into place around the inboard engine in order to begin immediate repairs. He then looked aft and saw his crew standing beside the plane. Gill and Bob Wilson were chuckling with one another toward the trailing edge of the wing, looking at the flak damage close up. Dusenberry and Ringwald were wrestling under the starboard waist gun. Eli was crouched down near the bomb bay looking at the wrinkled doors and Louis Dorenbush stood alone near the horizontal stabilizer. Raymond Dinger puffed away on his cigarette and looked across at the pilot. As their eyes met, Dinger made a deliberate gesture toward Witcomb with his right hand. He raised his arm slightly, then extended his thumb upward, signifying his pleasure with the landing. It was undoubtedly the bumpiest landing that Dinger had ever experienced with Pilot Witcomb, but it was also the most perilous flight of his young life. All things considered, Raymond Dinger was very pleased.

In the final analysis, it was difficult for the crew and the mechanics to understand how *Lassie Come Home* ever made it back to Thurleigh that day. The structural damage was significant, all of the control surfaces were compromised, the fuel system was riddled with holes, and the electrical and hydraulic systems were virtually nonexistent. It took much more than mere will to keep that aircraft aloft that day – it took the strength and determination of Bill Witcomb and Fred Hales. Both men lost 15 pounds of body weight in those six-and-a-half perilous hours of flying, which explained why they had to be extricated from their seats. Had their actions that day occurred a mere two years earlier, the United States would have awarded both men the Medal of Honor. Instead, they received a short bed rest and a chicken dinner.

The crew stoic, in his distinctively succinct way, summed up the mission like this:

March 22, 23 mission to German officers quarters in the Ruhr. Today was the first time I thought I had it. We got hit pretty bad. Both wings & bomb bay were full of holes. Altitude 26,000 -38° 711

Chapter 24

Thirty-Five

Day after day, mission after mission, the crew of *Lassie Come Home* gradually whittled away at the remains of their thirty-five mission obligation. On the days they didn't fly bombing missions, they flew sucker raids where they ventured into enemy skies to draw enemy fighters away from the main body of airplanes. These raids didn't count toward their mission requirement, despite the risk being almost as great as a regular bombing run. The stress and strain of combat bore in on each of them, naturally, but even flying sucker raids and transport hops in and around England was preferable to sitting on the ground doing nothing … waiting. At least in the air, each man was busy with his job. For Bill Witcomb, it was where he was the most comfortable. For the other members of the crew, it meant that they were doing something other than drilling on emergency procedures under their lieutenant/dictator.

In March, *Lassie Come Home* flew only seven credited combat missions to German targets, but they were in the air almost every day for one reason or another. Often they were tasked with flying spare parts to or from other bases, or ferrying a member of the command staff to places where generals gathered for high-level conferences.

On the last day of the month, Bill and his crew were assigned the Halle mission, along with nine other planes from the 368th. *Lassie Come Home* suffered a blowout on one of the main gear tires during run up, and that delayed takeoff considerably. This was another of the thousand bomber raids, and the assembly area for this mission was designated close to Thurleigh. The result was a lot of confusion during the formation of the bomber stream due to the large number of recognition flares going off. No one could tell who was who or which squadron was which, and by the time they were over the target, the Mighty 8th was a homogeneous mix of airplanes from all over the United Kingdom bombing as a single unit. It wasn't a tough target by recent standards; a little flak, but zero visibility. The Mickey equipment had failed, and the lead airplane abandoned the initial run and swung around in a full circle to run at the target a second time. Under normal conditions, this was the deadliest maneuver imaginable. Even with the subsequent run from the IP, the target was unattainable electronically and part of the formation moved on to bomb Leipzig. Bob Wilson labored over the Norden bombsight on both passes over the primary and couldn't acquire even a rudimentary fix on the target. He conveyed this to Bill on the flight deck, who coldly and dispassionately decided to forgo the bombing and bring the precious bombs back to Station 111.

Despite the overwhelming flood of war materiel that was now flowing into England from the States, standard 500-pound bombs were still a precious commodity. Many of the contracts to build the bombs and their fusing mechanisms had expired in the fall of 1944, and production had not only ceased, but some of the manufacturers had moved on to the production of other items. This put a new demand on the remaining plants to produce at even higher levels before their initial contracts expired. The Battle of the Bulge had thrown a monkey wrench into the works (or, a spanner into the gear box, as the English would say). Bomb producers were suddenly tasked with gearing up as they had never before had to do. The Germans were far from defeated, and a renewed effort was needed in order to terminate the hostilities.

Experienced air crews knew just how low the supply of bombs was in theater, and they did all they could to ensure that they'd have sufficient ammunition to drop on enemy targets. If a bombardier or a pilot made a decision not to drop a rack of bombs on an uncertain target, they were hailed for their good judgment instead of berated for it, as had been the case during the early years of the air war.

Flying home with a full load of bombs made for a nervous trip. Aside from the additional fuel that was needed to truck several tons of bombs to and from the target, there was the extra stress of what might happen should any one of those bombs detonate. Bob Wilson dutifully inserted the safety pins back into each bomb after *Lassie Come Home* turned off the bomb run and headed for home, but there was always the fear that one of the pins hadn't seated properly, leaving the bomb active and vulnerable to all kinds of external stimuli that might set it off. If the ship were hit by aerial gunfire or antiaircraft artillery from the ground, the explosion of a single bomb in the bomb bay would crack the airplane in half and doom the entire crew.

Tension aboard 43-38711 was high when they brought the bombs home that day. Dinger swiveled around in the ball, looking for fighters and wishing for them rather than having to worry about a bomb load all the way back to Thurleigh. Hales had asked Bill if they shouldn't go for another target, like much of the group did with Leipzig, but the 10/10tenths cloud cover over that city wouldn't have made Leipzig any easier to hit, with the sighting equipment not functioning properly. Bringing the bombs home was the only smart choice.

Three days later the boys were in the air again, headed to Kiel. The tail gunner got the date wrong in his diary, but he summed up the mission as a milk run: another mission without fighters or flak. Louis Dorenbush wrote:

> *April 2, 27th mission to Kiel. Target was sub manuf. A milk run. Easy mission but so darn cold. Alt. 26,000 temp -48° 711*

The next two weeks were filled with missions. The weather aloft was still frigid, even though conditions on the ground had begun to moderate somewhat. England was becoming downright livable for the American airmen in April. The frozen dank, damp, gray environment was gradually being replaced by occasional sunshine and rain that was only intermittent rather than endless. The skies over Germany were still a treacherous place to fly, between the icy conditions and fire from below, but Germany was drawing closer to defeat each day. The Luftwaffe was virtually nonexistent by then, and many of the 88-mm and 105-mm guns that had been spread throughout Germany were now withdrawn from outlying areas to defend the big targets, like Berlin, against the threatening Russian Army.

On March 28th, the 368th traveled to Berlin for the last time, so in April the squadron was no longer compelled to face the most heavily defended location in Europe. There was still flak to contend with at other targets, but damage from AA was limited compared to recent months, and the harrowing experiences of aircrews were now few and far between. Bombing accuracy increased as time went on and as the flak faded away.

– – –

On April 18th, Bill and his crew assembled at the revetment where Red and the Kid had *Lassie Come Home* ready to go. The airplane seemed to glisten, as though the ground crew had polished her up. This was to be mission thirty-five for Bill and his men. Fred Hales was assigned as pilot on another plane, so Bill Witcomb had yet another rookie copilot assigned to him. Pilot Witcomb inspected his crew, who stood at attention in front of their airplane for the last time. Several of them were smiling in formation, as though it was already over. But Bill promptly reminded them that this was the most important mission they would ever fly and it was vital that they all do their jobs better than ever before if it was to be a successful mission. The corner of Dinger's mouth smirked and Dusenberry smiled outright. Even Gill and Bob Wilson had grins on their faces at the thought that the war was about to end for them.

The target that day was Rosenheim and a marshalling yard. The 368th drew duty as the low squadron, and the lead was Lieutenant Martin. This was a low mission—10,000 feet—which meant little need for oxygen or heavy clothing. Gill was in dress uniform, as was Bob Wilson for the first time. On the way to the target, they were met by the Little Friends (P-51s) that provided air support. But fighters had no way of protecting the bombers from flak, and two planes of the 368th were hit over the target. Fred Hales had taken some flak damage to his airplane, but nothing serious. They flew home together and the group landed safely back at Station 111.

Upon landing, it took some time for the crew to emerge from the airplane. Unlike past flights where they couldn't get out the airplane fast enough, they remained at their stations for a bit, reflecting on the part they had played in the war. They were all tired from the on-again, off-again stress that was aerial combat. To a man, they were glad it was over. A jeep pulled up to the revetment where *Lassie Come Home* now sat idle. The young lieutenant driving yelled up to Bill Witcomb that he was to report to the CO after chow with his entire crew. Bill acknowledged the order and returned the salute from the junior officer.

And then, for the final time, he shut down all the switches on the panels before him and put the gallant lady to bed. She had been the office to which he reported almost every day, the home in the sky that had protected and shielded him during combat. The collection of metal, cables, wire, switches, and gauges was more than just an airplane to Bill Witcomb and his men. *Lassie Come Home* had a soul and a spirit, as though she were a living, breathing being. The folks at Boeing in Seattle had breathed life into her two short years before, and she had meant life to her crew from then on. For Bill and his men, it was like saying goodbye to a dear friend.

Louis Dorenbush omitted to note the altitude or the temperature in his last diary entry. Instead he wrote:

> *April 18, Last mission to Rosenheim. Target was transformer. Flak was light. Am I ever a happy warrior. 711 (Lassie Come HOME) & She sure did*

Outside the airplane, the crewmen hugged one another in congratulatory celebration. They had flown their thirty-five missions and it was now over. They enjoyed their chicken dinner, then, each in full-dress uniform, they assembled outside the orderly room with Lieutenant Witcomb for their audience with the commander. As they had done before, the nine men entered the commander's office and came to a full and precise attention. Bill called to present arms and the crew held their salute for the CO. The major rose to his feet, came to attention, and returned their salute. He then paced behind his desk and spoke of the end of the war being right around the corner. He recognized that they had done their part, but he still implored them to stick it out for a few more missions to see the thing through. Bill and the crew had talked of this many times, even as they could see the war coming to a close. It had been agreed that thirty-five times tempting fate was sufficient and that when they'd done their part, they would call it quits.

"Sir, with all due respect, we've done our job. We're tired and we're going home," said Bill, acting as spokesman for the entire crew. The major shook his head in understanding and walked to the front of his desk to shake each man's hand and thank him personally for a job well done.

"We'll miss you all," he said as he dismissed the group.

After filing into the outer office, Fred Hales stopped near the door and stared at Bill. Bill looked at him and asked, "What?"

"I want to see it through to the end, Bill," said Fred.

"Fred, you've done your share," said Bill.

"I want to do more." Bill smiled a warm understanding smile at his copilot and shook his hand.

"Good luck," said Witcomb.

Fred Hales remained behind to speak with the major separately about continuing to fly missions. He was a qualified pilot with six missions in the left chair and twenty-nine in the right. He was a welcome addition to the squadron roster for the finale. Bill and the rest of his crew slept in for the first time on a mission day, grabbing chow after the combat crews were finished. They all meandered out to the tarmac to watch as the 306th put up 38 aircraft on Patriot's Day, April 19th. Back in Newburyport, Massachusetts, people were celebrating the birth of a nation 170 years earlier. On that April morning in 1775, Americans first stood as a militia against European tyranny. The first American defeat was the rout at Lexington Green. The first American victory was in Concord, where Minutemen from all over Middlesex came together at the North Bridge and battled a regiment of the King's men. From that skirmish, colonists traversed the ridgeline along the road to Boston and repeatedly harassed the British troops from the cover of woods and rocks. How fitting it was that the very last mission of the 368th Bomb Squadron should occur on such an auspicious day.

Within a few weeks, Germany officially surrendered and airmen without sufficient mission credits were destined for the Pacific. Meanwhile, they flew mercy missions to Europe, delivering food and supplies to refugees and victims of the war. Mankind had laid waste to the entire continent, and it would take decades before the scars of the earth would heal enough to be pleasant to go for a walk again. The acrid smell of cordite and the pungent odors of war would take time to fade, but they would always remain fixed in the nostrils of those who fought. While the rebuilding of Europe was among the new mission priorities of the remaining members of the 8th Air Force, those who fulfilled their mission requirements and had sufficient points to go home were gradually being reassigned for shipment back to the States. Bill and his crew remained at Bedfordshire for a time, taking things easy and enjoying their absence from combat. During this time, Bill broke away from the base to visit his parent's family in Manchester and Birmingham. Just as his mother had done throughout the war, he brought Bundles for Britain with him when he went. The bundles were filled with tins of food, cigarettes, and pipe tobacco; everything that English civilians needed to enjoy postwar life a little better or to use as barter for other needed supplies.

Orders finally came through, and the nine men of *Lassie Come Home* were ordered to Southampton, where they boarded the *Ilê de France*. During the war, the beautiful luxury liner had been used for ferrying troops, and now it would serve as a taxi home for the crew. The five enlisted men were jammed into a cabin that was designed for two, and the officers shared a makeshift room of plywood that sat upon the forecastle deck of the ship. It was a long and uncomfortable trip home, but there was no longer the fear of German submarine attack. Besides, it was a trip home—what could be better?

Upon arrival in New York City, the nine men said their good byes and went their separate ways. Those who were destined for immediate discharge were mustered out with pay before heading toward home. Those who would remain on active duty until Japan was defeated were allowed a furlough home. Bill Witcomb would remain on active duty a while longer, reporting to Gunter Field to assist the base commander.

But on that muggy July morning in New York, the nine men of *Lassie Come Home* looked upon each other for the last time. They had flown thousands upon thousands of hours together as a crew, and almost three hundred of those hours were in combat. The married men had spent more time with their crew then they had with their wives. They had struck at the heart of Germany on each mission, and helped bring the European war to a swifter conclusion. And after all that, not one of them was killed, not one of them was captured, and amazingly, not one of them was ever wounded. Their skill at their jobs made them among the most effective weapons systems ever thrown into the war, striking deadly blows when they dropped bombs and bringing home precious bombs when the supplies were low. Had any of them been so inclined, they would have all easily qualified for a host of medals from the governments of the United States, Great Britain, and France. But none of these nine men went to war for medals, or even recognition. They were just nine young men in uniform, standing in a railroad station like so many other young men. They were the norm, nothing extraordinary, like most of their generation who served.

They said goodbye to each other, and especially to Bill Witcomb. Old Iron Ass had been a pain in their collective butts for nearly a year, but it was clear that his determination and skill had led them all to Grand Central Station safely. Eli Nelson shook his pilot's hand firmly and thanked him warmly. Eli knew, more than anyone, how Bill Witcomb's genius for flying had made the difference time and time again, and he was indeed grateful to Bill for getting them home. The crew departed that day, each taking a different train to a different place. Dinger jumped on the subway and shot back home on the Bronx Express. Bill Witcomb said a fond goodbye to copilot Fred Hales and boarded the northbound train for Boston. By suppertime he was in Newburyport, stepping off the Boston and Maine commuter that ran out of Boston just after 5:00 PM. He sat in the smoker car with the businessmen and nodded politely to those who smiled or spoke words of encouragement or praise to him. Within minutes of stepping onto the platform of the Newburyport station, Bill was being held in the warm embrace of his family. Bill Witcomb's war was finally over, even though his personal struggle to live life would last another fifty-seven years.

Chapter 25

Punctuation Marks

It's easy to glance over one's shoulders and evaluate the past with a scrutiny that puts everything into a geometric order that makes perfect sense. But living in any age requires the ability to navigate through uncharted shoal waters that disguise a host of dangers that are inherent to that age alone. It is for this reason that true students of history must evaluate much more than the mere recorded acts and deeds of those in the past. Only when those acts and deeds are placed into context with the environment in which the actors lived can we begin to understand their motivations and their reactions to what confronted them.

In *Crosses in the Sky* I have attempted to do just that. Much of the military history of World War II is well-chronicled and well-known. But those events that forever altered the world will be meaningless if we fail to comprehend everything that happened and everything that existed at that time.

When I set out to write this book, I was presented with assistance from many people. One such person was Joyce Dorenbush, widow of the late tail gunner aboard *Lassie Come Home*. Mrs. Dorenbush photocopied her husband's diary of his thirty-five missions and sent it along to me without hesitation or concern for remuneration. In a subsequent email from one of her family, I learned that there had been confusion about the notations Louis Dorenbush had made after each entry. He had written a three-digit numeric code that no one (including a member of Air Force cryptology) could figure out. It was simply that they had no context—no point of reference. Those three-digit numbers were, of course, the last three digits of the tail number of the airplane in which he flew that particular mission. Understanding the context was no less important in this instance than it is for those who study history in earnest. Here is a prime example of the importance of possessing all the facts in order for understanding to be complete.

To Joyce Dorenbush and her family, I extend my sincere thanks for taking a chance on a person they had never met and sharing the experience, wisdom, and wit of the family patriarch. Louis Dorenbush was a good husband, a good father, and a good airman at a time when America needed really good airmen, and I hope that my efforts here are worthy of him and his service to our country.

To Eli Nelson and Raymond Dinger, who granted me interviews by phone and their recollections by mail, I owe much. The feisty ball turret gunner has now passed, and the gentleman/flight chief continues to accumulate notches on his belt of retirement in his beloved Alabama. These two men represented the polar extremes of the crew of *Lassie Come Home* in many ways, but they were as united as two men could be in spirit, and in their dedication and fidelity to the cause of freedom.

I wish to extend to the 306th Bomb Group Historical Association a hearty well done for the publication in August of 1993 of the *Squadron Diary 368th Bombardment Squadron (H) 1942-1945*. Without their detailed record, my work would have been nearly impossible. The United States Department of Defense and my *alma mater*—The United States Air Force—were less-than-hospitable toward my overtures and seemingly indifferent to my literary pursuits, so I have no idea what their official records have to offer. Thank heaven that those squadron and group adjutants during World War II weren't so cavalier toward documenting combat history.

To my former fellow ambulance attendant, the late Bernie Harding of Milford, New Hampshire, I offer my special thanks.

Bernie was a B-24 pilot and prisoner of war of the Third Reich. For several years Bernie and I served together on a volunteer ambulance squad, but I never knew anything about his life during the war. It wasn't until I began to research this book in earnest that I discovered Bernie's past. He graciously granted me time and shared with me his experiences and the emotions that were with him during those years. Acquiring an understanding of the motivations that prompted young men and women to voluntarily throw themselves into the perils of war was essential for writing this story, and I couldn't have done it without Bernie.

Odd as it may seem, a special thanks must be expressed to the United States Coast Guard, and also to the Collings Foundation, for their assistance in providing a final punctuation mark to the life of Bill Witcomb. Bear with me; this is going to take some explaining.

In the summer of 2002 I received a telephone call from Bill's third-eldest daughter, Sandy. She indicated that Bill and Fran had made some decisions and that they wanted to see me. I subsequently learned that Fran had been diagnosed with terminal cancer and that she had been moved to a hospice center for more intense care. It was an odd experience for me to have a conversation with Bill alone that warm August afternoon, but I learned that he had made an unusual decision. Despite enduring a recent cardiac bypass operation that was going to prolong his life, Bill had decided to cease the kidney dialysis that he was undergoing three times a week and to accept whatever nature had in store for him. He insisted he had no intention of living a day longer than necessary without his beloved Fran, and his most fervent wish was to go at the same time she did. Fran was irate with the blasphemous nature of Bill's desire, suggesting that he was trying to instruct God what to do. But she forgave him and manifestly faced her own physical challenges with a smile on her face and a prayer on her lips. She was among the bravest women I've ever known.

On that last day that I met with Bill Witcomb, we resolved many things. My first concern was that my primary source of authoritative information about his experience in the war was no longer going to be available to me. I confessed my fear that I would not be able to properly craft the story without him. Bill winked at me with those cobalt blue eyes of his and said that he'd now and then sit upon my shoulder and whisper in my ear when I needed guidance or inspiration. When I asked, "What if that isn't enough?" Bill said he would instead give me a strong nudge or a good swift kick in the ass. I've often felt him there, pushing my fingers on the keyboard toward completing the story. On many occasions I've gone back and read material that I apparently wrote a few days or weeks prior, only to find it completely foreign to me, as though someone else was the actual author and I a mere typist. Indeed!

Bill Witcomb asked only two favors of me on that last day that we spoke. The first was that I never describe him or his crew as heroes. Like every veteran I've ever known, Bill and the others reserved that term for those who did not come home as they had done. I reluctantly agreed to his request, with the one proviso that I would merely relate the facts to my readers and if they decided that the crew of *Lassie Come Home* was comprised of heroes, then Bill would have to live with that. He bashfully and reluctantly agreed.

His second request was one that he had conveyed to his daughters, and he enlisted me as a co-conspirator. He told me that his last wish was that he and Fran be cremated after death and that their ashes be comingled. He then asked that they be buried at sea somewhere between Cape Ann and the Isle of Shoals (directly off the coast where lies the town of Newburyport, Massachusetts). He asked that this be accomplished by their ashes being dropped from the bomb bay of a B-17. Less than ten days after talking with Bill, my dear friend had passed on. His wife Fran died some ten days later. And two weeks after that, Bill's second daughter Nancy and I climbed aboard the B-17G "Nine-O-Nine" and conducted a formal burial at sea in the Atlantic Ocean between the Isle of Shoals and Cape Ann. The only part of his wish that we could not fulfill was dropping their ashes from the bomb bay. The prop wash would have blown everything back into the fuselage. I suspect, after the episode related to me about Wyatt Gillaspie and the urine pail, that Bill might have known what would happen, and I was happy that the crew chief of the Nine-O-Nine declined to use the bomb bay. Instead, the starboard door in the waist of the fuselage was used. The entire funeral was, as daughter Sandy so aptly put it, a surreal ending to the story.

And so, Petty Officer Mosher of the United States Coast Guard station at Portsmouth, New Hampshire provided assistance and information to me about tides, GPS coordinates, and probable locations for the unusual task that lay before us. I extend my thanks to the Coast Guard for all the help prior to the burial on September 18, 2002.

The Collings Foundation of Stow, Massachusetts, maintains and flies many vintage military aircraft. Among the many airplanes that are meticulously preserved, the foundation has the only B-24 Liberator in the world that is still flying. The "Wings of Freedom" tour is sponsored by Collings and crosses the United States each year visiting dozens upon dozens of locations from coast to coast. It was during a visit to Pease International Trade Port in Portsmouth, New Hampshire that Nancy Witcomb and I were able to board the "Nine-O-Nine" and carry out Bill and Fran's last request. To Richard Walsh (the pilot), his wife Connie, to Lucy Champion, Mike the crew chief, and the entire crew and staff of volunteers who worked with us that day, I extend my warmest thanks. Your reverence toward the sacred right of burial was laudable, and your professionalism and concern for the passing of a combat veteran and his wife was above and beyond the call of duty.

Although there is nothing specific that the Wright Museum of Wolfeboro, New Hampshire has contributed directly to this book, a special thanks needs to be given to that institution, and to the late David Wright, for continually indirectly inspiring me to harness the important memories of the past and commit them to paper. The Wright Museum is dedicated to the years 1939 through 1945 and deals with the overall national metamorphosis that occurred during that time to the United States of America. The primary theme of the museum surrounds the war at home, even though the trophies on display are the vintage vehicles and tanks that were used in the war. The only remaining Pershing tank from the battle at Ramagen, Germany is the centerpiece and pride of the museum's collection. But it was the air maps showing the flak fields between Thurleigh and Berlin, the instruction manual on display for the Norden bombsight, and the complete collection of *Life* magazine covers on display that managed to trigger my creative juices. Acquiring little-known statistics about the people I was studying helped me put things into their proper perspective. Facts such as: the four squadrons of the 306th Bomb Group flew 342 missions and sustained a loss of 171 aircraft. That may not seem like much flying, but Bill Witcomb and his crew flew more than 10 percent of the collective missions flown by all four squadrons—pretty impressive! More impressive is that *Lassie Come Home* was not one of the 171 airplanes lost.

To the family members of the crew of *Lassie Come Home* that I have heard from throughout the years that I have researched and written this book, I thank you for your encouragement and support. While your faith in me was truly welcomed, it is the very reason that it has taken so long to assemble this story. Each time I talked with any of you or received a letter or an email, the bar was suddenly elevated higher and higher for me. The importance of getting the story right grew exponentially with each contact. Despite the increased demand for accuracy due to my perception that stakes were being raised, knowing that you expected and deserved the truth made me a better historian.

Steve Bergholm—my college fraternity brother and one of my dearest friends—just happens to be the superintendent of buildings and grounds for the Newburyport, Massachusetts school district. He took the time and trouble to uncover the yearbook of the first graduating class and sent along the photograph and inscription attributed to Bill Witcomb, Class of 1938. Although this book was pretty much finished when Steve discovered this little treasure, the inclusion of the photo and text is a fitting capstone to the life of Bill Witcomb. To Steve I offer my heartfelt thanks.

To my family and friends, who have endured the endless telling and retelling of the tale of *Lassie Come Home*, I thank you for your patience. As you all know, I was born fifty years too late, so I'm relegated to writing about World War II rather than serving during it. Regardless, no writer creates in a vacuum and the stimulation, inspiration, and assistance you have all given me is greatly appreciated. This is your book as much as it is mine.

To the Witcomb girls—Susan, Nancy, Sandra, and Constance—thank you for sharing your parents with me. Thank you for the blind trust that you have invested in me. I truly hope that you each feel this work is worthy of that trust and that the reflection of your family's history contained in this volume is an honest representation.

To the late Fran Witcomb I offer my thanks for allowing me into her home and into her heart. Fran was among the most committed and directed people I have ever known, and the promise I made to her that last day that we met I hope I have now fulfilled. She was a wonderful lady, and she helped make Bill Witcomb a wonderful man. Just as she was true to him in every way, I have tried to be true to his memory and his actions, and, indeed, to hers.

And before this story can rightfully be closed, it is important to disclose the fate of that stalwart Boeing-built airplane that brought these nine young men home safely time after time. *Lassie Come Home* flew her last combat mission with Bill Witcomb at the controls. The airplane and crew, except for Fred Hales, stood down for the last combat mission of the war. Both crew and aircraft had done their fair share to win the war. During her service life, the airplane had a wing replaced on three different occasions, her number three engine replaced twice, her bomb bay thoroughly overhauled, and had battle damage patched up, welded, glued, and nailed back together after virtually every mission. In May of 1945, with her original crew now finished with combat flying, she was transferred to another crew—a crew of four men. *Lassie Come Home*, at the hands of a pilot, copilot, navigator, and flight engineer, flew relief missions into France from war's end until October of that year. Stripped of armaments, she would now haul vital supplies in order to help heal a badly wounded Western Europe. In the fall, the airplane was ordered home to Bradley Field where she was listed as officially retired.

On November 28, 1945, the Wednesday that followed Thanksgiving, *Lassie Come Home* was finally put to rest in a desolate corner of Kingman, Arizona. Her engines were all removed and her electronics and avionics were gutted from the airplane, her mighty propellers stacked in a heap with hundreds of others, and her tires pulled from the wheels, making her appear as though she wasn't fully dressed and standing on tiptoes. Her bomb bay doors were flung open to allow the arid desert air to circulate through the fuselage. There she sat alongside thousands of her sister B-17s—monuments to a time of self-sacrifice that later generations would never fully envision. Flying thirty-five formal missions and some twenty sucker raids, she had protected her crew like few other airplanes in World War II. Only a handful of the thousands of 8th Air Force crews that managed to complete their required missions would be able to boast as those of *Lassie Come Home* could. No one was killed, no one was captured, and not a single member of that lucky nine-man crew was ever wounded.

Under the care of the War Assets Administration, *Lassie Come Home* was eventually scrapped and melted down into aluminum ingots. That aluminum was later used to help rebuild American commerce. Some of it may have gone into new aircraft. Some was probably used in the construction of new buildings. Still another portion of it may be in the beverage can we drink from or the plumbing fixtures and appliances that we rely upon each day. Wherever it is, it is part of America and it continues to serve.

Finally, to Bill Witcomb—my friend—I extend my deepest thanks for everything you've done for me. When someone observed the stark contrast between our two political philosophies and began to make an issue of you being conservative and me being "liberal" (a term seldom associated with me by those who truly know me), you responded sternly. "Paul is neither a Republican nor a Democrat, he's an American!" Only a fellow veteran could comprehend the full value of that statement.

Over the course of the past few years, when I've felt low and uninspired, your spirit did indeed climb upon my shoulder and I heard you shouting in my ear to get moving. When I was lazy I felt your boot upon the seat of my pants, pushing me toward the computer. Although I was there on that surreal fall afternoon when Nancy and I buried your ashes at sea, you have never really left me for a moment. Your strong Yankee influence is now an integral part of me and I strive to live my life more by your terms each day. Having the strength of convictions and a commitment to a cause has become imbedded within my character, and I shall not stand idly by while those forces that you defeated more than half a century ago try to reemerge. I shall doubtless never achieve a fraction of what you did in your brief lifetime, but I consider myself a better man and truly blessed for having been afforded the opportunity to share the little time we had together. I will never forget the lessons that the living of your life has to offer. On behalf of a grateful nation, thank you for everything you and your crew did. On behalf of me, thank you for being my friend and, like it or not Bill, my hero.

Breinigsville, PA USA
20 September 2010
245685BV00002B/2/P